STUDIES IN HISTORY, ECONOMICS AND PUBLIC LAW

EDITED BY THE FACULTY OF POLITICAL SCIENCE
OF COLUMBIA UNIVERSITY

Volume XLII] [Whole Number 108

ATTITUDE OF AMERICAN COURTS IN LABOR CASES

A Study in Social Legislation

BY

GEORGE GORHAM GROAT, Ph.D.

Homer E. White Professor of Economics and Sociology
Ohio Wesleyan University

THE LAWBOOK EXCHANGE, LTD.

Clark, New Jersey
2003

ISBN 1-58477-308-1

Printed in the United States of America
On Acid-Free Paper

The Lawbook Exchange, Ltd.
33 Terminal Avenue
Clark, New Jersey 07066-1321

Please see our website
www.lawbookexchange.com
for a selection of our other publications and
fine facsimile reprints of classic works of legal history.

Library of Congress Cataloging-in-Publication Data

Groat, George Gorham, b. 1871.
Attitude of American courts in labor cases : a study in social legislation / by George Gorham Groat.
p. cm.
Originally published: New York: Longmans, Green & Co., 1911. (Studies in history, economics, and public law; v. 42, no. 108).
Includes bibliographical references and index.
ISBN 1-58477-308-1 (cloth: alk paper)
1. Labor laws and legislation—United States. I. Title. II. Studies in history, economics, and public law; no. 108.

KF3369 .G75 2003
344.7301—dc21 2002192202

STUDIES IN HISTORY, ECONOMICS AND PUBLIC LAW

EDITED BY THE FACULTY OF POLITICAL SCIENCE
OF COLUMBIA UNIVERSITY

Volume XLII] [Whole Number 108

ATTITUDE OF AMERICAN COURTS IN LABOR CASES

A Study in Social Legislation

BY

GEORGE GORHAM GROAT, Ph.D.

Homer E. White Professor of Economics and Sociology
Ohio Wesleyan University

New York
COLUMBIA UNIVERSITY
LONGMANS, GREEN & CO., AGENTS
LONDON: P. S. KING & SON
1911

To

E. W. S. G.

The Constitution of the United States was made for an undefined and expanding future, and for a people gathered and to be gathered from many nations and of many tongues. . . . We shall expect that the new and various experiences of our own situation and system will mold and shape it into new and not less useful forms.

JUDGE PARKER.

It must be remembered that even the constitutions we call rigid must take their choice between being bent and being broken. The Americans have more than once bent their Constitution in order that they might not be forced to break it. . . . And it has stood because it has submitted to a process of constant though sometimes scarcely perceptible change which has adapted it to the conditions of the new age.

JAMES BRYCE.

The true grounds of decision are considerations of policy and of social advantage, and it is vain to suppose that solutions can be attained merely by logic and general propositions of law which nobody disputes. Propositions as to public policy rarely are unanimously accepted, and still more rarely, if ever, are capable of unanswerable proof. They require a special training to enable any one even to form an intelligent opinion about them.

JUSTICE HOLMES.

PREFACE

THE purpose of this volume is to present the various views expressed by judges in their decisions in labor cases. They are stated as nearly as possible in the words of the judges themselves by means of liberal quotations from opinions. Intended for the student of social questions who is interested in the relations of capital and labor, it aims to show the political, economic and social principles that guide the courts in the solution of the problems that come before them. While it is true that courts always deal with particular cases and decide only specific questions, yet principles of necessity enter into their opinions and guide them to their conclusions. These principles this volume seeks to reveal by presenting in compact form the several lines of argument which support the decisions. It is believed that only by reading the views of the courts as expressed in their own words can they be clearly understood.

The discussion has been purposely restricted to those principles and problems that are still unsettled. The wide field in which principles are well established and where questions only of technical or minor significance are raised has not been entered. Since the purpose is to set forth the various conflicting views that obtain, the reader must be warned not to consult these pages for information as to the exact status of the law in any particular jurisdiction. Further it should be said that while in the discussion views may be expressed that are contrary to those advanced by judges in determining the law, it must be understood that no effort is made to urge that the law is not what it is.

What the law is, it is; and as such it must be obeyed. In the discussions of opinions it is only the views expressed and the reasoning adopted that is dealt with.

The extracts have been selected from more than five hundred opinions in cases dealing with various phases of the labor problem. The selections have been made with a view: (1) to giving the varied opinions held by different judges; (2) to bringing out both sides of the controversy; and (3) to emphasizing by the larger number of selections the extent of the acceptance of particular views. The length of the extract quoted should not, in every case, be taken as an index of its relative importance.

The material here presented has been limited to the opinions of the federal supreme and circuit courts and the state courts of last resort. A large number of intensely interesting and very significant opinions are undoubtedly found in the decisions of the lower state courts. To enter this vast field, however, would have extended the work beyond reasonable limits.

In Chapters IX, X and XVII the author has quoted freely and without special citation from his articles, "Precedent Versus Conditions in Court Interpretation of Labor Legislation,"[1] "Unionism and the Courts,"[2] and "Judicial Views of the Restriction of Women's Hours of Labor."[3] Exact references for all opinions cited are given in the alphabetically-arranged List of Cases (pp. 3-6).

It is hoped that the book may be found a useful supplement to text-books and lectures in courses on labor problems, as well as of service to those who are interested in

[1] Proceedings of the Third Annual Meeting of the American Association for Labor Legislation, Publication no. 9, p. 88. Dec., 1909.

[2] *Yale Review*, 19: 144, Aug., 1910.

[3] *Political Science Quarterly*, 25: 420, Sept., 1910.

these problems, but who have not sufficient time to consult the reports of the cases.

The author would be glad to thank individually the many from whom he has received helpful suggestions in the preparation of the work, but the list is too long. He is under special obligations, however, to Professor Seligman for his inspiration and encouragement, and to Professor Seager, not alone for advice and inspiration, but for the more arduous work that he has cheerfully undertaken of reading the manuscript.

George Gorham Groat.

October, 1911.

CONTENTS

PART I

INTRODUCTION

PART II

UNION ACTIVITIES

PART III

LEGISLATION

PART I

INTRODUCTION

LIST OF CASES

(The following is a list of the cases of most importance from the point of view of the principles discussed in the opinions. For each case the state and the year as well as the reference are given.)

Adair *v.* United States, U. S. Supreme Court, 1908, 208 U. S., 161.
Adams *v.* Brenan, Illinois, 1898, 52 N. E., 314.
Allis Chalmers Co. *v.* Iron Moulders' Union, U. S. Circ. Ct., 1906, 150 Fed., 155.
Arthur *v.* Oakes, U. S. Circ. Ct. of Ap., 1894, 63 Fed., 310.
Atchison T. & S. F. Ry. *v.* Gee, U. S. Circ. Ct., 1905, 139 Fed., 582.
Atkin *v.* State of Kansas, U. S. Sup. Ct., 1903, 191 U. S., 207.
Barr *v.* Essex Trades Council, New Jersey, 1894, 30 Atl., 881.
Beck *v.* Railway Teamsters, Michigan, 1898, 77 N. W., 13.
Berry *v.* Donovan, Massachusetts, 1905, 74 N. E., 603.
Bohn Mfg. Co. *v.* Hollis, Minnesota, 1893, 55 N. W., 1119.
Booth *v.* Burgess, New Jersey, 1906, 65 Atl., 226.
Boyer *v.* Western Union, U. S. Circ. Ct., 1903, 124 Fed., 246.
Braceville Coal Co. *v.* People, Illinois, 1893, 35 N. E., 62.
Broad, *In re,* Washington, 1904, 78 Pac., 1004.
Carew *v.* Rutherford, Massachusetts, 1870, 106 Mass., 1.
Carter *v.* Oster, Missouri, 1908, 112 S. W., 995.
Casey *v.* Typographical Union, U. S. Circ. Ct., 1891, 45 Fed., 135.
Cohn *v.* People, Illinois, 1894, 37 N. E., 60.
Commonwealth *v.* Carlisle, Court of Nisi Prius, Philadelphia, 1821, Brightley's Rep., 36.
Commonwealth *v.* Hamilton Mfg. Co., Massachusetts, 1876, 120 Mass., 383.
Commonwealth *v.* Hunt, Massachusetts, 1842, 4 Metcalf, 111.
Commonwealth *v.* Perry, Massachusetts, 1891, 28 N. E., 1126.
Cumberland Glass Mfg. Co. *v.* Glass Bottle Blowers' Association, New Jersey, 1899, 46 Atl., 208.
Curran *v.* Galen, New York, 1897, 46 N. E., 297.
Dalton, *In re,* Kansas, 1899, 59 Pac., 336.
Eden *v.* People, Illinois, 1896, 43 N. E., 1108.
Erdman *v.* Mitchell, Pennsylvania, 1903, 56 Atl., 327.
Farmers' Loan and Trust Co. *v.* No. Pacific Ry. Co., U. S. Circ. Ct., 1894, 60 Fed., 803.

Flaccus *v.* Smith, Pennsylvania, 1901, 48 Atl., 894.
Fletcher Co. *v.* International Association, New Jersey, 1903, 55 Atl., 1077.
Frorer *v.* People, Illinois, 1892, 31 N. E., 395.
Gillespie *v.* People, Illinois, 1900, 58 N. E., 1007.
Godcharles *v.* Wigeman, Pennsylvania, 1886, 6 Atl., 354.
Gray *v.* Building Trades Council, Minnesota, 1903, 97 N. W., 663.
Gulf Bag Co. *v.* Suttner, U. S. Circ. Ct., 1903, 124 Fed., 467.
Holden *v.* Hardy, Utah, 1896, 46 Pac., 756.
Holden *v.* Hardy, U. S. Sup. Ct., 1898, 169 U. S., 366.
Hopkins *v.* Oxley Stave Co., U. S. Circ. Ct. of Ap., 1897, 83 Fed., 912.
Hundley *v.* Louisville & N. Ry. Co., Kentucky, 1898, 48 S. W., 429.
International Text-Book Co. *v.* Weissinger, Indiana, 1902, 65 N. E., 521.
Jacobs, *In re*, New York, 1885, 98 N. Y., 98.
Jacobs *v.* Cohen, New York, 1905, 76 N. E., 5.
Jentzsch, *Ex parte*, California, 1896, 44 Pac., 803.
Jersey City Printing Co. *v.* Cassidy, New Jersey, 1902, 53 Atl., 230.
Johnson *v.* Goodyear Mining Co., California, 1899, 59 Pac., 304.
Jones *v.* VanWinkle, Georgia, 1908, 62 S. E., 236.
Jordahl *v.* Hayda, California, 1905, 82 Pac., 1079.
Karges Furniture Co. *v.* Wood-Workers' Union, Indiana, 1905, 75 N. E., 877.
King *v.* Ohio & Miss. Ry. Co., U. S. Circ. Ct., 1877, 7 Biss., 529.
Knoxville Iron Co. *v.* Harbison, U. S. Sup. Ct., 1901, 183 U. S., 13.
Lennon, *Ex parte*, U. S. Sup. Ct., 1897, 166 U. S., 548.
Lindsay & Co. *v.* Montana F. of L., Montana, 1908, 96 Pac., 127.
Lochner *v.* People of the State of New York, U. S. Sup. Ct., 1905, 198 U. S., 45.
Loewe *v.* California F. of L., U. S. Circ. Ct., 1905, 139 Fed., 71.
Loewe *v.* Lawlor, U. S. Circ. Ct., 1906, 148 Fed., 924.
Loewe *v.* Lawlor, U. S. Sup. Ct., 1908, 208 U. S., 274.
McCain *v.* State, Georgia, 1907, 58 S. E., 550.
McLean *v.* State, Arkansas, 1906, 98 S. W., 729.
McLean *v.* State, U. S. Sup. Ct., 1909, 29 Sup. Ct. Rep., 206.
Marx & Haas Co. *v.* Watson, Missouri, 1902, 67 S. W., 391.
Morgan, *In re*, Colorado, 1899, 58 Pac., 1071.
Muller *v.* State of Oregon, U. S. Sup. Ct., 1908, 208 U. S., 412.
National Protective Association *v.* Cumming, New York, 1902, 63 N. E., 369.
Newman, *Ex parte*, California, 1858, 9 Cal., 502.
O'Brien *v.* People, Illinois, 1905, 75 N. E., 108.
Old Dominion S. S. Co. *v.* McKenna, U. S. Circ. Ct., 1887, 18 Abbott N. C., 262.
O'Neil *v.* Behanna, Pennsylvania, 1897, 37 Atl., 843.

CHAPTER I

Introduction

To the thoughtful observer of the relations between employers and their employees, the conclusion is inevitable that American courts are taking a more and more active part in labor disputes. The number of cases carried into court for settlement is constantly growing, the variety and complexity of the questions raised for adjudication is becoming ever greater, and the importance of the interests involved is steadily increasing.

Until the end of the first quarter of the nineteenth century a labor dispute was rarely carried to court. Moreover, the few that were brought for adjudication were finally settled in the lower courts without appeal. Consequently, the outcome of these cases and the opinions of the judges who decided them excited little attention. Most of these cases arose under the law against conspiracies, and may now be studied in the recently-published *Documentary History of American Industrial Society.*

The second and third quarters of the century were somewhat richer in litigation between employers and employees, but even in this period the custom of appealing such cases had not been formed, and consequently the progress of the law was slow. It was only in the last quarter of the century that labor cases became really numerous. Since about 1875 the growth has been rapid. The difficulty in studying the opinions for this last period arises not from the dearth but from the wealth of the material. The perfected system of reporting brings into print the entire output of our whole court system, federal and state, and makes the study one to which but few can devote the necessary time.

At the present time, neither employer nor employee hesitates to appeal to the courts when he thinks it will be to his advantage. To each of the parties the court becomes a means of furthering its ends. It is probably not overstating the truth to say that while the appeals are made in the name of justice, they are in fact made in the hope of gaining an advantage without particular regard to justice. It will at once appear that the court is, as a result, placed in an exceedingly delicate position. Where two parties are seeking its aid for their own advantage, one of them is sure to be dissatisfied with the outcome. Each possesses its own peculiar political influence, and each is disposed to use that influence in its own cause. But the real importance of the court does not lie primarily in this phase of the situation. The court must stand between the parties and reduce the contest to a basis of justice, but it must also prevent the struggle from becoming one peculiar to the special interests involved and must keep it upon the broad and even level of all social conflict. Society cannot stand by and allow the struggle to become a specialized one. It can not permit the "rules of war" to become effective. This task of regulation must be assigned to the courts, and the courts must accomplish it in accordance with their own established methods of procedure. How are they succeeding in this difficult task? Is any progress evident? If so, along what lines and with what degree of speed? No categorical answers to these questions can be given. The many independent state courts of last resort do not agree. The numerous federal courts present the same situation, and the cases that have been carried up to the federal supreme court are comparatively few in number. This confusion is recognized by the courts themselves, as is shown by a few citations from their opinions:

> Many other illustrations might be given, but the foregoing suffice to show the confusion among different courts. (State *ex rel.* Zillmer *v.* Kreutzberg.)
>
> We are not inclined to follow the reasoning of the court in that case, although it is well considered and ably presented. (State *v.* Buchanan.)
>
> The case is well considered and ably presented, but is, we think, borne down by the weight of authority and sound reason. (State *v.* Muller.)
>
> While we entertain a profound respect for the courts of our sister states, we do not feel called upon to yield our conviction of right to a blind adherence to precedent; especially when they are, in our opinion, opposed to principle; and the reasoning by which they are endeavored to be supported is by no means satisfactory or convincing. (*Ex parte* Newman.)
>
> In *In re* Morgan it is contended by the learned judge . . . that the conclusion reached in Commonwealth *v.* Hamilton Mfg. Co. is in conflict with the later case by the same court in Commonwealth *v.* Perry. A careful analysis of the Perry Case makes it clearly apparent that there is no such conflict. It neither refers to, nor in any manner criticizes, the correctness of the conclusions reached in the Hamilton Case. (State *v.* Cantwell.)

The student desires a clear statement of underlying principles, but this the opinions never afford, or only as *obiter dicta*—the views of the writer of the opinion—having a more or less indirect bearing upon the case at bar. As one judge expresses it, the court is not

> called upon to lay down general rules by which labor organizations should be governed in their relations to the business interests of the country and to society. We are to deal alone with the facts presented in this particular case, and the prin-

ciples of the law by which they shall be governed. (Jordahl *v.* Hayda.)

The lawyer insists that such utterances of general principles or discussions of principles, unless they have a very direct bearing on the case at bar, have no weight. Doubtless *as law* they have none; and recognition of this fact is important to one who seeks to sustain his contention before a court by citing legal authority. The *obiter dicta,* however, are of great importance for the light they throw upon the development of principles. A suggestion made by one judge, entirely aside, it may be, from the main issue, has its influence upon another judge, who reads the opinion. The *obiter* may be accepted by him and woven into the fabric of his argument on another case, or it may be noticed only for purposes of refutation. So by degrees it works its way into the general field of discussion and, possibly quite unconsciously, becomes a part of the mental attitude of judges toward similar cases as they arise. At last it may receive recognition as an accepted legal principle. It is because of the possibility of such development that *obiter dicta* are of consequence. Viewed in this light the animadversions of judges on social, political or economic topics take on a peculiar interest. For this reason they have been inserted in the extracts in addition to the more generally accepted rules of law.

Decided cases are, in some sense, evidence of what the law is. We say in some sense, because it is not so much the decision as it is the reasoning upon which the decision is based, which makes it authority, and requires it to be respected. (Bryan *v.* Berry.)

But obiters have a value, for they show the drift of the judicial mind, and indicate what the decisions will be when certain questions get fairly before the courts. (Cogley, *The Law of Strikes, Lockouts, and Labor Organizations*, p. 229.)

When read in this light, the decisions reveal a most interesting variety in points of view, in lines of argument, and in the emphasis assigned to particular considerations. In the midst of such variety there is slowly developing, however, a uniformity of underlying principle, and it is this line of development that is of utmost importance. No concise statement can yet be made of these deep-seated, far-reaching principles, for their formulation is not yet perfected. That the principles are being developed, however, through which fundamental ideas of justice may be applied to the ever new and ever more complex conditions of industrial life, no one who studies the opinions will deny. This process will be of increasing importance, for the principles so evolved must prevail; they can be set aside only by a revolution of our form of government and society. These basic principles, newly stated, sum up the political, economic and social philosophy of the past and apply it to the present. Upon the courts then we must rely for the slow but finally satisfactory solution of many of the difficulties involved in our industrial strife.

The following study of the opinions in labor cases reveals three facts of tremendous importance:

(1) The judges of our courts have been too greatly influenced by precedents set in decisions applicable to conditions that have passed away.

(2) There is clearly discernible a tendency on the part of many influential judges distributed rather widely among state courts of final appeal and the federal courts to give more attention to actual present conditions.

(3) The law is being adapted to these new conditions by reading new meaning into the phrases of the constitutions, thus making formal constitutional amendments unnecessary.

The second and third tendencies afford ground for congratulation, and it is to be hoped that they may become even more pronounced, stopping only just short of the point that would endanger our fundamental institutions.

The study further shows, (1) that there are some exceedingly delicate problems involved in these controversies; and (2) that beyond all question a very encouraging degree of progress has been made toward their settlement. That courts so frequently settle particular difficulties in a peaceable way before the conditions have become so acute as to cause serious trouble; or even that they so frequently step in and assume authority after serious trouble has begun—these are not the acts that entitle them to greatest respect. Such work is certainly not to be ignored in any casting up of their credits. But far ahead of this in real importance is the steady progress that has been made in the development of principles and of recognized rules of law. These rules and principles will guide in the decision of future cases. They will also become generally known and recognized as valid among the leaders in the community, thus obviating the necessity of so many appeals to the courts in the future.

A reading of early cases and comparison of them with later ones indicate the substantial progress that has already been made. Organizations of laborers are no longer in themselves conspiracies, looked upon with suspicion and condemned almost without a hearing. As has been said in a recent decision: " We do not find it necessary to enter upon a discussion of the right of labor to organize for mutual benefit and self-protection. All sane-thinking persons concede this right." (Jordahl *v.* Hayda.)

This gain it is difficult to appreciate. Even the members of labor organizations themselves sometimes fail to realize it, so intent are they upon developing their plans for the future. In addition to the full recognition of the right to organize there are running through the decisions statements that would grow wearisome in the frequent repetition were it not for their fundamental importance. Such statements give expression to the idea of equality in an almost infinite variety of form. "Equality of capitalist and laborer before the law;" "The law recognizes neither the capitalist nor the laborer but the man;" "Every one is entitled to the equal and impartial protection of the law." Such expressions and many others of like import may be found in abundance. Some persons may be pessimistic enough to say that they are mere high-sounding phrases, beautiful to hear but empty of meaning, as a very little observation of practical life will show. Even admitting the truth of the statement, there still remains great consolation in the existence of such statements merely as the expression of ideals. But one does not have to admit the charge. While the ideal has not yet been realized in all its fullness, certainly some very real progress has been made. The practical point gained, then, is the recognition of the right of the laborer to do as any other man would do, to act always as a citizen, whether in pursuit of his interest as a laborer or of any other special interest.

At this point the difficulty increases by the very fact of progress made. Granted the right to organize and to act with others in organization, the question then arises, What may be done by the organizations? Here one enters the field of union activity in its great variety and becomes aware of the infinite complexity of its problems.

Here it is that propositions that seem simple to start with become involved in confusion and disagreement at the end. The courts, always guided by precedent where precedent can be found, search for it here in vain. New situations must be met, and in the absence of precedents the course adopted is to seize upon older principles and revise them to meet the new conditions. This has been a slow process, as courts have been reluctant to pass upon any principle further than its application to the particular case at bar. Success has certainly attended their efforts though it has come at times with exasperating slowness. Yet a difficulty has remained that seems as yet not to have been met very satisfactorily. The courts have been modifying and restating the principles of individual rights to meet the case of the aggressive unionist, the striker, the boycotter and the picketer. During this time capital has been concentrated under the control of the corporation and the corporation has loomed up as the rival of the employee, in place of his former rival, the individual employer. Corporation law has had its development in a more uninterrupted way until the corporation, a powerful aggregation in fact, comes to the bar as a "person" claiming all the rights of persons and opposes its strength to that of the laborer as a person but a physical person only. The various methods by which the several courts have met this difficult situation are discussed in Part II.

Efforts to cut the Gordian knot by legislation have presented new questions to the courts. Laws must be constitutional. The application of the constitutionality test has filled many pages of court reports. For a restless, active people, who look upon their government as their own, it is easy to regard legislation as the most effective means of remedying undesirable situations. When the laborers are worsted in a contest for shorter hours, or the more regular payment of wages, or when the community becomes impressed with the evil conditions that surround the laboring classes, the most direct and effective way of settling the matter satisfactorily seems to be to enact legislation. But experience has shown that it is much easier to convince the legislature that a measure is necessary than to convince the courts that it is constitutional. Here again the ancient and time-honored principles formulated by the "fathers" are brought forward as the standard for testing the new legislation. "Life, liberty and property" are to be protected, as required by the constitution, and no one is to be deprived of any one of them except by "due process of law." The development of the property concept is extended to include right to contract, right to labor, right to business profits. These and other "rights" have become "property rights," and thus are protected as constitutional. At this point the court faces a difficulty of importance. From a legal and constitutional point of view it is of great consequence that consistency be preserved between the general provisions of the fundamental law and the various enactments of the legislatures. To the community at large, the importance of such a matter seems insignificant in face of the crying need for reform presented by some of our industrial conditions. Thus arises a conflict between two forces. The legislature seeks to secure the laws at the expense, if necessary, of consistency; while the courts often insist that consistency be preserved at the expense, if necessary, of needed legislation.

Of course very much legislation of this character has been enacted and has been sustained by the courts. The laws that usually come under the general term "factory legislation," and deal with sanitation, safety devices, child labor, and other similar topics are admittedly constitutional. Such statutes are not often attacked in court. When they are, it is usually on a technicality and the decision does not discuss the principle involved. The police power is given a constantly-widening significance and admittedly covers such legislation when the health, safety or welfare of the public is concerned. The issue arises at the margin where the health, safety or welfare of the public merges into that of the individual. The difficulty of drawing this marginal line appears in more cases than one. The battle has been fiercely waged at this point. That some progress has been made is evident. That much remains to be done is shown by the fact that on practically the same issue the courts of final appeal in different states adopt directly opposite lines of argument. The instances of this are numerous and will be found illustrated in Part III.

The decisions when taken in connection with conditions at times lead to great inconsistencies, and even seem to place the court in the position of standing actually in the way of those whose rights they seek to protect. The conservatism of the courts keeps them close to the literal statements of the constitution. Through the legislature the changing conditions of progress work themselves into law often clearly suited to meet the difficulties arising from such conditions. In such instances we have the spirit of progress working out through legislation which the spirit of conservatism working through the courts practically annuls. How to reconcile these conflicting tendencies is a problem not for the courts alone but for society itself to solve. The courts in bringing all legislation into conformity with the fundamental law are but doing the work traditionally and constitutionally assigned to them, but they are doing it in some cases altogether too effectively. It is necessary to adapt to the changing conditions and increasingly complex relations of modern industrial life the abstract principles of personal liberty which were formulated over a century ago and which are embodied in our constitutions.

The courts often manifest a strange dislike for legislation because of what it may lead to as a precedent. In some instances the entire objection reduced to a word seems to be that it opens the way for paternalism. The denunciation is not because of the evil inherent in the law itself nor because of its clear unconstitutionality, but because it may make possible other laws that would be open to such objection. The argument urged by those who advocate such measures is, of course, that each such law should stand or fall upon its own merits, not be accepted solely because it resembles some law already in force nor be rejected solely because some measure similar but more radical may follow. It is rare for the courts to accept this reasoning. Here is a situation where, on the one hand, a law is urged as fitted to meet a positive need, and on the other hand, is opposed as opening the way to laws not needed and dangerous.

A situation still more anomalous may easily be found. It is in connection with freedom of contract. While courts generally admit that such a right is not an absolute one, they are still very reluctant to recognize any new limitation. That is the general principle upon which they rest. The laborer must have the same liberty of contract that others have. Now the legislature charters a corporation, giving it in many respects greater powers than are possessed by an individual. These powers the corporation will use to its own advantage in bargaining with laborers and as a result laborers are virtually coerced into accepting such conditions of employment as are offered. Or it may not be a corporation that has the advantage. An employer may be in position to dictate the terms and conditions upon which employment will be given, the employee being left to accept the conditions without modification or to reject them and go without work. A one-industry locality under centralized control furnishes the clearest instance of this. The inequality of bargaining becomes evident and a law is enacted to equalize the situation. It may be to shorten hours of labor in the interests of health, to require the payment of wages in money or at certain specified intervals, or to forbid Sunday work in certain occupations. Both the community and the laborers concerned may have been active in securing such a statute. But the employer appeals to the court. The basis of his appeal is that the rights of the laborer have been infringed in that he is not left free to agree to work as long as his employer may wish him to, or under the conditions that the employer may see fit to furnish. Then the court hands down its opinion to the effect that any law that prevents a laborer from selling his labor as he thinks best is an infringement of his constitutional privileges and therefore not only void but vicious. Such cases are not brought to trial by the laborer. They are pushed by the employer. Yet seldom has the court appeared to recognize the peculiar phase of the situation: an employer so concerned in preserving the constitutional and inalienable rights of his employees to enjoy the utmost liberty of entering freely and voluntarily into contracts. The concern is so great that he is willing to incur the expense necessary to carry the issue to the highest state courts and, if necessary, to the federal supreme court also. Instead of sustaining a law clearly demanded by the conditions and useful in restoring to the laborer something of an equality of bargaining power, the empty phrase about freedom of contract is repeated and the laborer is in fact turned over to the employer with no possible choice but to work for the terms and conditions offered. It is perhaps at this point that the courts have most to accomplish before the desired degree of progress will be attained.

CHAPTER II

The Courts

A discussion of the attitude of the courts toward labor legislation might be expected to begin immediately with an analysis of cases. But the difficulties of such an analysis arise not merely from the subject-matter of the laws or the legal principles involved in the trials, but from the character and function of the courts themselves. To understand this branch of the government at the outset is of prime importance. This leads to the broad question of the court's duty toward legislation and to its place in our system of government as one of the three grand divisions of our governmental machinery. Thus at the outset the problem takes us far into the principles of political science and their application to the art of government. Obviously it would be impossible as well as unnecessary in this work to enter into a discussion of these principles and their application. It does not seem wise, however, to pass the topic without some consideration.

The work of discussing and perhaps of criticizing the courts is one that must be entered upon with extreme caution. There is need, in the first place, of a spirit of honesty and fairness. Our courts occupy a peculiar position in our governmental polity. Absolute separation and independence of function is impossible. In a very direct and important way the judiciary exercises a deep influence over each of the other two divisions. The courts of America have a right to command, and they do, in fact, command the highest respect of all citizens. To them we owe a political debt that is beyond computation. Without detracting from the force of this statement it should also be recognized that reverence and respect for the courts do not preclude a discussion of their activity coupled with honest and tempered criticism. A worshiping of the court as something superhuman, on the one hand, and an unbridled, indiscriminate criticism on the other, are alike to be avoided. Tempered, discriminating criticism fairly and honestly offered is what is needed and what is attempted in the following pages.

It is a trite statement that courts are bound by precedent. Many excellent reasons have been urged why this should be so and of these reasons many are thoroughly sound. To the constitutional lawyer there can be no important countervailing considerations. Many cases have been decided solely on precedent, even when reason seemed to dictate to the judge an opposite view. A striking instance of the force of precedent is shown in the case of Willcutt *v.* Bricklayers' Union. The decision was made by a majority in accordance with a principle held by the same court in a former case. Two members, the Chief Justice and one other, dissented and a third member of the court, Judge Loring, wrote a separate opinion setting forth the reason for his voting with the majority. In this he says:

For the reasons stated in the opinion of Mr. Justice Sheldon, I should agree with the conclusion there reached [the dissenting opinion] were it not for the recent decision made by this court . . . In my opinion the decision in [the former case] ought not to be overruled in the case at bar although it was wrong, provided laborers and labor unions will not suffer injustice from our standing by it. The evils which ensue from overruling a wrong decision where no injustice is involved in following it are greater than those which come from standing by it. It would be hard to measure the disastrous consequences to the administration of justice if it were thought that a change in the personnel of the court is to be the occasion for rearguing what has been decided.

Apparently the same view is held by Chief Justice Cullen of the New York court of appeals. In the opinion in People *v.* Grout he points out the great variety of labor cases that come before the court and the full discussion that had been given to the principles involved. It is admitted that the arguments used to support the propositions are not in agreement among themselves. "There are at times found in the opinion in one case *dicta* in conflict with that found in the opinion in another." Yet "there is not inconsistency in the several decisions made by us, so far as the propositions actually determined are concerned." Having admitted thus the variety of view and at the same time emphasized the consistency of decisions actually made, the justice adds that in the case at bar it seems that

> no good purpose would be subserved by now reopening the whole discussion of the subject, nor does there appear much prospect that by such action we would finally reach harmony among ourselves. I think the wise course is to adhere strictly to the decisions actually made by the court without further examination of the general questions involved, and regardless of the individual opinions of our several members.

The argument in the opinion concludes that the decision in the case can stand only on the ground of precedent, and adds, "I feel it my duty to follow it regardless of my own opinion on the question."

Courts of one state in the absence of precedent within the state often follow opinions expressed by courts of another jurisdiction when such opinions are acceptable in principle. The instances of this are numerous. The rule however is not universal. It appears to rest very much in the discretion of the court what the influence of such opinions shall be. That is the same as saying that it depends upon the personal factor of the individual judge. Professional courtesy may temper the criticism or the reason for rejecting the view, to be sure, yet the rejection is none the less sure.

While we entertain a profound respect for the courts of our sister states, we do not feel called upon to yield our conviction of right to a blind adherence to precedent; especially when they are, in our opinion, opposed to principle; and the reasoning by which they are endeavored to be supported is by no means satisfactory or convincing.

This view was expressed by the California supreme court in 1858. At that time a dissenting opinion was written. In 1861 in another case the same court accepted as the prevailing view the dissenting opinion of 1858.

In 1889 the supreme court of California was called upon to consider the validity of a statute. In the argument the judges' attention was called to the fact that "this very statute" had been upheld by the circuit court of the United States. The court refused to accept the binding force of this as a precedent, declaring that "while we have the greatest respect for the able judge who wrote the opinion, yet it is not binding on us as a precedent, and the reasoning therein does not convince us of its correctness, nor, in our opinion, do the authorities therein cited support it." Somewhat more non-committal is the following utterance, from the same court, "Decided cases are, in some sense, evidence of what the law is. We say, in some sense, because it is not so much the decision as it is the reasoning upon which the decision is based, which makes it authority, and requires it to be respected."

That previous cases decided in the same state are generally binding is beyond question. That cases decided in other states may or may not be binding is evident. That courts never reverse themselves is of course contrary to fact. The basis then of this binding force of precedent must be finally the reasonableness of the position taken and the relative advantage of reversal or conformity. This lies entirely for the judges to determine, and the conclusion is necessarily affected by the personal equation. The endeavor to conceal or minimize a reversal of opinion may contribute to legal continuity. It is doubtful if the advantage so gained is not more than offset by a loss of respect on the part of those who honor the facts and truth even more than consistency.

What attitude the court shall assume toward the legislature is a question upon which various views are expressed in the opinions. It is also a question of far-reaching importance. The adjustment of power between legislature and court in a government like ours is a delicate matter. It is also difficult to preserve after it has once been made. That adjustment is made in the constitution. Its preservation is largely, if not entirely, in the hands of the court. Constitutionally the question is important. It is of no less importance socially, since it involves the protection and the advancement of social welfare, and the relative ability of legislature and court to secure those advantages. On this question there is no serious disagreement among the courts. At any rate when discussing the proposition as a general one there is always practical agreement. It is when an application of the principle is to be made that declarations appear which indicate an attitude of mind not always in accordance with the theory. Naturally the court will be jealous of any infringement upon what it conceives to be its rights. Further, it will naturally be more ready to claim, than other departments will be to concede, that certain matters come within its province. This adjustment from the practical side has been progressing from the beginning and has been assisted by a variety of cases, not being confined to labor decisions alone. Here again a complete discussion lies outside the present purpose. The determination to exercise their own right is a topic upon which the courts in their written opinions seldom touch. When reverted to the statements are brief but positive that the court will discharge its duty. In such situations there is often implied in the expressions a conviction of superior insight. The legislature may think that it is right. That does not make it right. "Although the legislature," says Chief Justice Zane of Utah, quoting the New York court of appeals, "may declare [the right] to be public, that does not necessarily determine its character. It must, in fact, be public, and, if it be not, no legislative fiat can make it so." This is a typical statement illustrative of the attitude of many judges that the view of the court is the absolute right, while the legislature is making a futile effort to declare wrong to be right. What is really said, of course, is that the view that the court entertains is not the same as that of the legislature, and as the court decides which is most likely to be right, the verdict is in favor of itself.

One other instance of this attitude is found in the opinion of the United States supreme court. The so-called Bakeshop law had been passed by the legislature of New York state and had been upheld by the courts of that state. The United States supreme court annulled the law. Such laws, writes Justice Peckham,

are not saved from condemnation by the claim that they are passed in the exercise of the police power and upon the subject of the health of the individual whose rights are interfered with, unless there be some fair ground, reasonable in and of itself, to say that there is material danger to the public health, or to the health of the employees.

The ground for such a law must not only seem reasonable to legislators, and even to judges of state courts, it must actually be in and of itself reasonable. If the statement has any meaning, it must be that what appears reasonable to others must also appear reasonable to the court. That may seem rather finite, but it certainly sounds more rational to the reader of the opinion. It can hardly be possible that a court can be endowed with a special faculty for determining between the absolute and the relative, and for declaring positively what the absolute is. It is doubtful if courts could retain the respect to which they are entitled, if such expressions were frequent, and really indicated the mental attitude of judges as a body.

It is encouraging to turn to other opinions and there find other views. The danger seems to be recognized by the court itself in Minnesota when Judge Mitchell admits that courts,

> influenced by such terms of illusive meaning as "monopolies," "trusts," "boycotts," "strikes," and the like, may be led to transcend the limits of their jurisdiction, and, like the court of king's bench in Bagg's Case assume that, on general principles, they have authority to correct or reform everything which they may deem wrong, or, as Lord Ellsmere puts it, "to manage the state."

But some courts go further than the expression of a fear that they may become reformers. In a large number of instances there is positively expressed a recognition of the legislature's function as a representative body. Many interesting and suggestive extracts might be inserted to show the wholesome tendency on the part of many judges to recognize that the legislature has a certain province quite apart from that of the court and which the court should not enter. In Parkinson *v.* Building Trades, Chief Justice Beatty of California finds an instance where the matter is "outside the province of the courts, and as with regard to other questions of economic or political aspect, the remedy, if a remedy is needed, must be found by the legislature." In another opinion in the same case, Judge Sloss says: "If there be, in such combinations, evils which should be redressed, the remedy is to be sought, as to some extent it has been sought, by legislation. If the conditions require new laws, those laws should be made by the lawmaking power, not by the courts."

The difficulty of course reaches its climax when the legislature has deemed a law to be necessary, and the courts are asked to pass upon it. That doubt should be dissolved in favor of the law is a principle that has the authority of the United States supreme court. Chief Justice Marshall is quoted as saying in the Dartmouth College case: "In nò doubtful case would [the court] pronounce a legislative act to be contrary to the constitution." The same court in another case (Sinking Fund Cases) is quoted: "Every possible presumption is in favor of the validity of a statute, and this continues until the contrary is shown beyond a rational doubt." (Holden *v.* Hardy.)

Judge Lucas of West Virginia refers to a former opinion of that court in an extract of some length. In their former opinion, declares the judge, it was held:

(1) It is the duty of a court to uphold a statute when the conflict between it and the constitution is not clear, and the implication which must always exist, that no violation has been intended by the legislature, may require in some cases, where the meaning of the constitution is in doubt, to lean in favor of such a construction of the statute as might not, at first view, seem most obvious and natural. Where the meaning of the

constitution is clear, the court, if possible, must give the statute such a construction as will enable it to have effect. (2) It is always to be presumed that the legislature designed the statute to take effect, and not be a nullity. (3) Wherever an act of the legislature can be so construed and applied as to avoid a conflict with the constitution, and give it the force of law, such construction will be adopted by the court. . . . . (6) The expediency or inexpediency of an act is a question for the legislature, and not for the court. . . . (14) The judiciary cannot inquire into the motives and necessities which may have superinduced the passage of an act. (15) The courts have no right to set aside, to arrest, or nullify a law passed in relation to a subject within the scope of the legislative authority, on the ground that it conflicts with their notions of natural right, absolute justice, or sound morality.

These principles, thus clearly announced by this court, are sustained by all the best authorities, by the elementary writers, and by the supreme court of the United States.

Judge Barnes of Nebraska, after referring to the functions of the three departments of government, asserts that

courts should never usurp legislative functions, and before declaring a law unconstitutional, we should be fully convinced that it clearly conflicts with some provision of the fundamental law . . . If after a careful consideration of the question in all of its bearings, the matter is left in doubt, we should resolve such doubt in favor of the law. . . . There is little reason, under our system of government, for placing a narrow interpretation on [the police] power, or restricting its scope so as to hamper the legislature in dealing with the varying necessities of society and new circumstances as they arise, calling for legislative intervention in the public interest. The moment the police power is destroyed or curbed by fixed or rigid rules, a danger will be introduced into our system which would be far greater than the results arising from an occasional mistake by legislative bodies in exercising such power.

Other brief extracts will serve to show the views of other judges.

This statute was evidently conceived and enacted for the purpose of correcting some evil. . . The legislature is always presumed to have intended a constitutional exercise of power; and laws will be so construed as to make their provisions lawful if possible. (Shaffer & Munn *v.* Union Mining Co.)

The courts are frequently confronted with the temptation to substitute their judgment for that of the legislature. A given statute, though plainly within the legislative power, seems so repugnant to a sound public policy as to strongly tempt the court to set aside the statute, instead of waiting, as the spirit of our institutions requires, until the people can compel their representatives to repeal the obnoxious statute. (People *v.* Lochner.)

Whether or not this be wise legislation it is not the province of the court to inquire. Under our systems of government the courts are not concerned with the wisdom or policy of legislation. (Harlan, dissenting view, Lochner *v.* People.)

So, also, if it be said that a statute like the one before us is mischievous in its tendencies, the answer is that the responsibility therefor rests upon legislators, not upon the courts. No evils arising from such legislation could be more far-reaching than those that might come to our system of government if the judiciary, abandoning the sphere assigned to it by the fundamental law, should enter the domain of legislation, and, upon grounds merely of justice or reason or wisdom, annul statutes that had received the sanction of the people's representatives. We are reminded by counsel that it is the solemn duty of the courts in cases before them to guard the constitutional rights of the citizen against merely arbitrary power. That is unquestionably true. But it is equally true—indeed, the public interests imperatively demand—that legislative enactments should be recognized and enforced by the courts as embodying the will of the people, unless they are plainly and palpably, beyond all question, in violation of the fundamental law of the Constitution. (Atkin *v.* State.)

The law may have been unwise or injudicious; with that we have nothing to do. If it were passed by the legislature in the exercise of a police power, then we have no authority to annul the act. (Peel Splint Co. *v.* State.)

A somewhat different angle is taken in the opinion in Wenham *v.* State. It is inserted to close this section.

The members of the legislature come from no particular class. They are elected from every portion of the state, and come from every avocation and from all the walks of life. They have observed the conditions with which they are surrounded, and know from experience what laws are necessary to be enacted for the welfare of the communities in which they reside.

Though in so many ways the courts have given expression to their opinion that the legislature has a distinct and separate province, and that when acting within that province it is not to be interfered with, yet it must not be concluded that this recognition causes all difficulties to disappear. There is the line of demarcation to be established, and that task lies almost, if not quite entirely, with the courts. " It is not for the legislature alone to declare public policy," insists Justice Dodge in State *v.* Kreutzberg. Public policy comes so intimately in touch with constitutionality that it needs but the decision of the court that constitutionality is involved and the court has jurisdiction. That decision will necessarily rest in part at least upon the personal views of the individuals who sit as judges.

The declarations that have been cited above are all in general terms. Some of them led the court to decide in favor of the law before it, others were stated preceding the rendering of an opinion that the legislature had exceeded its authority. The statements of course have some binding force as being the views of judges stated in general terms.

It is to be presumed that these judges would be bound by them in a decision. Yet in practice there is always room for such individual interpretation as will result in setting aside the principle entirely in the case and siding against the legislature.

One other point must be mentioned. It must not be overlooked in any discussion of courts in relation to that portion of social legislation that is called labor legislation that courts have in our political polity a definite field marked out for them.

It is the province of the courts, when the question is properly presented, to define and protect the rights of those brought within their jurisdiction. In discharging this duty, judges can only decide on established principles and rules, and are not empowered to create rights or initiate new powers or privileges. That is a legislative, not a judicial, function. It would seem to be unnecessary to state such elementary truths, were it not that other views appear to be entertained by some. (Barr *v.* Essex Trades Council.)

Chief Justice Grant of Michigan insists upon the same point when he says:

The aim of the courts has been, not to introduce into their decisions new principles, but to apply old and well-established ones, for the equal protection of all persons, [and quotes Judge Ashurst in saying] "Where cases are new in their principle, then I admit that it is necessary to have recourse to legislative interposition in order to remedy the grievance; but where the case is only new in the instance, and the only question is upon the application of a principle recognized in the law to such new case, it will be just as competent to courts of justice to apply the principle to any case which may arise two centuries hence as it was two centuries ago. If it were not so, we ought to blot out of our law books one-fourth part of the cases that are to be found in them." (Beck *v.* Railway Teamsters.)

To what extent courts are amenable to public opinion is a matter of great importance, and one that has not been passed entirely without comment. Judge Vann of New York says:

The prejudice said to exist in some minds against interference by courts of equity in labor disputes should not be heeded; for if, upon well-settled principles, the courts have jurisdiction, they must exercise it, or refuse to do their duty. Public opinion may express itself in legislation, but not in judicial decisions.

Justice Holmes says, in dissenting from the majority opinion of the United States supreme court which held against the New York Bakeshop law,

This case is decided upon an economic theory which a large part of the country does not entertain. If it were a question whether I agree with that theory, I should desire to study it further and long before making up my mind. But I do not conceive that to be my duty, because I strongly believe that my agreement or disagreement has nothing to do with the right of a majority to embody their opinions in law. It is settled by various decisions of this court that state constitutions and state laws may regulate life in many ways which we as legislators might think as injudicious, or if you like as tyrannical, as this, and which, equally with this, interfere with the liberty to contract. . . . Some of these laws [instances of legal infringement on right to contract just referred to] embody convictions or prejudices which judges are likely to share. Some may not. But a Constitution is not intended to embody a particular economic theory, whether of paternalism and the organic relation of the citizen to the state or of *laissez faire*. It is made for people of fundamentally different views, and the accident of our finding certain opinions natural and familiar, or novel, and even shocking, ought not to conclude our judgment upon the question whether statutes embodying them conflict with the Constitution of the United States.

Further in indicating this conformity to a public opinion there is the recent utterance of Chief Justice Cullen of New York:

I fear that the many outrages of labor organizations, or of some of their members, have not only excited just indignation, but at times have frightened courts into plain legal inconsistencies, and into the enunciation of doctrines, which, if asserted in litigations arising under any other subject than labor legislation, would meet scant courtesy or consideration.

Judge Holmes, when sitting on the Massachusetts bench, spoke of "judicial reasonings" as seeming to him "often to be inadequate."

The true grounds of decision are considerations of policy and of social advantage, and it is vain to suppose that solutions can be attained merely by logic and general propositions of law which nobody disputes. Propositions as to public policy rarely are unanimously accepted, and still more rarely if ever are capable of unanswerable proof. They require a special training to enable anyone even to form an intelligent opinion about them.

To bring this chapter to a close and also to come back to the point of starting, perhaps the whole matter of difficulty has been expressed best by Chief Justice Parker of New York. After stating the view already quoted in this chapter to the effect that the court is bound to consider favorably the opinions of legislatures, he refers to the courts in more general terms.

In the early history of this country eminent writers gave expression to the fear that the power of the courts to set aside the enactments of the representatives chosen to legislate for the people would in the end prove a weak point in our governmental system, because of the difficulty of keeping the exercise of such great power within its legitimate bounds. So far in our judicial history it must be said that the courts have, in the main, been conservative in passing upon legislation attacked as unconstitutional; but occasionally, and especially when a case is one on the border line, it is quite possible that the judgment of the court that the legislation is unwise may operate to carry the decision to the wrong side of that border line. Certain it is that the courts have greatly extended their jurisdiction over many administrative acts that were originally supposed not to present cases for the court to pass upon, and in that way the courts have come to play a very important part in state and municipal administration.

Confronted with the varied expressions quoted in the preceding pages, one is justified in concluding that the courts are not sure of themselves and that there is lack of unanimity in their views. This must not be attributed to the inefficiency of the courts. The courts are feeling their way into new fields. The whirl and eddy of reform confuse judges as they confuse all of us. It is difficult to distinguish the real current that embodies the forward movement. Naturally the responsibility that goes with the heavy duty of deciding these weighty questions tends to conservatism. It is natural as it is right that courts should adopt for a motto: "It is better that a thing should be done rightly than that it should be done quickly." In an effort to refute the "criticism of the law's obsolete and archaic features" the critics are reminded that "the law in altering its wonted usage or in deviating from its fixed policies resembles time somewhat which, as Bacon says, 'innovateth greatly but slowly and by degrees scarce to be perceived.'"[1]

[1] Mahon, "The Law an Expansive Science," *American Law Rev.*, vol. xli, p. 685, Sept.-Oct., 1907.

It is doubtless true that many judges, as well as other citizens, view the courts as the bulwark against extremes of radicalism, paternalism, or even socialism. Insofar as the courts serve this purpose they are of inestimable value. When judges, however, go so far as to insist on the necessity of a literal preservation of the ideas of the past unchanged, there immediately arises grave danger that the bulwark of defense may become an engine of obstruction. Much of the past is of value, but the present loudly demands changes in the direction of a greater degree of socialization and an acceptance of newer ideas of justice and equality. Yet a conserving force in the midst of these changes is necessary. Things social must be held together while they are progressing. The social unity so far as it has been attained must be preserved. Considering how difficult it is to strike a balance between preserving the good that has been achieved in the past and keeping the way open for greater good in the future, we must recognize the valuable service which our courts are performing. The responsibility which rests upon them is enormous, and it is only in the light of this responsibility that their decisions can fairly be judged. It is with full recognition of these considerations that the work of the following chapters is now entered upon.

CHAPTER III

EARLY CASES—1800-1850

LABOR trials are now so frequent that they often fail to receive the attention they deserve. It was not so in the beginning of our national history. During the half-century between 1800 and 1850 less than two score trials occurred of which record has been preserved. In variety too the contrast is striking. Every possible phase of difficulty comes finally to the courts in these days. The early cases dealt with but one problem, conspiracy.[1]

The circumstances of most of these early cases were similar. The workingmen had formed an association. They had refused to work except for the wages that they demanded or for any master who employed a non-member of their association. One case, however, presented novel features. The masters had joined together and undertaken to restore wages to the level prevailing before they had been advanced by a successful strike. Since the same arguments were advanced in this case as in the others, it was no exception so far as the application of the law was concerned. These cases were not decided in elaborate opinions written by the court. Most of them were jury trials and in its charge to the jury the court usually explained its interpretation of the law. In the arguments by the counsel for

[1] A complete record of these cases is available in volumes iii and iv of *A Documentary History of American Industrial Society.* The Arthur H. Clark Company. In these volumes may be found either the record of or the reference to every known labor case that occurred prior to 1842.

each side elaborate statements of the conflicting claims were often given, however, and some of these have been preserved.

The organizations that were particularly aggressive in these early days were among boot and shoe workers, hat makers, spinners and weavers. Eight cases were against cordwainers, or boot and shoe makers, and were tried in various cities in Pennsylvania, New York, Maryland and Massachusetts.

In the very first of these cases, 1806, involving some cordwainers in Philadelphia—the first known trial of wage earners for conspiracy in this country—opposing views of counsel appear in the following statements. The prosecution contended

> that no man is at liberty to combine, conspire, confederate, and unlawfully agree to regulate the whole body of workmen in the city. The defendants are not indicted for regulating their own individual wages, but for undertaking by a combination to regulate the price of the labor of others as well as their own.[1]

The defense asserted that the refusal of the workmen to labor for any master employing a journeyman who infringed the rules of the society to which they belonged was no offense.

> There is no crime in my refusing to work with a man who is not of the same association with myself. Supposing the ground of my refusal to be ever so unreasonable or ridiculous, . . . to be in reality, mere caprice or whim, . . . still it is no crime. The motive for my refusal may be illiberal, but it furnishes no legal foundation for a prosecution: I cannot be indicted for it. Every man may choose his company, or re-

[1] *Doc. Hist.*, vol. iii, p. 68.

fuse to associate with any one whose company may be disagreeable to him, without being obliged to give a reason for it: and without violating the laws of the land.[1]

Each side sought then to establish that the law supported his proposition as against that of his opponent. The English law was cited freely to show that the acts charged came within the English common law of conspiracy and that the English common law held in the state. The defense set up the claim that the English common law of conspiracy was not clear and that the precedents cited did not cover the case at bar. More than that it opened the whole question of the applicability of the common law of England to the states in view of the recent political separation and the breaking-off of certain connections of common law. The difference in the spirit of the law toward working men in the two countries was also emphasized. Finally, the patriotism of the court was appealed to to uphold American liberty rather than British tyranny.

The line of reasoning followed in the earliest case was pursued in substance by the opposing parties in all of the cases. Two questions were always present. (1) To what extent did the common law of England apply? (2) Admitting its applicability, what was the value or even the validity of the precedents cited? The second of these questions was brought more prominently to the front in the earlier cases. In later cases, the earlier decisions were appealed to as precedents.

The law of conspiracy was held by the courts to apply to these cases throughout the period, the only difference being with reference to the extent of its application. In the charge to the jury in the first of these cases the Recorder stated that

[1] *Doc. Hist.*, vol. iii, pp, 150, 151.

a combination of workmen to raise their wages may be considered in a two fold point of view: one is to benefit themselves; the other is to injure those who do not join their society. The rule of law condemns both. If the rule be clear, we are bound to conform to it even though we do not comprehend the principle upon which it is founded. We are not to reject it because we do not see the reason of it. It is enough, that it is the will of the majority. It is law because it is their will—if it is law, there may be good reasons for it though we cannot find them out. . . . One man determines not to work under a certain price and it may be individually the opinion of all: in such a case it would be lawful in each to refuse to do so, for if each stands alone either may extract from his determination when he pleases. In the turn-out of last fall, if each member of the body had stood alone, fettered by no promises to the rest, many of them might have changed their opinion as to the price of wages and gone to work; but it has been given to you in evidence, that they were bound down by their agreement, and pledged by mutual engagements, to persist in it, however contrary to their own judgment. The continuance in improper conduct may therefore well be attributed to the combination. The good sense of those individuals was prevented by this agreement, from having its free exercise. . . . The court . . . all stand independent of both parties. . . . They have given you the rule as they have found it in the book, and it is now for you [the jury] to say whether the defendants are guilty or not. The rule they consider as fixed. They cannot change it.[1]

The counsel for the defense in the New York Cordwainers' Case, 1809, was at great pains to point out the absurdity of some phases of the common law and attempted to show the unreasonableness of holding the customs of generations before to be still binding. The charge of the court, given by the mayor, referred particularly to this

[1] *Doc. Hist.*, vol. iii, pp. 233-236.

view and made it clear that he did not agree with it. The English common law was the birthright of "our immediate ancestors." They had appealed to it in their opposition to England. Further than this, the constitution of the state made the matter perfectly clear when it declared that such parts of the common law of England as well as the statute law and the acts of the legislature of the colony of New York as together formed the law of the colony at the time of its independence and as were not repugnant to the constitution were to continue the law of the state until the legislature should see fit to alter them. By the law as thus established the principles of conspiracy were clear. According to this principle, he maintained,

> there were two points of view in which the offence of a conspiracy might be considered; the one where there existed a combination to do an act unlawful in itself to the prejudice of other persons; the other where the act done or the object of it was not unlawful, but unlawful means were used to accomplish it. As to the first, there could be no doubt that a combination to do an unlawful act was a conspiracy. The second depended on the common principle, that the goodness of the end would not justify improper means to obtain it. . . . The court did not mean to say, nor did the facts in the case require them to decide, whether an agreement not to work, except for certain wages, would amount to this offence without any unlawful means taken to enforce it.[1]

To the mind of the mayor the unlawfulness and the conspiracy lay in the means that were employed by the strikers to force those who did not belong to the society to become members.

A similar view was expressed by the judge in the Pittsburgh Cordwainers' Case, 1815.

[1] *Doc. Hist.*, vol. iii, pp. 382, 383.

> It is not for demanding high prices, that these men are indicted, but for employing unlawful means to extort those prices; for using means prejudicial to the community . . . Upon the whole, that this is an indictable offense at the common law, we have no doubt. It was never doubted but "that where diverse persons confederate together by indirect means to impoverish or prejudice a third person, or to do acts unlawful or prejudicial to the community" they are indictable at the common law, for a conspiracy.[1]

This extreme view reached its fullest expression in the New York Hatters' Case in 1823.

> Journeymen confederating and refusing to work, unless for certain wages, may be indicted for a conspiracy, . . . for this offense consists in the conspiracy and not in the refusal; and all conspiracies are illegal though the subject matter of them may be lawful. . . . The object of a conspiracy . . . may be (1) to injure public trade, (2) to affect the public health, (3) to violate public police, (4) to insult public justice. Journeymen may each singly refuse to work, unless they receive an advance in wages, but if they refuse, by preconcert or association, they may be indicted and convicted of conspiracy. . . . The gist of a conspiracy is the unlawful confederacy, and the offence is complete when the confederacy is made, and any act done in pursuit of it is no constituent part of the offence.

A milder view of the law is found in the opinion in the Master Ladies' Shoemakers' case of Pennsylvania, 1821, written by a judge of the supreme court of that state. He called in question the authorities that had in former cases been accepted. In these no general principle had been distinctly asserted. To follow English precedent seemed unsound policy for the reason that in England workmen had been put

[1] *Doc. Hist.*, vol. iv, pp. 81, 86.

under restrictions so severe, by statutes that were never extended to this country that we ought to pause before we adopt their law of conspiracy, as respects artisans, which may be said to have, in some measure indirectly received its form from the pressure of positive enactment, and which therefore may be entirely unfitted to the condition and habits of the same class here. . . .

The unsettled state of the law of conspiracy has arisen . . . from a gradual extension of the limits of the offence; each case having been decided on its own particular circumstances, without reference to any pre-established principle. When a combination had for its direct object to do a criminal act; as to procure the conviction of an innocent man (the only case originally indictable, and which afterwards served as a nucleus for the formation of the entire law of the subject) the mind at once pronounced it criminal. So where the act was lawful, but the intention was to accomplish it by unlawful means; as where the conviction of a person known to the conspirators to be guilty, was to be procured by any abuse of his right to a fair trial in the ordinary course. But when the crime became so far enlarged as to include cases where the act was not only lawful in the abstract, but also to be accomplished exclusively by the use of lawful means, it is obvious that distinctions as complicated and various as the relations and transactions of civil society, became instantly involved, and to determine on the guilt or innocence of each of this class of cases, an examination of the nature and principles of the offence became necessary. This examination has not yet been very accurately made; for there is in the books an unusual want of precision in the terms used to describe the distinctive features of guilt or innocence. It is said the union of persons in one common design is the gist of the offence: but that holds only in regard to a supposed question of the necessity of actual consummation of the meditated act; for if combination were, in every view, the essence of the crime, it would necessarily impart criminality to the most laudable associations. It is said in Leach's note to Hawkins that the conspiracy is the gist of the charge, and that to do a thing lawful in itself by conspiracy, is unlawful; but that is begging the very question, whether a conspiracy exists, and leaves the inquiry of what shall be said to be doing a lawful act by conspiracy, as much in the dark as ever. Mr. Chitty, in his Criminal Law, the best compilation on the subject extant, very truly says, there are many cases in which an act would not be cognizable by law, if done by an individual, that would, nevertheless, be the subject of an indictment if effected by several with a joint design: yet he, too, says the offence depends on the unlawful agreement, and not on the act which is to follow it: the act when done being but evidence of the agreement. From this it might be inferred that an act can operate only to show that an agreement of some sort has taken place, but not by its nature or object to stamp the character of guilt on it; but Chitty himself admits that it is impossible to conceive a combination, merely as such, to be illegal. It will therefore be perceived that the motive for combining, or, what is the same thing, the nature of the object to be attained as a consequence of the lawful act is, in this class of cases, the discriminative circumstance. Where the act is lawful for an individual, it can be the subject of a conspiracy, when done in concert, only where there is a direct intention that injury shall result from it, or where the object is to benefit the conspirators to the prejudice of the public or the oppression of individuals, and where such prejudice or oppression is the natural and necessary consequence. . . .

I take it, then, a combination is criminal wherever the act to be done has a necessary tendency to prejudice the public or to oppress individuals by unjustly subjecting them to the power of the confederates, and giving effect to the purposes of the latter, whether of extortion or mischief. According to this view of the law, a combination of employers to depress the wages of journeymen below what they would be, if there was no recurrence to artificial means by either side, is criminal. (Commonwealth *v.* Carlisle.)

Rivalry between individuals cannot perceptibly disturb the equilibrium of society. They will fall within the limits of fair competition. But combination increases power. That power may become mischievous to the public at large. "It is the employment of an engine so powerful and dangerous that gives criminality to an act that would be perfectly innocent, at least in a legal view, when done by an individual." (Commonwealth *v.* Carlisle.)

Again a more liberal view of conspiracy is found, this time expressed by the supreme judicial court of Massachusetts. (Commonwealth *v.* Hunt, 1842.) Two years previous, the case had been tried by the lower court in the city of Boston. There the more extreme view had been adopted and the defendants had been found guilty. On appeal the decision was reversed by the supreme court. None of the earlier trials of which records have been found had been held in the Massachusetts courts. They were therefore free from any legal obligation to accept the opinions expressed in previous cases. The general rules of the common law, says the opinion, are in force in this state. At the same time it is true that although the same rule of law may be in force in England and in Massachusetts, "it must depend upon the local laws of each country to determine, whether the purpose to be accomplished by the combination, or the concerted means of accomplishing it, be unlawful or criminal in the respective countries." The laws of England regulating wages and other matters pertaining to laborers,

> not being adapted to the circumstances of our colonial condition, were not adopted, used or approved, and therefore do not come within the description of the laws adopted and confirmed by the provision of the constitution already cited. This consideration will do something towards reconciling the English and American cases, and may indicate how far the

principles of the English cases will apply in this Commonwealth, and show why a conviction in England, in many cases, would not be a precedent for a like conviction here.

While "as a general description" a combination to do an unlawful act is punishable as conspiracy, it is clear that not every such combination is punishable as such. The justice quotes with approval Chitty's statement that "we can rest, therefore, only on the individual cases decided, which depend, in general on particular circumstances, and which are not to be extended." A review of American cases next follows and brings the court to the conclusion that they "are not much more satisfactory." So far as general conclusions are concerned the opinion accepts, of course, the same fundamental rules of law that were laid down in all former opinions.

A reader of the opinions delivered by the various judges during the entire period prior to 1842 looking for economic reasoning, will find very little to reward his search. The situation was regarded as purely a legal one. Such advantage as the workmen were able to secure was only in the limitation of the applicability of the English law, and the not very positive uncertainty of the validity of the English authorities cited. The question of the effect of strikes on trade was raised in several of the trials. In the Philadelphia Cordwainers' case, 1806, the Recorder raised the question whether the advance in wages would not force up prices and thus injure the business of the city and limit exports. The idea of a natural price as against an artificial price is also explained, and it is pointed out that a natural price of wages cannot prevail where they are thus fixed by the will of the few who are interested.[1] In the Pittsburgh Cordwainers' case, 1815, the judge referred to the restraint

[1] *Doc. Hist.*, vol. iii, pp. 102, 228, 229.

on trade that resulted from such an organization. As Pittsburgh is "a trading and manufacturing town" it is especially important that the freedom of all artisans should be protected.[1] Such references as these are rather incidental to the case and one feels from reading the entire account that they did not have very great weight in determining the outcome.

The first extensive reference to this phase of the question was in the case of the shoemakers of Geneva, brought under the statute of the state of New York. (People *v.* Fisher, 1835.) The revision of 1828 had included the law of conspiracy. According to the statute "two or more persons conspiring to commit any act injurious to trade or commerce shall be deemed guilty of a misdemeanor." In the second part of this opinion the real legal question is raised: "is a conspiracy to raise the wages of journeymen shoemakers an act injurious to trade or commerce?" By a course of reasoning somewhat fully elaborated the question is answered in the affirmative.

The raising of wages, runs the argument, is a matter in which the public have a deep interest. The products of labor compose a large proportion of the materials with which trade is carried on. Boots and shoes are articles of trade and commerce.

> If journeymen bootmakers, by extravagant demands for wages, so enhance the price of boots made in Geneva, for instance, that boots made elsewhere, in Auburn for example, can be sold cheaper, is not such an act injurious to trade? It is surely so to the trade of Geneva in that particular article, and that I apprehend is all that is necessary to bring the offence within the statute.

All combinations to affect wages, continues the argument,

[1] *Doc. Hist.*, vol. iv, p. 81.

are injurious to the public at large, in that they dictate what others shall or shall not work for. If combinations of this kind are lawful in Geneva they are so elsewhere. If bootmakers can fix the wage at one dollar a pair they can fix it at fifty dollars. Bakers would do the same, also tailors and others.

Such combinations would be productive of derangement and confusion, which certainly must be considered "injurious to trade." . . . It is true, that no great danger is to be apprehended on account of the impracticability of such universal combinations. But if universally or even generally entered into, they would be prejudicial to trade and to the public; they are wrong in each particular case.

In the arguments before the court in the case of the Hudson shoemakers, 1836, the discussion above cited was referred to by counsel for the defendants, and a rather extended refutation of its soundness presented. This is so modern in its thought that it should be reproduced at length.

Look at the consequences of your decision! If against the accused, you place them at the mercy of their employers—you forbid to them that union which alone can enable them to resist the oppressions of avarice—you condemn them to constant labor for such a pittance as others may choose—you refine upon even ancient cruelty. The time was when the rate of wages was fixed by the legislature or the local magistrates, but you will commit it to those whose interest it is to reduce it. . . . If, however, your decision should be in favor of the accused, you will repudiate this common law doctrine which has been so unnecessarily pressed into the cause of the prosecution. In this you will but imitate the conduct of the legislature. You will leave trade to regulate itself by the mutual freedom from partial restraints of both the employer and his workmen. You will leave to one side the same union which practically exists upon the other, and you will restrain both no farther than public, not private, considerations will justify. . .

To justify a conviction the injury must be to the trade of the whole community. Although Mosier and Sattock may have sold less, yet other masters sold more. The same number were made and consumed. The defendants did not cease to work at all, though they left the employ of particular masters. If they had abandoned all work because they could not get their prices, then there would have been a subtraction of so much from the productive labor of the country. Still the question would remain, upon whom should the blame rest—upon him who refused to pay, or him who refused to work until he was paid? I cannot comprehend how an injury to the trade of one part and a corresponding benefit to another part, can operate to the injury of the whole. I can see the injury and its corresponding advantage, but I can see no subtraction from the sum total. . .

Nor can I see the great danger which some anticipate from these combinations—if the mechanic gets greater pay, I can see how we, who are not mechanics, have more to pay. We may become poorer, but he will be just so much the richer. Yet I can see no diminution from the aggregate wealth of the community. It appears to me that the thing, if left alone, will regulate itself. If the journeymen tailors, by means of their combinations get the prices of their work so high that we cannot afford to pay them, we shall not go without clothes, we shall make them ourselves as you do now and for the same reason, because it is our interest to do so. Nor will our whole city be without bread, because the journeymen bakers are extravagant in their demands. We will make it ourselves, as many of us do now. If they persist in their extravagance, they must either starve from their obstinacy, adopt some other calling or retrace their steps until they find the proper level with other things in the community. If the farmer raises the price of provisions, the mechanic will raise the price of his fabrics and thus the whole matter will regulate itself. The mischief is, when everything else is enhanced in value, that you will attempt to keep any one class down to old values and thus exclude them from a just participation in the general prosperity. This you cannot do by positive enactments or judicial decisions without causing heart burnings and discontent. In our country the protection against such a partial operation of the laws is to be found in our courts of justice and though the remedy may be delayed for a while, the good sense and true patriotism which pervade our whole community render it ultimately certain.[1]

The main reliance of the prosecutors in all these cases was their ability to bring the acts within the law of conspiracy. This they succeeded in doing. In some of the cases the defendants were freed, but not so much because of differences of opinion as to what constituted a conspiracy as because of some mitigating circumstance which in the minds of the jurors made the law inapplicable to the case. There can be no question, then, that the activities of the laborers when carried on through their organized societies were very greatly limited. One man might, of course, stop work. But when several stopped at the same time and for the same cause that was almost *prima facie* evidence of conspiracy.

Feeling on both sides was intense. Each side saw in the success of the other the defeat of those principles of liberty and eternal justice for which the nation had been established. The most impassioned appeals were made to the jurors and every opportunity seized for impressing them with the extreme gravity of the situation. It will not be possible to reproduce these flights. Indeed the reporters themselves confess their inability to catch more than the substance of the rhetoric that was used in the "higher and sublime flights of the imagination, or in their impassioned

[1] *Doc. Hist.*, vol. iv, pp. 303-307.

and enthusiastic addresses to the feelings." Two brief extracts will indicate something of the depth of the feeling. In the preface to the report of the Pittsburgh Cordwainers' case, tried in 1815, is found the following comment made by the reporter.

The verdict of that jury is most important to the manufacturing interests of the community; it puts an end to those associations which have been so prejudicial to the successful enterprise of the capitalists of the western county. But this case is not important to this country alone; it proves beyond the possibility of doubt, that notwithstanding the adjudications in New York and Philadelphia, there still exists in those cities combinations which extend their deleterious influence to every part of the union. The inhabitants of those cities, the manufacturers particularly, are bound by their interests, as well as the duties they owe the community, to watch those combinations with a jealous eye, and to prosecute to conviction, and subject to the penalties of the law, conspiracies so subversive to the best interests of their country.[1]

On the other hand, the title-page of the report of the Hudson Shoemakers' case contains the following:

Trial of . . . Journeymen Shoemakers of the City of Hudson for an alleged combination and conspiracy . . . where twelve patriotic jurymen set aside by their verdict the decision of Chief Justice Savage, thus rescuing the rights of mechanics from the grasp of tyranny and oppression.[2]

The period that is under review came to a close with the law of conspiracy still applicable to strikes and still highly detrimental to the interests of organized workmen. The courts did not succeed in reaching a practical solution of the questions involved. So fully under the influence of the rules of law were they that they failed to discern a new

[1] *Doc. Hist.*, vol. iv, pp. 16, 17.

[2] *Ibid.*, p. 277.

movement. The spirit of medievalism with its antagonism to the working classes and its ingrained feeling that in some way the laborer must be controlled by his employers, somewhat after the manner of a serf by his lord or an apprentice by his master, survived. The ideas of personal liberty, of independence in industry, of *laissez faire* were new. They had been developed by the industrial leaders. These ideas those leaders could express and enforce in matters pertaining to themselves. They did not see that logic and fairness required their application to journeymen as well as to masters. So far as the new nation had adopted them, they were essentially political, not industrial. The period does not reveal to us much progress toward the realization of the idea that in every expression where the word political was used the word industrial must be inserted also, that political freedom before it could be freedom in any real sense must be industrial freedom as well.

The final conclusion to be drawn from these cases has been left for the end of the chapter, since it marks in one respect a transition to more modern conceptions. The assumption had usually been that evil purposes were behind all workingmen's associations. That they could exist for any laudable purpose seemed inconceivable to the courts.

It is in Commonwealth *v.* Hunt, 1842, that is to be found the first judicial appreciation of the possible good in labor organizations, the first suggestion that even a violation of law by their members should not be made an occasion for denouncing the association as such. This portion of the opinion is so important that it is quoted at length.

The manifest intent of the association is, to induce all those engaged in the same occupation to become members of it. Such a purpose is not unlawful. It would give them a power which might be exerted for useful and honorable purposes, or for dangerous and pernicious ones. If the latter were the real and actual object, and susceptible of proof, it should have been specially charged. Such an association might be used to afford each other assistance in times of poverty, sickness and distress; or to raise their intellectual, moral and social condition; or to make improvement in their art; or for other proper purposes. Or the association might be designed for purposes of oppression and injustice. But in order to charge all those, who become members of an association, with the guilt of a criminal conspiracy, it must be averred and proved that the actual, if not the avowed object of the association, was criminal. An association may be formed, the declared objects of which are innocent and laudable, and yet they may have secret articles, or an agreement communicated only to the members, by which they are banded together for purposes injurious to the peace of society or the rights of its members. Such would undoubtedly be a criminal conspiracy, on proof of the fact, however meritorious and praiseworthy the declared objects might be. The law is not to be hoodwinked by colorable pretences. It looks at truth and reality, through whatever disguise it may assume. But to make such an association, ostensibly innocent, the subject of prosecution as a criminal conspiracy, the secret agreement, which makes it so, is to be averred and proved as the gist of the offence. But when an association is formed for purposes actually innocent, and afterwards its powers are abused, by those who have the control and management of it, to purposes of oppression and injustice, it will be criminal in those who thus misuse it, or give consent thereto, but not in the other members of the association. In this case, no such secret agreement, varying the objects of the association from those avowed, is set forth in this count of the indictment.

Nor can we perceive that the objects of this association, whatever they may have been, were to be attained by criminal means. The means which they proposed to employ, as averred in this count, and which, as we are now to presume, were established by the proof, were, that they would not work for a person, who, after due notice, should employ a journeyman not a member of their society. Supposing the object of the association to be laudable and lawful, or at least not unlawful, are these means criminal? The case supposes that these persons are not bound by contract, but free to work for whom they please, or not to work, if they so prefer. In this state of things, we cannot perceive, that it is criminal for men to agree together to exercise their own acknowledged rights, in such a manner as best to subserve their own interests. One way to test this is, to consider the effect of such an agreement, where the object of the association is acknowledged on all hands to be a laudable one. Suppose a class of workmen, impressed with the manifold evils of intemperance, should agree with each other not to work in a shop in which ardent spirit was furnished, or not to work in a shop with any one who used it, or not to work for an employer, who should, after notice, employ a journeyman who habitually used it. The consequences might be the same. A workman, who should still persist in the use of ardent spirit, would find it more difficult to get employment; a master employing such an one might, at times, experience inconvenience in his work, in losing the services of a skillful but intemperate workman. Still it seems to us, that as the object would be lawful, and the means not unlawful, such an agreement could not be pronounced a criminal conspiracy. . . . It is perfectly consistent with every thing stated in this count, that the effect of the agreement was, that when they were free to act, they would not engage with an employer, or continue in his employment, if such employer, when free to act, should engage with a workman, or continue a workman in his employment, not a member of the association. . . .

It acknowledges the established principle, that every free man, whether skilled laborer, mechanic, farmer or domestic servant, may work or not work, or work or refuse to work with any company or individual, at his own option, except so far as he is bound by contract. But whatever might be the force of the word "compel," unexplained by its connexion, it is disarmed and rendered harmless by the precise statement of the means, by which such compulsion was to be effected. It was the agreement not to work for him, by which they compelled Wait to decline employing Horne longer. On both of these grounds, we are of opinion that the statement made in this second count, that the unlawful agreement was carried into execution, makes no essential difference between this and the first count.

The court does not overlook the concern of the workman who was discharged because the members of the organization refused to work with him. This was however a result of legitimate competition.

We think, therefore, that associations may be entered into, the object of which is to adopt measures that may have a tendency to impoverish another, that is, to diminish his gains and profits, and yet so far from being criminal or unlawful, the object may be highly meritorious and public spirited. The legality of such an association will therefore depend upon the means to be used for its accomplishment. If it is to be carried into effect by fair or honorable and lawful means, it is, to say the least, innocent; if by falsehood or force, it may be stamped with the character of conspiracy. It follows as a necessary consequence, that if criminal and indictable, it is so by reason of the criminal means intended to be employed for its accomplishment, and as a further legal consequence, that as the criminality will depend on the means, those means must be stated in the indictment.

PART II

UNION ACTIVITIES

CHAPTER IV

The Strike

First among the methods of unions is the strike. It is the method that has been championed by labor leaders and put into practice by unions until it is one of the most familiar of unionist activities.

But few opinions can be read, however, before it becomes evident that in strikes two separate considerations are involved. These are: (1) the strike as the mere act of stopping work, and (2) the strike as a means of forcing an employer to yield, often accompanied by riotous proceedings through which property and even life are endangered. Some opinions make it clear that this distinction has been kept clearly in mind while others show quite as clearly that the stopping of work and the destruction of property were not distinguished either in the decision or in the opinion justifying it. It is in connection with some of the most riotous strikes that the distinction has received no attention and doubtless there was much in the evidence presented to show that it was of no practical importance in the case.

A discussion of the definition of the term was entered upon most fully by Circuit Judge Jenkins in Farmers' Loan and Trust Co. *v.* Northern Pacific Railroad Co, and by Circuit Justice Harlan in Arthur *v.* Oakes. These cases arose out of the railroad strikes of 1894 and the violence attending them doubtless influenced the views expressed in the opinions. The answer to the question before the court, said Judge Jenkins, "must largely depend upon the proper definition of the term." Definitions are then quoted from a number of authorities.

This part of the motion presents the issue whether a strike is lawful. The answer must largely depend upon the proper definition of the term. It has been variously defined. By Worcester, "To cease from work in order to extort higher wages as workmen;" by Webster, "To quit work in a body, or by combination in order to compel their employers to raise their wages;" the Encyclopedia Dictionary, "The act of workmen in any trade or branch of industry when they leave their work with the object of compelling the master to concede certain demands made by them,—as an advance of wages, the withdrawal of a notice of reduction of wages, a shortening of the hours of work, the withdrawal of any obnoxious rule or regulation, or the like;" the Imperial Dictionary, "To quit work in order to compel an increase or prevent a reduction of wages;" the Century Dictionary, "To press a claim or demand by coercive or threatening action of some kind; in common usage, to quit work along with others, in order to compel an employer to accede to some demand, as for increase of pay, or to protest against something, as a reduction of wages; as to strike for higher pay, or shorter hours of work." Bouvier defines it: "A combined effort of workmen to obtain higher wages or other concessions from their employers by stopping work at a preconcerted time." The definition sanctioned by the court of appeals of New York in Railway Co. *v.* Bowns, and embodied by Mr. Anderson in his Law Dictionary, is: "A combination among laborers, or those employed by others, to compel an increase of wages, change in the hours of labor, a change in the manner of conducting the business of the principal, or to enforce some particular policy in the character or the number of men employed, or the like." Mr. Black, in his Law Dictionary, defines it to be: "The act of a party of workmen employed by the same master, in stopping work all together at a preconcerted time, and refusing to continue, until higher wages or shorter time or some other concession is granted to them by the employer." Whichever definition may be preferred,—and possibly no one of them is precisely accurate,—there are running through all of them two controlling ideas: First, by compulsion to extort from the employer the concession demanded; second, a cessation of labor, but not the abandonment of employment. The stoppage of work is designed to be temporary, continuing only until the accomplishment of the design, and upon its accomplishment the resumption of employment. The cessation of labor is not a bona fide dissolution of contractual relations and an abandonment of the employment, but is designed as a means of coercion to accomplish the desired result. The cessation of labor is prearranged by the body of men through their organizations, and is to take effect simultaneously at a stated time, for the purpose of preventing the master from continuing his business, and to compel him to submit to the dictation of his servants. The definition of the term proffered to the court at the argument, recognized by the labor organizations of the country, was this: "A strike is a concerted cessation of or refusal to work until or unless certain conditions which obtain or are incident to the terms of the employment are changed. The employee declines to longer work, knowing full well that the employer may immediately employ another to fill his place; also knowing that he may or may not be re-employed or returned to service. The employer has the option of acceding to the demand and returning the old employees to service, of employing new men, or of forcing conditions under which the old men are glad to return to service under the old conditions." This latter definition recognizes the idea of cessation of labor, but not an abandonment of employment. It suggests that the latter may result at the option of the master. It does not, in terms, declare a combination to extort, or to oppress, or to interfere in any way with the business of the employer, except as injury might result as an incident to the cessation of service. If the latter be the correct definition of a strike, society has been needlessly alarmed. I doubt if, in the light of the history of strikes, the child would be recognized by this baptismal name. . . .

Of the ideal strike, in the definition proposed at the argument, the only criticism to be indulged is that it is ideal, and never existed in fact. Undoubtedly, in the absence of restrictive contract, workmen have a right by concerted action to cease work to procure better terms of service, no compulsion being used except that incident to the cessation; subject, however, to the qualification, at least with respect to those employments that directly concern the public welfare, that reasonable notice of the quitting should be given. But such is not the strike of history. The definition suggested is misleading and pretentious. To my thinking, a much more exact definition of a strike is this: A combined effort among workmen to compel the master to the concession of a certain demand, by preventing the conduct of his business until compliance with the demand. The concerted cessation of work is but one of, and the least effective of, the means to the end; the intimidation of others from engaging in the service, the interference with, and the disabling and destruction of, property, and resort to actual force and violence, when requisite to the accomplishment of the end, being the other, and more effective, means employed. It is idle to talk of a peaceable strike. None such ever occurred. The suggestion is impeachment of intelligence. From first to last, from the earliest recorded strike to that in the state of West Virginia, which proceeded simultaneously with the argument of this motion, to that at Connellsville, Pa., occurring as I write, force and turbulance, violence and outrage, arson and murder, have been associated with the strike as its natural and inevitable concomitants. No strike can be effective without compulsion and force. That compulsion can come only through intimidation. A strike without violence would equal the representation of the tragedy of Hamlet with the part of Hamlet omitted. . . . It has well been said that the wit of man could not devise a legal strike, because compulsion is the leading idea of it. A strike is essentially a conspiracy to extort by violence; the means employed to effect the end being not only the cessation of labor by the conspirators, but the necessary prevention of labor by those who are willing to assume their places, and, as a last resort, and in many instances an essential element of success, the disabling and destruction of the property of the master; and so, by intimidation and by the compulsion of force, to accomplish the end designed. I know of no peaceable strike. I think no strike was ever heard of that was or could be successful unaccompanied by intimidation and violence. . . .

" The common rule," says Mr. Justice Brewer, " as to strikes is this: Not merely do the employees quit the employment, and thus handicap the employer in the use of his property, and perhaps in the discharge of duties which he owes to the public, but they also forcibly prevent others from taking their places. It is useless to say that they only advise; no man is misled."

These extreme views and the definition of a strike as formulated by Judge Jenkins came up for discussion in the appeal that was taken of this case to the circuit court of appeals. Justice Harlan wrote the opinion. Since the case had arisen over the violation of an injunction against a strike, the justice raises the question, "What is to be deemed a strike, within the meaning of the order of the circuit court?" The definitions in the former opinion are then quoted in review. The conclusion is:

We are not prepared, in the absence of evidence, to hold, as matter of law, that a combination among employees, having for its object their orderly withdrawal in large numbers or in a body from the service of their employers, on account simply of a reduction in their wages, is not a " strike " within the meaning of the word as commonly used. [Quoting Sir James Hannan (of the Queen's Bench) in support of this modified view], A " strike " is properly defined as a " simultaneous cessation of work on the part of the workmen."

As a result of the difference of definition, the injunction

issued by Judge Jenkins was modified by Justice Harlan, so as to indicate more clearly what acts in connection with the strike were enjoined.

The above cases enter more fully into the discussion of the definition of a strike than do any others. The statements of Judge Jenkins here quoted indicate a more extreme view than would be accepted by the judges in general. The views of others must be gathered, however, by inference from their opinions. Typical statements are the following: "to cease working in a body by prearrangement until a grievance is redressed." (Cumming Case.) "A combination not to work for an employer, that is to say, of a strike." (Reynolds *v.* Davis.)

Accepting, as the courts generally do, the more liberal definition of a strike, evidence is not lacking that it is not in itself illegal. Unless accompanied by acts that are in themselves unlawful the strike is not denounced by the courts. "It is settled, however," says Judge Loring of Massachusetts, "that laborers have a right to organize as labor unions to promote their welfare. Further, there is no question of the general right of a labor union to strike. On the other hand, it is settled that some strikes by a labor union are illegal." (Pickett *v.* Walsh.) And again the same judge states: "It is settled in this commonwealth that the legality of a combination not to work for an employer, that is to say, of a strike, depends upon the purpose for which the combination is formed—the purpose for which the employees strike." (Reynolds *v.* Davis.)

Judge Mitchell of Minnesota has defended the strike on individualist grounds in the following words:

It is perfectly lawful for any man (unless under contract obligation, or unless his employment charges him with some public duty) to refuse to work for or to deal with any man or class of men, as he sees fit. This doctrine is founded upon the fundamental right of every man to conduct his own business in his own way, subject only to the condition that he does not interfere with the legal rights of others. And as has been already said, the right which one man may exercise singly, many, after consultation, may agree to exercise jointly, and make simultaneous declaration of their choice. This has been repeatedly held as to associations or unions of workmen, and associations of men in other occupations or lines of business must be governed by the same principles. (Bohn Mfg. Co. *v.* Hollis.)

Another basis for justification appears in some opinions resting on the implied right derived from the right to organize. "The law," says Judge Sheldon in his dissenting opinion,

does not do so vain a thing as to allow the formation of labor unions and to declare their right to initiate and by lawful means to carry on a justifiable strike, and then refuse them the use of the only practical means by which their acknowledged rights can be secured. (Willcutt *v.* Bricklayers.)

"If it be true," argues Judge Holmes, from the Massachusetts bench,

that workingmen may combine with a view, among other things, to getting as much as they can for their labor, just as capital may combine with a view to getting the greatest possible return, it must be true that, when combined, they have the same liberty that combined capital has, to support their interests by argument, persuasion, and the bestowal or refusal of those advantages which they otherwise lawfully control. (Vegelahn *v.* Guntner.)

One of the most comprehensive statements of this right is in the National Protective Association Case in the New York court of appeals. The statement is made in the dissenting opinion of Judge Vann and is adopted by Chief Justice Parker in his prevailing opinion.

It is not the duty of one man to work for another unless he has agreed to, and if he has so agreed, but for no fixed period, either may end the contract whenever he chooses. The one may work or refuse to work at will, and the other may hire or discharge at will. The terms of employment are subject to mutual agreement, without let or hindrance from any one. If the terms do not suit, or the employer does not please, the right to quit is absolute, and no one may demand a reason therefor. Whatever one man may do alone, he may do in combination with others, provided they have no unlawful object in view. Mere numbers do not ordinarily affect the quality of the act. Workingmen have the right to organize for the purpose of securing higher wages, shorter hours of labor, or improving their relations with their employers. They have the right to strike (that is, to cease working in a body by prearrangement until a grievance is redressed), provided the object is not to gratify malice, or inflict injury upon others, but to secure better terms of employment for themselves. A peaceable and orderly strike, not to harm others, but to improve their own condition, is not a violation of law.

After quoting these words Judge Parker continues:

Stated in other words, the propositions quoted recognize the right of one man to refuse to work for another on any ground that he may regard as sufficient, and the employer has no right to demand a reason for it. . . The same rule applies to a body of men, who, having organized, for purposes deemed beneficial to themselves, refuse to work. Their reasons may seem inadequate to others, but, if it seems to be in their interest as members of an organization to refuse longer to work, it is their legal right to stop. The reason may no more be demanded, as a right, of the organization than of an individual, but if they elect to state the reason, their right to stop work is not cut off because the reason seems inadequate or selfish to the employer or to organized society. And if the conduct of the members of an organization is legal in itself, it does not become illegal because the organization directs one of its members to state the reason for its conduct.

The extract above quoted from Judge Vann is adopted by Chief Justice Beatty of California in Parkinson *v.* Building Trades Council. After quoting it at length Justice Beatty adds: "This is a most conservative statement of the law. It embraces nothing that is not conceded at this day by even the most determined opponents of the principle of the strike." The view stated here is quite generally accepted by the courts as satisfactory. The additions made by Chief Justice Parker are not however so generally accepted. That Chief Justice Beatty is willing to adopt them is shown in his own statement that follows his comment on Judge Vann's paragraph. "In case of a peaceable and ordinary strike," he says, "without breach of contract, and conducted without violence, threats, or intimidation, this court would not inquire into the motives of the strikers. Their acts being entirely lawful, their motives would be held immaterial."

The strike, as such, then, has come to be generally regarded by the courts in very much the same light as the labor union. Much of the same conditions and qualifications are asserted in the making of their declarations. In Willcutt *v.* Bricklayers Union, Judge Hammond found that the strike which the court was asked to consider had four objects. (1) Increase of wages; (2) wages paid during working hours, amounting "merely to a demand for a shorter day;" (3) all foremen to be members of the union; (4) business agents of unions to be allowed to visit any building under construction. Of these four, states the opinion, the first and second were "properly enforceable by a strike." The third and fourth raise "more difficult questions." The conclusion is interesting. "It is unnecessary under the circumstances to determine these questions [the third and fourth demands] as the plaintiff [the employer] replied with a bare refusal of all the demands. We are of opinion therefore that this strike must be regarded as simply a strike for higher wages and a shorter day."

The point is clearly put by Justice Harlan (Arthur *v.* Oakes) in the quotation there referred to from Sir James Hannen.

I am of opinion that strikes are not necessarily illegal. . . . Legality or illegality must depend on the means by which it is enforced, and on its objects. It may be criminal, as if it be a part of a combination for the purpose of injuring or molesting either masters or men; or it may be simply illegal, as if it be the result of an agreement depriving those engaged in it of their liberty of action; . . . or it may be perfectly innocent, as if it be the result of the voluntary combination of the men for the purpose only of benefiting themselves by raising their wages, or for the purpose of compelling the fulfillment of an engagement entered into between employers and employees, or any other lawful purpose.

There is no question, then, of "the general right of the labor union to strike." But a general right is often a vague right, and courts do not deal with rights that are general and vague. What may organizations of laborers strike for? Here again the answer is not as specific as one would desire to find it. If the object be to secure better terms of employment, it is one that courts will endorse generally. Yet when strikes lead to litigation and courts are called upon for an opinion, the general principles laid down do not vary materially but the particulars modify the application so greatly that the result after all is generally confusing rather than clarifying. The reasoning in the various opinions wherever expressed at all fully is very uniform. One of the longest utterances illustrating this point is found in the oral opinion of Justice Brewer, sitting in the circuit court in 1885. The effort is made to set forth to the strikers in the simplest possible form of expression the underlying principles. It is as follows:

I think a few preliminary considerations, in reference to the common rights which we all have as free men in this country, may not be amiss. Every man has a right to work for whom he pleases, and to go where he pleases, and to do what he pleases, providing, in so doing, he does not trespass on the rights of others. And every man who seeks another to work for him has a right to contract with that man, to make such an agreement with him as will be mutually satisfactory; and unless he has made a contract binding him to a stipulated time, he may rightfully say to such employee at any time, "I have no further need for your services."

Now, it is well to come down to simple things. Supposing Mr. Wheeler has a little farm of 20 acres. He comes to Mr. Orr and says to him, "Here, work for me, will you?" and Mr. Orr goes to work for him under some contract. Now, every one of us realizes the fact that if Mr. Orr is tired of working there, if he does not think the pay is satisfactory, or if it is a mere whim of his, he has a right to say, "Mr. Wheeler, I won't work for you any more," and Mr. Wheeler would have no right to do anything. Mr. Orr is a free man, and can work for whom he pleases, and as long as he pleases, and quit when he pleases; and that right which Mr. Orr has Mr. Wheeler has also. The fact that Mr. Wheeler happens to be an employer does not abridge his freedom. If he is tired of Mr. Orr's work, or if he dislikes the man, or if he does not want any more of his assistance on his place, he can say to Mr. Orr, and say very properly, "I have paid you for all the time you have worked; now you can leave, and seek work elsewhere." Those are common, every-day, simple rules of right and wrong we all recognize. Nobody doubts that. Nobody would think for a moment, in a simple case of that kind, of questioning the right, either of Mr. Orr to quit or of Mr. Wheeler to say, " You may leave." And that which is true in these simple matters where there is a little piece of property, and a single owner and a single laborer, is just as true when there is a large property, a large number of employees, and a corporation is the owner. Rules of right and wrong, obligations of employer and obligations of employee, do not change because the property is in the one instance a little bit of real estate, and in the other a large railroad property; and if we apply these simple, commonplace rules of right and wrong, we avoid, oftentimes, a great many of the troubles into which we come.

Moving on a little further to another matter. Supposing Mr. Wheeler had two men employed, and that he finds that in the management of his little farm he is not making enough so that he can afford to employ two laborers, and he says to one of them: " I will have to get along without your services, and I will do with the services of the other," and the one leaves. That is all right. Supposing the one that leaves goes to the one who has not left and says to him: " Now, look here; leave with me,"—giving whatever reasons he sees fit, whatever reasons he can adduce,—and the other one says: " Well, I will leave," and he leaves because his co-laborer has persuaded him to leave,—has urged him to leave; that is all right. Mr. Wheeler has nothing to say; he may think that the reasons which the one that is leaving has given to the one that he would like to have stay are frivolous, not such as ought to induce him to leave, but that is those gentlemen's business. If the one whom he would like to have stay is inclined to go because his friend has urged him, has persuaded him, has induced him to leave, Mr. Wheeler cannot say anything. That is the right of both these men,—the one to make suggestions, give reasons, and the other to listen to them, and act upon them.

But supposing . . . one is discharged and the other wants to stay, is satisfied with the employment; and the one that leaves goes around to a number of friends and gathers them, and they come around, a large party of them,—a party with revolvers and muskets,—and the one that leaves comes to the one that wants to stay and says to him: "Now, my friends are here; you had better leave; I request you to leave;" the man looks at the party that is standing there; there is nothing but a simple request,—that is, so far as the language which is used; there is no threat; but it is a request backed by a demonstration of force, a demonstration intended to intimidate, calculated to intimidate, and the man says: "Well, I would like to stay, I am willing to work here, yet there are too many men here, there is too much of a demonstration; I am afraid to stay." Now, the common sense of every man tells him that that is not a mere request,—tells him that while the language used may be very polite and be merely in the form of a request, yet it is accompanied with that backing of force intended as a demonstration and calculated to make an impression; and that the man leaves, really because he is intimidated.

If I take another illustration I will make it even more plain. Supposing half a dozen men stop a coach, with revolvers in their hands, and one man asks the passengers politely to step out and pass over their valuables; and they step out and pass over their valuables; and supposing those men should be put on trial before any court for robbery, would not you despise a judge that would say, "Why, there was no violence; there were no threats; there was simply a request to those passengers to hand over their valuables, and they handed them over; it was simply a request and a loan of their valuables." Would not the common sense of every man say that that request, no matter how politely it was expressed, was a request backed by a demonstration of force that was really intimidation, and made the offense robbery? Would not you expect any judge to say that? Would not you despise any one that would say otherwise? . . .

Then there is another proposition that comes in,—a familiar rule of law,—that where a party of men combine, with the intent to do an unlawful thing, and in the prosecution of that unlawful intent one of the party goes a step beyond the balance of the party, and does acts which the balance do not themselves perform, all are responsible for what the one does. In order to make that rule of law applicable, there must be a concert of action; an agreement to do some unlawful thing. If there is no such agreement, no such preconcert of action, why then each individual is responsible simply for what he does. Thus, for instance, if there should happen to gather here on the street 50 or 100 or 200 men, with no preconcert of purpose, accidentally meeting here, and a street fight should develop in their midst, all of that crowd are not responsible for it; that would be unjust; that would be unfair; because they did not go there, they did not meet together, with a preconcerted purpose to do anything unlawful, and, although something unlawful may be done in that crowd, yet only they are at fault who do the unlawful thing. But if they all met, as I said, for the purpose of doing some unlawful act, having formed beforehand the purpose to do it, and are present there to carry that purpose into effect, then every man, by virtue of uniting in that preconceived purpose to do the unlawful tl ing, makes himself responsible for what any one does.

A familiar illustration which often comes before a court is this: Supposing three or four men form a purpose to commit burglary, and break into a house for the purpose of committing that burglary; that is all they had intended to do; that is the unlawful act, and the single unlawful act, which they had set out to accomplish; they get into the house and somebody wakes up, and one of the party shoots and kills. Now, the three or four persons who went into that house never formed beforehand the intent to kill anybody; they simply went in there to commit burglary; but, combining to do that unlawful thing, in the prosecution of that burglary, and to make it successful, one of the party shoots and kills, and the law comes in and says: "All of you are guilty of murder; we do not discriminate between you; you broke into that house to commit burglary; in prosecution of that burglarious entrance one of your party committed murder; all are guilty."

Now that is a reasonable rule, when you stop to think of it; it is not a mere harsh, arbitrary, technical rule which the courts have laid down, and the statutes have established; it is a rule intended to prevent combinations or conspiracies to do an unlawful thing, and where there are many together it is often difficult to distinguish the one who does any particular act.

In 1877 Judge Drummond of the United States circuit court wrote an opinion in which he entered fully into this point. (King *v.* Railway Co.) The strike was one for the purpose of securing higher wages from the railroad and the strikers had succeeded in stopping traffic. Reference is made in the opinion to the fact that wages cannot be fixed arbitrarily by either party.

In the case of labor, between the man who seeks the employment of a man who wants to employ him, [the fixing of wages] is a matter of agreement and must always be. Therefore, it may as well be impressed upon these defendants, as upon all other persons, that it is not possible that they can say precisely how much they shall have for the service they perform, they have no right to dictate to their employers what they shall receive, nor has the employer any right to dictate to them what he shall give. It is a matter of common bargain and agreement, and unless it can be settled in this way we have to destroy all the relations of life. You cannot go into the store of a merchant in this city and say, I will give you such a price for an article, and leave the money and remove it from the store. No; the owner of the article has a right to say what he will take for it, as well as the purchaser what he will give, and unless they agree the article must remain there.

This view is illustrative of the reasoning that may be found in practically all of the decisions where the question is considered. Of course it does not settle anything.

If the employer yields to the employee, then the employee has prevailed. If the employee yields, then the employer has prevailed. If each yields in part, then a compromise is reached. The right to bargain has been exercised by both in all of these instances, and the difficulties are settled out of court. But when one party persists stubbornly and the other resists as stubbornly, neither one yielding to the other, what are the rights of each party? To say that the employer may manage his business as he pleases and then, by the authority of the court, force the employee against his wishes, is obviously no more right than would it be to say that the laborer may work or not, as he pleases, and then, by the authority of the court, force the employer against his wishes. The question that the court has to determine is how far either party may go in its attempts to coerce the other to meet its demands.

Until the recent past, the advantage has rested pretty uniformly with the employer. But with the more effective organization and more intelligent direction of workingmen the employer does not retain the advantage that he once had. The contest is more nearly equal. With the closer approximation to equality has come stiffer fighting, with consequences far more serious following in its wake. What are the rules of the fight? What may be done by means of a strike?

As to one point there is no lack of agreement. Laws must not be violated. Well-established rights must not be invaded. Strikes do not change the lawful organization of society. Strikers still have only the rights of all men; no others.

It must be borne in mind (what sometimes seems to be forgotten by the actors upon each side of such controversies) that the controversy is not a warfare in the sense that for the time being the usual rules of conduct are changed, as in the case of an actual war between two countries. There is no martial law in these cases, no change in the ordinary rules of society, but these rules remain the same as before, commanding what was theretofore right and prohibiting what was theretofore wrong. (Willcutt *v.* Bricklayers Union.)

This position is so obvious and rational that it will not be necessary to cite other extracts to illustrate it. Uniformly the courts stand against lawlessness in all forms, and particularly in the form of destruction of property and the invasion of personal rights.

The purposes of a strike that are lawful are usually stated as Judge Vann stated them in the extract that has been quoted at length. These are to secure higher wages, shorter hours, to improve their relations with their employers. The right to strike is conceded provided the object be "not to gratify malice or inflict injury upon others, but to secure better terms of employment for themselves;" "not to harm others but to improve their own condition." In commenting on this statement, Chief Justice Parker in the same opinion insists that "the enumeration is illustrative rather than comprehensive," and holds that the securing of the reemployment of an employee whom they regard as having been improperly discharged, and employment for those of their union who are out of employment is valid reason for a strike.

These purposes are open to question and the courts are by no means entirely agreed on the list. It is true that certain purposes are admitted to belong to the recognized list, but probably no one would contend that the list is a closed one. One or two instances of this difficulty will indicate its extent. In Pickett *v.* Walsh, Judge Loring found that the strike involved other important rights than those existing between employer and employee. His opinion is, in part, as follows:

That strike has an element in it like that in a sympathetic strike, in a boycott and in a blacklisting, namely: It is a refusal to work for A., with whom the strikers have no dispute, because A. works for B., with whom the strikers have a dispute, for the purpose of forcing A. to force B. to yield to the strikers' demands. . . . That passes beyond a case of competition. . . . It is a combination by the union to obtain a decision in their favor by forcing third persons who have no interest in the dispute to force the employer to decide the dispute in [the defendant union's] favor. Such a strike is not a justifiable interference with the right of the plaintiffs to pursue their calling as they think best. In our opinion organized labor's right of coercion and compulsion is limited to strikes on persons with whom the organization has a trade dispute; or to put it in another way, we are of opinion that a strike on A., with whom the striker has no trade dispute, to compel A. to force B. to yield to the strikers' demands, is an unjustifiable interference with the right of A. to pursue his calling as he thinks best.

Judge Taft holds that even the right to quit an employment is not absolute. On this point he has spoken in two opinions.

(1) All the employees had the right to quit their employment, but they had no right to combine to quit in order thereby to compel their employer to withdraw from a mutually profitable relation with a third person for the purpose of injuring that third person, when the relation thus sought to be broken had no effect whatever on the character or reward of their service. It is the motive for quitting, and the end sought thereby, that makes the injury inflicted unlawful, and the combination by which it is effected, an unlawful conspiracy. The distinction between an ordinary lawful and peaceable strike entered upon to obtain concessions in the terms of the strikers' employment and a boycott is not a fanciful one, or one which needs the power of fine distinction to determine

which is which. Every laboring man recognizes the one or the other as quickly as the lawyer or the judge. (Thomas *v.* Cincinnati & C. Ry. Co.)

(2) But it is said that it cannot be unlawful for an employee either to threaten to quit or actually to quit the service when not in violation of his contract, because a man has the inalienable right to bestow his labor where he will, and to withhold his labor as he will. Generally speaking, this is true, but not absolutely. If he uses the benefit which his labor is or will be to another, by threatening to withhold it or agreeing to bestow it, or by actually withholding it or bestowing it, for the purpose of inducing, procuring, or compelling that other to commit an unlawful or criminal act, the withholding or bestowing of his labor for such a purpose is itself an unlawful and criminal act. The same thing is true with regard to the exercise of the right of property. A man has the right to give or sell his property where he will, but if he give or sell it, or refuse to give or sell it, as a means of inducing or compelling another to commit an unlawful act, his giving or selling it or refusal to do so is itself unlawful.

Herein is found the difference between the act of the employees of the complainant company in combining to withhold the benefit of their labor from it and the act of the employees of the defendant companies in combining to withhold their labor from them, that is, the difference between the strike and the boycott. The one combination, so far as its character is shown in the evidence, was lawful, because it was for the lawful purpose of selling the labor of those engaged in it for the highest price obtainable, and on the best terms. The probable inconvenience or loss which its employees might impose on the complainant company by withholding their labor would, under ordinary circumstances, be a legitimate means available to them for inducing a compliance with their demands. But the employees of defendant companies are not dissatisfied with the terms of their employment. So far as appears, those terms work a mutual benefit to employer and employed. What the employees threaten to do is to deprive the defendant companies of the benefit thus accruing from their labor, in order to induce, procure, and compel the companies and their managing officers to consent to do a criminal and unlawful injury to the complainant. Neither law nor morals can give a man the right to labor or withhold his labor for such a purpose. (Toledo &c. Ry. Co. *v.* Pa. Co.)

These various views may be summed up in the statement of two positions. The first deals with the right to strike, and may be expressed as follows: A man's right to stop work when he chooses or to accept or reject conditions as he chooses is a part of his personal rights. He can not be compelled to work against his wishes (contract conditions and conditions of crime of course being exceptions). This right is elementary. With the right to form organizations for purposes of improving working conditions conceded, it follows that combinations may be formed to do what one may do. That is to say, the rights that one man has with reference to choice of conditions of labor many in combination have. If one stops working because he chooses to, many working under the same conditions, or organized for mutual advantage, may do the same because they choose, even if it is through the organization that they have learned of the advantage and because of it that they have made their choice. The advantage of acting in concert is an advantage that belongs to all combination; combination of capital, of employers, and of all others as well as of laborers.

The second statement concludes that the strike is not lawful, reasoning by the following stages: The common law of England inherited by the United States holds that combination to affect wages is an injury to trade and therefore an unlawful conspiracy. Whether or not a man may cease work depends upon what his motive is. But as one man cannot commonly do much harm by ceasing to work even with an evil motive, the matter yields to the personal right of such a man to cease work anyway. When many unite to cease at the same time the chance of accomplishing the unlawful motive becomes greater. This becomes a basis for holding that the motive makes the strike wrong. Or again, the acts of many in combination increase the chances for success and therefore undue pressure is brought to bear upon the employer. This may be coercion and the wrong lies in the combination of many to do what one alone might do. This may be illustrated by an extract from Pickett *v.* Walsh.

A successful strike by laborers means, in many if not most cases, that for practical purposes the strikers have such a control of the labor which the employer must have that he has to yield to their demands. A single individual may well be left to take his chances in a struggle with another individual. But in a struggle with a number of persons combined together to fight an individual, the individual's chance is small, if it exists at all. It is plain that a strike by a combination of persons has a power of coercion which an individual does not have.

Further discussion would involve the consideration of motive and combination. These points will be dealt with in another place.

These differences find their way into the discussions written by legal authorities. As it is no part of the present object to decide the question of the legality of strikes, it will be sufficient to indicate this difference by two references. Cogley, in *The Law of Strikes, Lockouts, and Labor Organizations,* makes a distinction between a strike and a stopping of work.

While a strike is quitting work, yet it is accompanied with

the distinguishing feature of being done by prearrangement between many workmen to cease working simultaneously at a given time and for the express purpose of injuring or crippling, in some way, the employer in his business. . . . It is evident from the nature of things that the purpose of a strike is to extort, by force of numbers, intimidation and coercion, and by crippling his business by quitting at the busiest season and preventing other employees from taking their places, some concession from the master. . . . From the definitions given, all strikes are illegal. The wit of man could not devise a legal one. Because compulsion is the leading idea of a strike.[1]

Stimson, in *Hand-book to the Labor Law of the United States,* takes the opposite view.

A recent text-book upon strikes and boycotts goes so far as to say that there can be no such thing as a legal strike. The truth is probably the exact opposite. Instead of saying no strikes are legal, we should now say all strikes are legal; that is, all plain and simple combinations to quit work when there is no breach of a definite time-contract in so doing, and where it is not complicated with any element of boycotting, or marked by any disorder or intimidation. When these latter exist, it is the boycotting, disorder, or intimidation that is illegal, and may be punished or prevented by injunction; not the strike.[2]

The development of the court's attitude is evident. Bound at first to the precedent of conspiracy, there has been a steady movement toward a more liberal view. Personal rights have been more fully recognized as applicable. Prob-

[1] Pp. 2, 3, 223. For fuller discussion of Cogley's view see the following pages, 1-6, 98-103, 223-247.

[2] P. 194. See further pp. 177-179, 194-222. This same subject is well treated in an article by Darling, Recent American Decisions and English Legislation Affecting Labor Unions, *American Law Rev.*, vol. 42, p. 200, Mch.-Apl., 1908. See especially pp. 209-228.

ably the rights will be still further extended. "Every man, as I have stated," wrote Judge Drummond, of the circuit court in 1877,

has a right to leave the service of his employer if he is not satisfied with the wages he gets, but men ought not to combine together and cause at once a strike among all railroad employees, so as to prevent the running of trains, because the injury there is public in its character.

This statement written at that comparatively early date, may be regarded as a remnant of the idea that there was something wrong in the combination, something that savored of conspiracy: Men ought not to combine together and do what every man has a right to do. This view is not to be found in later opinions. It gave way to the typical view of the next stage in the development, the view that the Massachusetts courts have developed most fully. In the words of Judge Loring, as late as 1908:

It is settled in this commonwealth, that the legality of a combination not to work for an employer, that is to say, of a strike, depends(in case the strikers are not under contract to work for him) upon the purpose for which the combination is formed — the purpose for which the employees strike. (Reynolds *v.* Davis.)

The most advanced position is that adopted by Chief Justice Parker and the majority of the New York court of appeals in the National Protective Association case. The opinion was written in 1902, six years earlier than the Massachusetts case just referred to. Yet it states in the most unqualified way that laborers may strike for any reason that seems to them sufficient. They need not state their reasons. If, however, they choose to state them

their right to stop work is not cut off because the reason seems inadequate or selfish to the employer or to organized society. And if the conduct of the members of an organization is legal in itself, it does not become illegal because the organization directs one of its members to state the reason for its conduct.

This view is more radical than many judges are yet ready to accept. In several instances they have declined to accept it as authority when cited by counsel in briefs. It probably will be more widely accepted as time passes. The development of judicial opinion as expressed in the cases that have been reviewed certainly tends toward it, rather than toward a less liberal view.

CHAPTER V

THE BOYCOTT

THE term boycott has come to be so familiar in the industrial world that it would seem quite unnecessary to pause to define it. The fact is, however, that while in general use the word has no universally accepted definition. For ordinary conversation this vagueness is not a serious drawback. But when the courts have to use the term the necessity for a clearer definition is apparent. "The most casual observation," wrote Judge Halloway of Montana, as late as 1908, "will disclose that scarcely any two courts treating of the subject formulate the same definition." (Lindsay & Co. *v.* Montana F. of L.) Reference is made in this opinion to three definitions, as follows:

(1) A combination of many to cause a loss to one person by coercing others, against their will, to withdraw from him their beneficial business intercourse, through threats that, unless others do so, the many will cause similar loss to them. (2) An organized effort to exclude a person from business relations with others by persuasion, intimidation, and other acts which tend to violence, and thereby coerce him, through fear of resulting injury, to submit to dictation in the management of his affairs. (3) A combination between persons to suspend or discontinue dealings or patronage with another person or persons because of the refusal to comply with a request of him or them.

"We prefer," adds Judge Halloway, "a broader definition, and one we deem more consonant with present-day conditions," and cites the following from another case:

> I think that the verb "to boycott" does not necessarily signify that the doers employ violence, intimidation, or other unlawful coercive means; but that it may be correctly used in the sense of the act of a combination, in refusing to have business dealings with another until he removes or ameliorates conditions which are deemed inimical to the welfare of the members of the combination, or some of them, or grants concessions which are deemed to make for that purpose.

In Barr *v.* Essex Trades Council Vice Chancellor Green refers to the sense in which the term is used by the unions. The counsel for the unionists claimed that the word boycott

> does not in any way mean, indicate, or imply any threats, violence, intimidation, or coercive action. . . . that such word has a technical meaning in the said labor organizations, and simply expresses and implies that the members of the said organizations should simply refrain from trading or dealing with those persons who oppose such organizations by their own actings and doings; that the use of the word . . . merely advises and encourages those who have earned their money, by giving their services and labor, to spend such money among those who are friendly to fair trade and fair dealings, and are in sympathy with the efforts of organized labor to advance its own interests and welfare by peaceable, proper, and lawful means, and not otherwise.

To this the judge pointed out that

> the difficulty is that these communications were addressed to the public, and indiscriminately circulated. They were not intended only for members of the order by whom a technical signification would be given to the word "boycott," but for the general public, who would read them, and give the word its

accepted meaning. [What that meaning is appears from the following definitions]:

"An organized attempt to coerce a person or party into compliance with some demand, by combining to abstain, or compel others to abstain, from having any business or social relations with him or it; an organized persecution of a person or company, as a means of coercion or intimidation, or of retaliation for some act, or refusal to act in a particular way." (Century Dictionary.) "A conspiracy formed and intended directly or indirectly to prevent the carrying on of any lawful business, or to injure the business of any one by wrongfully preventing those who would be customers from buying anything from, or employing the representatives of, said business, by threats, intimidation, or other forcible means." (Am. and Eng. Encyclopedia of Law.) "A combination between persons to suspend or discontinue dealings or patronage with another person or persons, because of refusal to comply with a request of him or them. The purpose is to constrain acquiescence or to force submission on the part of the individual who, by noncompliance with the demand, has rendered himself obnoxious to the immediate parties, and perhaps to their personal and fraternal associates." (Anderson's Law Dictionary.) "The word in itself implies a threat. In popular acceptation, it is an organized effort to exclude a person from business relations with others by persuasion, intimidation, and other acts, which tend to violence, and they coerce him, through fear of resulting injury, to submit to dictation in the management of his affairs." (Brace *v.* Evans., Pennsylvania's leading case.)

Judge Carpenter of Connecticut (State *v.* Glidden), in discussing the meaning of the term, says,

That word is not easily defined. It is frequently spoken of as passive merely,—a let-alone policy; a withdrawal of all business relations, intercourse, and fellowship. If that is its only meaning, it will be difficult to find anything in it criminal. We may gather some idea of its real meaning, however, by a reference to the circumstances in which the word originated.

Here follows a paragraph from McCarty's *England under Gladstone,* describing the experiences of Captain Boycott as agent of Lord Earne, in attempting to collect rents. The judge then adds:

If this is a correct picture, the thing we call a boycott originally signified violence, if not murder. If the defendants, in their hand-bills and circulars, used the word in its original sense, . . . there can be no doubt of their criminal intent. . . . We prefer, however, to believe that they used it in a modified sense. As an importation from a foreign country, we may presume that they intended it in a milder sense,—in a sense adapted to the laws, institutions, and temper of our people. In that sense it may not have been criminal. But even here, if it means, as some high in the confidence of the trades union assert, absolute ruin to the business of the person boycotted unless he yields, then it is criminal.

Chief Justice Grant of Michigan (Beck *v.* Railway Teamsters) also cites several references to definitions. He does not believe that the term " has no authoritative meaning." On the contrary he states that " the term has been defined by lexicographers and courts."

This list of definitions may be closed with that given by Judge Taft in Toledo &c. Ry. Co. *v.* Penn. Co., and widely cited in both state and federal courts.

As usually understood, a boycott is a combination of many to cause a loss to one person by coercing others, against their will, to withdraw from him their beneficial business intercourse, through threats that, unless those others do so, the many will cause similar loss to them. Ordinarily, when such a combination of persons does not use violence, actual or threatened, to accomplish their purpose, it is difficult to point out with clearness the illegal means or end which makes the combination an unlawful conspiracy; for it is generally lawful for the combiners to withdraw their intercourse and its benefits from any person, and to announce their intention of doing so, and it is equally lawful for the others, of their own motion, to do that which the combiners seek to compel them to do. Such combinations are said to be unlawful conspiracies, though the acts in themselves and considered singly are innocent, when the acts are done with malice, i. e., with the intention to injure another without lawful excuse.

So far as these legally-accepted definitions go, those authorities that express some doubt as to the exact meaning of the term seem to be right. Those who admit of no vagueness would have to reject some of the definitions that others accept.

That the weight of opinion is on the side of the illegality of the boycott seems not to be open to question. Cogley, in the work already referred to, has no doubt on the subject.[1] "A boycott," he says, "is one of the most serious forms of intimidation resorted to during strikes." To the definitions that have been quoted in the preceding pages he adds one from Black's Law Dictionary:

> A conspiracy formed and intended directly or indirectly to prevent the carrying on of any lawful business, or to injure the business of any one by wrongfully preventing those who would be customers from buying anything from or employing the representatives of said business, by threats, intimidation, or other forcible means.

He declares that a boycott, in the sense in which he understands the term, is an intimidation, an "illegal conspiracy at common law and punishable." That this writer has allowed his feelings to influence him somewhat is evident

[1] Pp. 249-290.

from the way in which he characterizes boycotters. He says:

> Undoubtedly every person has the right to select those upon whom they wish to bestow favors or their patronage. But men who will wantonly conspire to boycott inanimate objects, simply because men of their own trade and calling who did not belong to their associations built them, are monsters who place themselves outside the pale of the law and should be exterminated from the face of the earth. They place themselves on a level of the anarchist, whose religion and creed is the destruction of all existing systems of property, society, government and religion.

The sentences that follow grow more rather than less extreme.[1] Much more satisfactory to read are the statements of Stimson in his *Hand-book*.[2] His conclusions are that the boycott belongs to the class of unlawful conspiracies "wherein the intent becomes of importance." It is a combination primarily to injure. "The prime question in the law of boycott is that of intent." From his study of the cases and the laws upon which they rest his conclusion is that "just as simple strikes are nearly always lawful, so boycotts are nearly always unlawful." He uses the word boycott as "meaning exclusively an unlawful conspiracy." [3]

While what has been said above would lead one to believe that there is no divided opinion on the legality of boycotting, the reading of the opinions does not fully justify such a conclusion. There are two quite distinct lines of reasoning, one positively hostile to the boycott, and another tolerant and in some respects even friendly. In the para-

[1] *Cf.*, pp. 253-254. [2] *Cf.*, pp. 222-290.

[3] See also Darling, "Recent American Decisions and English Legislation Affecting Labor Unions, *American Law Rev.*, vol. 42, p. 200, Mch.-Apl., 1908.

graphs that follow will be found the expression of these two distinct lines of reasoning.

The fundamental idea is briefly expressed by Judge Brown of Minnesota (Gray *v.* Building Trades Council.)

A boycott, as generally understood, is held by nearly all the authorities to be an unlawful conspiracy. . . . [The courts] have very generally condemned those combinations usually termed "boycotts," which are formed for the purpose of interfering, otherwise than by lawful competition, with the business affairs of others, and depriving them, by means of threats and intimidation of the right to conduct the business in which they happen to be engaged according to the dictates of their own judgment. . . . The authorities proceed on the theory that they are unlawful interferences with property rights.

Emphasis is laid in many opinions upon the fact that the business is the property of the owner, and that organized refusal to buy is malicious intention to destroy that property. Thus Judge Carpenter of Connecticut in one of the strongest of the anti-boycott opinions exclaims:

It seems strange that in this day and this free country—a country in which law interferes so little with the liberty of the individual—that it should be necessary to announce from the bench that every man may carry on his business as he pleases, may do what he will with his own so long as he does nothing unlawful, and acts with due regard to the rights of others; and that the occasion for such an announcement should be, not an attempt by government to interfere with the rights of the citizen, nor by the rich and powerful to oppress the poor, but an attempt by a large body of working-men to control, by means little if any better than force, the action of employers. . . . The principle, if it once obtains a foothold, is aggressive, and is not easily checked. It thrives on what it feeds, and is insatiate in its demands. More requires more. If a large body of irresponsible men demand and receive power outside of law, over and above law, it is not to be expected that they will be satisfied with a moderate and reasonable use of it. . . .

They [the boycotters] had not the right to say: "You shall do this, or we will ruin your business." Much less had they a right to proceed to ruin its business. In such a case the direct and primary object must be regarded as the destruction of the business. The fact that it is designed as a means to an end, and that end, in itself considered, a lawful one, does not divest the transaction of its criminality. (State *v.* Glidden.)

Again, Vice Chancellor Green enforces the point in the following words:

Mr. Barr's business of publishing the paper, with the incidents of its circulation and advertising, was as much his property as were the type and presses upon which the paper was printed. A harmful interference with the circulation and with the advertising in his paper was therefore an injury to his property. . . . The acts of the defendants directly infringe upon the exercise of this right by Mr. Barr. True, explicitly in words, they recognize the right, and protest earnestly that they have no wish to interfere with him in the management of his business, with such means as he may select; but is it not perfectly apparent that the only purpose of the movement is to force him to abandon his determination to use plate matter in the make up of his newspaper? (Barr *v.* Essex Trades Council.)

The writer pauses to recognize the right of the printers to strike, even to "combine to leave the service of their employer." But the strikers did not stop there. They enlisted the aid of the Essex Trades Council, "which boasts (and I have no doubt truly) of a purchasing power of $400,000 a week." Through the organized activity of the Council the members withheld their patronage from the paper and its advertisers. This was done through a "moral intimidation" to "further cripple the paper."

> To say that this is only advice or an intimation to the advertiser, for his guidance if he sees fit to accept it, is trifling with the language. Advice, behind which lurks the threat of the withdrawal of such a volume of business, could have no other effect than to intimidate and coerce.

The importance of the fact of combination is emphasized in the same opinion.

> It is said that [the boycott] was only the exercise by each person of his right to spend his money as his own will dictated. The fallacy of this is apparent. It loses sight of the combination, the whole strength of which lies in the fact that each individual has surrendered his own discretion and will to the direction of the accredited representative of all the organizations. He no longer uses his own judgment, but by entering into the combination agrees to be bound by its decree.

Of the question of motive or intent and its bearing on the boycott, there is also some discussion. Still reading from the opinion that has just been quoted the following paragraph appears:

> This renders necessary an inquiry as to the intent of the defendants, to ascertain if the case falls within the class in which it is held that a malicious motive in the defendant may make an act which would not be wrongful without the malice a wrongful act when done with malice. From the authorities, the test is, has the injury been inflicted intentionally and without legal excuse? When we speak, in this connection, of an act done with a malicious motive, it does not necessarily imply that the defendants were actuated in their proceedings by spite or malice against the complainant Mr. Barr, in the sense that their motive was to injure him personally, but that they desired to injure him in his business in order to force him not to do what he had a perfect right to do. In this case the defendants have, I doubt not, no personal spite against Mr. Barr individually, and no desire to do him a personal injury.

Nor do I suppose they wish to permanently injure his enterprise, for they undoubtedly want re-employment for those who left him. They only wish, by crippling his business, to compel him to accede to their views as to materials he shall use in the make up of his paper. They in fact claim that they had no intention to injure the business of the complainant, and that their only desire was for the protection of themselves. If the injury which has been sustained, or which is threatened, is not only the natural, but the inevitable, consequence of the defendants' acts, it is without effect for them to disclaim the intention to injure. It is folly for a man who deliberately thrusts a firebrand into a rick of hay to declare, after it has been destroyed, that he did not intend to burn it. If a person deliberately discharges a loaded pistol at pointblank range, directly at the person of another, it is useless for him to say that he did not intend to maim his victim. The law, as a rule, presumes that a person intends the natural result of his act; and this is true with reference to civil as well as criminal acts.

One of the most elaborate opinions against the boycott is that by Judge Taft. It was first written from the bench of the Cincinnati superior court, in general term, with the intention, as President Taft has since said, of attempting "to explain what was the illegality of the boycott." [1] The case was appealed to the supreme court of Ohio and there affirmed without opinion. Presumably the view of the lower court was approved. The view there expressed was later quoted at length by Judge Taft himself when circuit judge, in Thomas *v.* Cincinnati N. O. & T. P. Ry. Co. This view has been widely accepted and is one of the most authoritative statements of the illegality of the boycott.

We are dealing in this case with common rights. Every man, be he capitalist, merchant, employer, laborer, or profes-

[1] *McClure's Mag.*, vol. xxxiii, p. 204, June, 1909.

sional man, is entitled to invest his capital, to carry on his business, to bestow his labor, or to exercise his calling, if within the law, according to his pleasure. Generally speaking, if, in the exercise of such a right by one, another suffers a loss, he has no ground for action. Thus, if two merchants are in the same business in the same place, and the business of the one is injured by the competition, the loss is caused by the other's pursuing his lawful right to carry on business as seems best to him. In this legitimate clash of common rights the loss which is suffered is damnum absque injuria. So it may reduce the employer's profits that his workmen will not work at former prices, and that he is obliged to pay on a higher scale of wages. The loss which he sustains, if it can be called such, arises merely from the exercise of the workman's lawful right to work for such wages as he chooses, and to get as high rate as he can. It is caused by the workman, but it gives no right of action. Again, if a workman is called upon to work with the material of a certain dealer, and it is of such a character as either to make his labor greater than that sold by another, or is hurtful to the person using it, or for any other reason is not satisfactory to the workman, he may lawfully notify his employers of his objection, and refuse to work it. The loss of the material man in his sales caused by such action of the workman is not a legal injury, and not the subject of action. And so it may be said that in these respects what one workman may do, many may do, and many may combine to do without giving the sufferer any right of action against those who cause the loss. But on this common ground of common rights, where every one is lawfully struggling for the mastery, and where losses suffered must be borne, there are losses willfully caused to one by another in the exercise of what otherwise would be a lawful right, from simple motives of malice.

The normal operation of competition in trade is the keeping away or getting away patronage from rivals by inducements offered to the trading public. The normal operation of the right to labor is the securing of better terms by refusing to contract to labor except on such terms. . . . If the workmen of an employer refuse to work for him except on better terms, at a time when their withdrawal will cause great loss to him, and they intentionally inflict such loss to coerce him to come to their terms, they are bona fide exercising their lawful rights to dispose of their labor for the purpose of lawful gain. But the dealings between Parker Bros. and their material men, or between such material men and their customers, had not the remotest natural connection either with defendants' wages or their other terms of employment. There was no competition or possible contractual relation between plaintiffs and defendants where their interests were naturally opposed. The right of the plaintiffs to sell their material was not one which, in its exercise, brought them into legitimate conflict with the rights of defendants to dispose of their labor as they chose. The conflict was brought about by the effort of defendants to use plaintiffs' right of trade to injure Parker Bros., and, upon failure of this, to use plaintiffs' customers' right of trade to injure plaintiffs. Such effort cannot be in the bona fide exercise of trade, is without just cause, and is, therefore, malicious. The immediate motive of defendants here was to show to the building world what punishment and disaster necessarily followed a defiance of their demands. The remote motive of wishing to better their condition by the power so acquired will not, as we think we have shown, make any legal justification for defendants' acts.

A rather unusual line of argument dealing with the boycott as it influences parties three or four stages removed from those concerned in the controversy is traced by Vice Chancellor Stevenson of New Jersey. (Booth *v.* Burgess.)

Coming now to the facts of the case before the court, we find at the beginning of the line of dealers whose right to contract and right to a free market must be recognized, the complainant, a manufacturer and an employer of labor, on the one hand, and a free combination of about twenty-five former employees of the complainant on the other. No one has suggested in this case that these two parties are not wholly within their respective rights in the conduct which they have voluntarily pursued. The motives of the free combination of employees for refusing to renew their contracts of employment, whether moral or immoral, "malicious" or benevolent, are entirely beyond judicial inquiry. Passing a step further, we find the customers of the complainant, the boss carpenters and contractors of Hudson county. If these boss carpenters voluntarily combine to refrain from purchasing goods from the complainant, they would thereby violate no right of the complainant, and the complainant would have no action at law or in equity against them, notwithstanding the fact that this combined action, this entirely voluntary boycott, might cause great damage to the complainant in its business. These boss carpenters might notify the complainant that if it employed nonunion workmen they would cease to deal with it, or they might by their threat of a voluntary removal of their custom in any other way dictate to the complainant how its business should be conducted, and in fact coerce the complainant to discharge its nonunion hands and re-employ the strikers. That such coercion cannot constitute the tort with which we have to deal has sometimes been overlooked. In such case the plaintiff's right of free market is not violated. The boss carpenters are simply exercising their absolute right to refrain from contracting. Each of the two dealers is free, and each has the full advantage of the freedom of the other. Passing still a step further, we come to the employees of the boss carpenters. We have now four parties to the affair in hand, and the situation has become more complex, but after all there is no difficulty, it seems to me, in solving the problems which the situation presents. The employees of the boss carpenters, in the exercise of their absolute, unquestionable right to refrain from being employed, and their further unquestionable right to do this thing in voluntary combination, may from good motives or bad motives notify the boss carpenters that if they take "unfair" material from the complainant they will cease to renew their contracts of employment, and thus the boss carpenters may be coerced to refrain from dealing with the complainant, and this coercion may in turn coerce the complainant to discharge its nonunion men and take back the strikers. Still we have no case of coercion which can constitute the tort with which we are dealing, because at the very basis of the entire series of transactions which we are examining we find only a free combination of dealers exercising their absolute right to refrain from dealing, so that all inquiry into motives is excluded. The tort under consideration, which necessarily involves coercion, consists in a violation of some dealer's right to a free market. In the case which we have now reached, there is no such right belonging to the complainant or to its customers, the boss carpenters, which is in any way invaded. Coercion which results, however directly and intentionally, from the exercise of the absolute right to refrain from contracting, cannot possibly be a tort, because it violates no legal right; it is a mere incidental result of the assertion and enjoyment of a right. Taking one more step, at last we come to the defendants. If it appeared that these defendants individually or in free combination were merely exercising their right to refrain from contracting, then, no matter how damaging to the complainant such conduct might be, no right of the complainant would be violated, and the defendants would be guilty of no tort. I know of no reason why the chain which I have been following up link by link might not be indefinitely extended. The employees of the boss carpenters in turn might be constrained by a most powerful coercion to refrain from continuing in the employ of their masters by a voluntary combination of other dealers in labor or merchandise, but if this last set of dealers were merely exercising their absolute right to refrain from contracting with the employees of the boss carpenters, unless these employees submitted to their dictation, it seems to me beyond all question that we have not yet reached any tort or found any one liable to an action at law or in equity for the relief of any of the parties in this long chain, no matter how enormous the pecuniary damage of such party may be. But in fact we have come to the end of the chain, and we find that the powerful coercive force originating there which draws dealers away from the complainant at the other end of the chain is not the voluntary exercise of the right to refrain from contracting. The pull at the far end of the chain is given by the defendant Burgess, the business agent of this powerful labor organization in Hudson county, when he snaps his fingers and the employees of the boss corpenters against their will are coerced to refrain from renewing their contracts for labor with their employers by the fear of fines, expulsion from their labor unions, social ostracism, and poverty.

The United States supreme court has passed upon the boycott, but its decision was based on its interpretation of the anti-trust act of 1890 rather than on a statement of common-law principles. The case was that of Loewe *v.* Lawlor. It was held that the terms of the law were such as to include all combinations, whether of laborers or others, if there was restraint of trade. Whether or not the court finds in the statute its only reason for condemning the boycott is left somewhat in doubt by the insertion into the opinion of the following:

The combination charged falls within the class of restraints of trade aimed at compelling third parties and strangers involuntarily not to engage in the course of trade except on conditions that the combination imposes; and there is no doubt that (to quote from the well-known work of Chief Justice Erle on Trade Unions) "at common law every person has individually, and the public also has collectively, a right to require that the course of trade should be kept free from unreasonable obstructions."

Judge Powers of Vermont took a position as indicated in the following extract:

That evils exist in the relations of capital and labor, and that workmen have grievances that oftentimes call for relief, are facts that observing men cannot deny. With such questions we, as a court, have no function to discharge further than to say that the remedy cannot be found in the boycott. (State *v.* Stewart.)

While the references quoted and the cases referred to make it clear that the weight of authority is against the boycott, at the same time opinions have been expressed by some courts that lead to the opposite conclusion. These views have for the most part been declared quite recently, and show a tendency to greater freedom from the idea that coercion and intimidation are a necessary part of the boycott. There is one exception to the statement that these opinions are recent. That is the case of Payne *v.* Western Atlantic Railroad Co., decided by the supreme court of Tennessee in 1884. In the opinion the principle of the boycott is fully discussed. It is interesting to note however that the contention was between the railroad company and certain stores. The railroad had posted the following notice: "Any employee of this company on Chattanooga payroll who trades with L. Payne from this date will be discharged." Payne brought action for damages against the road. The employees were not directly concerned. It will be noticed that much of the argument deals with the right to strike and the right to discharge, but the fundamental principle of the boycott as a legal act runs through the entire section.

The novelty, interest and importance of the questions demand a careful examination of the cases and the principles involved. The case turns upon the common law. The first question is: Is it unlawful for one person, or a number of persons in conspiracy, to threaten to discharge employees if they trade with a certain merchant? Would it be unlawful to discharge them for such reason? If not, it surely would not be unlawful to "threaten" it. . . .

For any one to do this without cause is censurable and unjust. But is it legally wrong? Is it unlawful? May I not refuse to trade with any one? May I not forbid my family to trade with any one? May I not dismiss my domestic servant for dealing, or even visiting, where I forbid? And if my domestic, why not my farm-hand, or my mechanic, or teamster? And if one of them, then why not all four? And if all four, why not a hundred or a thousand of them? The principle is not changed or affected by the number. And if it were, who should say how many it would be lawful and how many unlawful to forbid? Nor can it be better determined by effect than by number. To keep away one customer might not perceptibly affect the merchant's trade; deprived of a hundred of them, he might fail in business. On the contrary, my own dealings may be so important that if I cease to trade with him, he must close his doors. Shall my act in keeping away a hundred of my employees be unlawful, because it breaks up the merchant's business, and yet it be lawful for me to accomplish the same result by withholding my own custom?

Obviously the law can adopt and maintain no such standards for judging human conduct; and men must be left without interference to buy and sell where they please, and to discharge or retain employees at will for good cause or for no cause, or even for bad cause, without thereby being guilty of an unlawful act *per se*. It is a right which an employee may exercise in the same way, to the same extent, for the same cause or want of cause as the employer. He may refuse to work for a man or company, that trades with any obnoxious person, or does other things which he dislikes. He may persuade his fellows, and the employer may lose all his hands and be compelled to close his doors; or he may yield to the demand and withdraw his custom or cease his dealings, and the obnoxious person be thus injured or wrecked in business. Can it be pretended that for this either of the injured parties has a right of action against the employees? Great loss may result, indeed has often resulted from such conduct; but loss alone gives no right of action. Great corporations, strong associations, and wealthy individuals may thus do great mischief and wrong; may make and break merchants at will; may crush out competition, and foster monopolies, and thus greatly injure individuals and the public; but power is inherent in size and strength and wealth; and the law cannot set bound to it, unless it is exercised illegally. Then it is restrained because of its illegality, not because of its quantity or quality. The great and rich and powerful are guaranteed the same liberty and privilege as the poor and weak. All may buy and sell when they choose; they may refuse to employ or dismiss whom they choose, without being thereby guilty of a legal wrong, though it may seriously injure and even ruin others.

Railroad corporations have in this matter the same right enjoyed by manufacturers, merchants, lawyers and farmers. All may dismiss their employees at will, be they many or few, for good cause, for no cause, or even for cause morally wrong, without being thereby guilty of legal wrong. *A fortiori* they may "threaten" to discharge them without thereby doing an illegal act, *per se*. The sufficient and conclusive answer to the many plausible arguments to the contrary, portraying the evil to workmen and to others from the exercise of such authority by the great and strong, is: They have the right to discharge their employees. The law cannot compel them to employ workmen, nor to keep them employed. If they break contracts with workmen they are answerable only to them; if in the act of discharging them they break no contract, then no one can sue for loss suffered thereby. Trade is free, so is employment. The law leaves employer and employee to make their own contracts; and these, when made, it will enforce; beyond this it does not go. Either the employer or employee may terminate the relation at will, and the law will not interfere, except for contract broken. This secures to all civil and industrial liberty. A contrary rule would lead to a judicial tyranny as arbitrary, irresponsible and intolerable as that exercised by Scroggs and Jeffreys. . . .

If defendants, by means of "threats and intimidation," have driven away plaintiff's customers and thus destroyed his trade, they have injured him by an unlawful act, and are liable to him in damages whether they did it wickedly and maliciously or not. For it is unlawful to threaten and intimidate one's customers; and the loss of trade is the natural and proximate result of such acts. But "threats and intimidations" must be taken in their legal sense. In law a threat is a declaration of an intention or determination to injure another by the commission of some unlawful act; and an intimidation is the act of making one timid or fearful by such declaration. If the act intended to be done is not unlawful, then the declaration is not a threat in law, and the effect thereof is not intimidation in a legal sense. So too of the alleged conspiracy. A conspiracy is an agreement between two or more persons to do an unlawful act. If the act to be done is not unlawful then the agreement or combination is not a conspiracy. . . .

The question then is, is an act not unlawful rendered actionable to the one suffering injury therefrom, because it is committed willfully, wickedly and maliciously, and in pursuance of a conspiracy to do the injury suffered? Does one render himself liable in damages for maliciously and wickedly exercising his right or denouncing his intention of so doing, if thereby he injures another? . . .

Plaintiff appeals with confidence to the legal maxim: There is no wrong without its remedy. Far be it from us to shake the public and professional confidence in this venerable maxim of the English common law. Its influence has long been and will long continue most wholesome in preventing the private redress of real and imaginary wrongs. But as it is a legal maxim it must be taken in a legal sense. So taken it can obviously mean no more than that there is a legal remedy for every legal wrong, *i. e.* every injury suffered as the consequence of an unlawful act or a lawful act done in an unlawful manner. Neither is shown here. Defendants have merely warned their employees not to trade with plaintiff; if they do they must give up their employment. They had the right to discharge them on this ground; it was not unlawful, but highly proper therefore to give them warning of their intention. The manner of giving the warning was not unlawful or even censurable. The posted notice contained no word of slander, libel or reproach upon the character of plaintiff; no charge or insinuation that he was dishonest or unfair in his dealing. Omitting any attack on plaintiff's character as a man or trader, defendants, in the usual manner, and in a few harmless words, told its employees to stop trading with him or they must stop working for them. The common law does not forbid such an act, nor has our legislature yet endeavored to make such an act unlawful by statute, as has been done in some of the States, and probably in England. No legal wrong has been done; therefore there is no legal remedy. For the moral wrong of the act, if there be any, defendants may be called to account in another tribunal. Courts administering the civil law cannot punish sin or wickedness unless it be committed in violation of the civil law, which is the measure of their jurisdiction.

Nor will the maxim "*sic utere tuo, ut alienum non laedas*" aid the plaintiff in his contention. As commonly translated, "So use your own as not to injure another's," it is doubtless an orthodox moral precept; and in the law too it finds frequent application to the use of surface and running water, and indeed generally to easements and servitudes. But strictly even then it can mean only: "So use your own that you do no legal damage to another's." Legal damage, actionable injury, results only from an unlawful act. This maxim also assumes that the injury results from an unlawful act, and paraphrased means no more than: "Thou shalt not interfere with the legal rights of another by the commission of an unlawful act," or "Injury from an unlawful act is actionable." This affords no aid in this case in determining whether the act complained of is actionable, that is, unlawful. It amounts to no more than a truism: An unlawful act is unlawful. This is a mere begging of the question; it assumes the very point in controversy, and cannot be taken as a *ratio decidendi.*

A majority of the court therefore conclude that the act done, *i. e.*, the publication of the notice that the company would discharge employees who traded with plaintiff, was not an unlawful threat nor an unlawful act; was not a libel; and though done wickedly and maliciously, and in pursuance of a wicked design, is still not actionable, because it was not an unlawful act, nor an act done in an unlawful manner.

There are three other prominent cases that take a favorable legal view of the boycott, all written since the beginning of the present century: Marx & Haas Jeans Clothing Co. *v.* Watson, Missouri, 1902; Lindsay & Co. *v.* Montana F. of L., Montana, 1908; Parkinson Co. *v.* Building Trades Council, California, 1908. The first of these decisions deals largely with printed notices of boycott, and the constitutional right of free speech. The state constitution declares that "No law shall be passed impairing the freedom of speech; that every person shall be free to say, write or publish whatever he will on any subject, being responsible for all abuse of that liberty." Concerning this declaration the court says:

The two ideas—the one of absolute freedom "to say, write or publish whatever he will on any subject," coupled with responsibility therefor, and the other idea of preventing any such free speech, free writing, or free publication—cannot coexist. And just here it must be observed that the right of free speech, free writing, or free publication was not created by the constitution, which recognizes those rights as now existing, and only seeks their protection and perpetuation.

The same right is also implied in another section of the constitution: "that no person shall be deprived of life, liberty or property without due process of law." Following this citation the court continues:

In other words, free speech is an inevitable concomitant and adjuvant of personal liberty,—as necessary to the latter's existence as vital air to the lungs, or locomotion to the body. . . . These terms, "life," "liberty," and "property," are representative terms, and cover every right to which a member of a body politic is entitled under the law. Within their comprehensive scope are embraced the right of self-defense, freedom of speech, religious and political freedom, exemption from arbitrary arrests, the right to buy and sell as others may; all our liberties,—personal, civil, and political; in short, all that makes life worth living; and of none of these liberties can any one be deprived, except by due process of law.

The next point dealt with is the claim that the injury done is irreparable because of the insolvency of those by whom it is inflicted. This point has often been accepted as decisive by some courts; the damage cannot be recovered from workingmen because they have no property which can be attached. The case before us takes a different view.

It is obvious that, if this remedy be given on the ground of the insolvency of the defendant, the freedom to speak and write, which is secured by the constitution of Missouri to all its citizens, will be enjoyed by a man able to respond in damages to a civil action, and denied to one who has no property liable to an execution . . . [The Section] makes no distinction, and authorizes no difference to be made by courts or legislatures, between a proceeding set on foot to enjoin the publication of a libel, and one to enjoin the publication of any other sort or nature, however injurious it may be, or to prohibit the use of free speech or free writing on any subject whatever; because, wherever the authority of injunction begins, there the right of free speech, free writing, or free publication ends. . . . Nor does it in any way change the complexion of this case by reason of its being alleged in the petition "that the defendants, and each of them, is without means, and has no property, over and above the exemption allowed by law, wherefrom the plaintiff might secure satisfaction for the damages resulting to it from the acts aforesaid." The constitution is no respecter of persons. The impecunious man "who hath not where to lay his head" has as good right to free speech, etc., as has the wealthiest man in the community. The right to enjoin in the former's case is precisely the same as in the latter's—no greater and no less. . . . The authority to enjoin finds no better harbor in the empty pocket of the poor man than in the full pocket of the rich man. And such authority to enjoin can have no existence in circumstances such as the present case presents, if the constitution is to be obeyed. If these defendants are not permitted to tell the story of their wrongs, or, if you please, their supposed wrongs, by word of mouth, or with pen or print, and to endeavor to persuade others to aid them by all peaceable means in securing redress of such wrongs, what becomes of free speech, and what of personal liberty? The fact that in exercising that freedom they thereby do plaintiff an actionable injury does not go a hair toward a diminution of their right of free speech, etc., for the exercise of which, if resulting in such injury, the constitution makes them expressly responsible. But such responsibility is utterly incompatible with authority in a court of equity to prevent such responsibility from occurring.

On the same subject of freedom of speech, Judge Halloway of Montana writes (Lindsay *v.* Montana F. of L.) after reference to the constitution,

It cannot be said that a citizen of Montana is free to publish whatever he will on any subject, while an injunction preventing him from publishing a particular item upon a particular subject hangs over his head like a sword of Damocles, ready to fall with all the power which can be invoked in contempt proceedings, if he does the very thing the section of the constitution says he may do. It is impossible to conceive the idea that the individual has an absolute right to publish what he pleases, subject to the restriction mentioned, and at the same time to entertain the idea that a court may prevent him from doing so. The two ideas cannot possibly coexist.

On the subject of financial responsibility, this court takes the view of the case last quoted.

The constitution does not discriminate among men according to the amount of their possessions. The guaranty of this section extends as fully to the poorest as to the wealthiest citizen of the state: and, though an abuse of the liberty so guaranteed may result in loss for which there cannot be any adequate compensation, the framers of our constitution in preparing it, and the people in adopting it, doubtless concluded that it was better that such results be reached in isolated cases, than that the liberty of speech be subject to the supervision of a censor. To declare that a court may say that an individual shall not publish a particular item is to say that the court may determine in advance just what the citizen may or may not speak or write upon a given subject—is, in fact, to say that such court is a censor of speech as well as of the press.

Judge Taft, in his opinion in Thomas *v.* Cincinnati N. O. & T. P. Ry. Co., treats this subject of freedom of speech in a different manner. In this case the boycott had been against connecting railroads. The injunction had already been issued and the case was one of contempt for violation.

Something has been said about the right of assembly and free speech secured by the constitution of Ohio. It would be strange, indeed, if that right could be used to sustain the carrying out of such an unlawful and criminal conspiracy as we have seen this to be. It never has been supposed to protect one from prosecution or suits for slander, or for any of the many malicious and tortious injuries which the agency of the tongue has been so often employed to inflict. If the obstruction to the operation of the road by the receiver was unlawful and malicious, it is not less a contempt because the instrument which he used to effect it was his tongue, rather than his hand.

Though the second case, the Lindsay case, dealt with the topics already referred to, the main part of the opinion defended the boycotting act principally on other grounds. In establishing the boycott the unions had passed resolutions to that effect at their meetings and the following circular had been issued:

All laboring men and those in sympathy with organized labor are requested not to patronize Lindsay & Co. who are engaged in the wholesale fruit business, also distributers for cigars and vegetables of all kinds in Billings and vicinity, as they are unfair. We urge the retail merchants, laboring men, and all who are in sympathy with organized labor to place themselves in position to patronize friendly wholesalers. We further desire to call attention to the fact that Lindsay & Co. are operating peddling wagons throughout this city, and we ask the people to guard against patronizing these wagons. We ask this for your own protection and the protection of organized labor.

This circular had the effect of turning trade away from the boycotted firm, "with the result that the business of the company in Billings was practically paralyzed and great financial loss resulted." An injunction had been granted by the lower court and the supreme court was asked to dissolve it. The court found that "only two acts of any consequence are shown to have been committed by the defendants: (1) They declared Lindsay & Co. unfair, or, in the language of respondent, boycotted the company; and (2) they published the circular set forth above, that is, they caused it to be printed and circulated." The court asks itself the question, What is a boycott? and answers by accepting the broader definitions that have already been quoted. It then proceeds:

But what is there unlawful in the act of the union workingmen of Billings in withdrawing their patronage from the plaintiff? Certainly it cannot be said that Lindsay & Co. had a property right in the trade of any particular person. In this country patronage depends upon good will, and we do not think that it will be contended by any one that it was wrongful or unlawful, or violated any right of the plaintiff company, for any particular individual in Billings to withdraw his patronage from Lindsay & Co., or from any other concern which might be doing business with that company, and that, too, without regard to his reason for doing so. . . . If the act done is lawful, the combination of several persons to commit it does not render it unlawful. In other words, the mere combination of action is not an element which gives character to the act. . . . .

We hold, then, that a labor organization may employ the boycott as herein defined in furtherance of the objects of its existence. If, however, the means by which it enforces the boycott are illegal, then it may render its members amenable to the processes of the law, but, if they are not, the courts are powerless to render assistance to the person or firm boycotted, even though financial loss results as the direct consequence of the boycott. It may be true that, speaking generally, no one has the right intentionally to do an act for the purpose of injuring another's business; but injury, however, in its legal significance, means damage resulting from the violation of a legal right, and it is the violation of the legal right which renders an act wrongful in the eye of the law and makes it actionable. If, then, these defendants and their associates did not violate any legal right of the plaintiff in withdrawing their patronage from the company, or in agreeing to withdraw their patronage from any one who might patronize Lindsay & Co., they cannot be enjoined from continuing the boycott in force, so long as the means employed to make the boycott effective are not illegal. The evidence shows that the only means used in this instance was the publication of the circular in question.

This brings the court to the consideration of the right to

publish the circular. That an individual has that constitutional right is made clear in the paragraph that has already been quoted. That this individual right is not lost in the combination is asserted at the conclusion of the opinion. "If any one of these individuals could publish this circular, they may with equal security all join in its publication."

The last of these cases, the Parkinson case, was that of a boycott organized by the building trades against the employers of these laborers. The opinion is one of the longest that has been written on the subject, there being three concurring opinions and one dissenting. The notice that the plaintiff was "unfair" had been printed and circulated, with the effect that a majority of contractors had ceased to deal with him. "Can it be said," asks the court, "that the defendants entered into a conspiracy for the purpose of compelling the plaintiff, by coercion and intimidation, to subject its business to their control? Can it be said that they entered into a conspiracy at all? This question is then answered in the following words:

A combination there certainly was, but it had no reference to the plaintiff except as the business of the plaintiff put it into the general class (employers of labor) who would necessarily be affected by the enforcement of the regulations of the unions. Their object was to secure higher wages, shorter hours, and more favorable conditions generally than employers of labor might be willing to concede, and just so far as they might be successful in accomplishing this object it may be assumed that employers, as a class, the plaintiff included, would incur a corresponding loss. But assuming all this, would that constitute the combination a conspiracy? . . . To support the conclusion that these defendants were guilty of a conspiracy, it must be held that their purpose was at least unlawful if not criminal, or their purpose being lawful that they proposed to attain it by the employment of some unlawful means.

Limiting our consideration for the present to this question of conspiracy, it is clear that the avowed object of these organizations—the several unions of working men and the council in which they were combined—was in no sense unlawful, and the discussion may be confined to the question whether the means proposed for its attainment were unlawful, a question as to which there is a wide divergence of view disclosed by the decisions of the courts of different jurisdictions, and often by the differing opinions of judges of the same court.

The argument then takes up the question of motive in connection with the acts done by the defendants. The interpretation of the New York court of appeals is adopted, as stated in the National Protective Association case, and other authorities, and the conclusion reached is that the motive is not material. The unions had adopted the rule that its members should not work for employers who handled unfair material. The printed circular was simply the notice to all employers that this rule was binding and that it would be enforced by the unions.

The contractors were working in harmony with the unions (as indeed the plaintiff had previously done), and fair dealing required that the council, representing and acting for the unions, should protect such contractors from any loss they might incur if left in ignorance of the action it had taken. If they had not sent the notices some of those contractors who felt constrained to stop dealing with plaintiff when informed that it had been declared unfair might have purchased material which they could not have used, and it is only upon the assumption that such purchases would have been made that the plaintiff can base a claim that it was damaged by the notices. But can plaintiff make such a claim as a ground for equitable relief? It seems very clear that it cannot; for, with full knowledge that it had been declared unfair and of all the consequences flowing from that declaration, it would not have been justified in selling material to a contractor employing union men without disclosing a fact so material to his freedom of contract. And, if good faith and fair dealing imposed an equal obligation upon the plaintiff and the council to inform the contractors of what the plaintiff knew, it is difficult to see what right of plaintiff was infringed by the sending of the notices. Their only effect was to enable the contractors and plaintiff to conduct their future dealings on equal terms. . . .

The fact that the business agent of the council in the course of the dispute . . . told Mr. Parkinson that they would drive him out of business if he refused to observe their rules is material only in so far as it is an item of evidence tending to show that the course pursued by the council was dictated by a malicious purpose to injure the plaintiff, and not by a desire to benefit its members. . . . Conceding that it might have warranted the superior court in concluding that the motives of defendants were tinctured with malice, it cannot be denied that all the acts of the council and its affiliated unions were lawful, and that they were adapted to the promotion of the plans devised by them for bettering the condition of the members. Being so adapted, and being lawful in themselves, they could not be rendered actionable by the mere fact that some feeling of animosity had been engendered in the course of the controversy between the parties.

One of the concurring opinions was written by Judge Sloss. While agreeing with the judgment of the court he was not prepared to assent to everything that was said in the main opinion.

The opinion of the Chief Justice appears to proceed upon the theory that, since the defendants had bound themselves to act in a certain way in the event of a controversy of this kind, it was not only proper, but laudable, for them to notify contractors of their intended action and of the consequences which would follow to contractors who should continue to deal with the plaintiff. More than this, that it was in some way incumbent upon plaintiff to notify contractors dealing with him that a continuance of their patronage would be likely to result in loss to them. I cannot agree to the proposition that the rights of the parties are in any way affected by such considerations. If the defendants' course of conduct amounted to an unlawful interference with plaintiff's rights, it was not made lawful by the fact that the defendants had decided, in advance, to act in this way whenever an occasion should present itself.

Their action, he further argued, was not unlawful, since the defendants had a right to cease to work and the reason for their ceasing was wholly immaterial.

It is said [the defendants] are bringing to bear upon the Parkinson Company, with which they have a controversy, the pressure of loss inflicted by third persons, not connected with the main dispute, and are, by holding over these third persons the risk of financial loss, compelling them against their will to inflict upon Parkinson the damage resulting from a cessation of their patronage. This is the argument commonly advanced to establish the illegality of what has been called, in much of the recent discussion of the subject, a "secondary," rather than a "primary" boycott. I do not see that we are helped to a solution of the question of the illegality of the defendants' acts by looking into the "motive" or "intent" with which they acted. . . . The defendants were seeking in all they are shown to have done to secure employment by the plaintiff for themselves, to the exclusion of those not associated with them, and to secure that employment upon terms deemed satisfactory or advantageous to them. That is the effort of every dealer in goods. It is the struggle of competition, and is no more to be frowned upon where the subject of trade is labor than where it is a specific commodity. The uniting or combining of a number of persons to accomplish a lawful object by lawful means will not per se render the conduct of the many any more unlawful than would be the same conduct on the part of any one of them. . . .

The injunction, then, must rest upon the principle that it is unlawful, in an effort to compel A. to yield a legitimate benefit to B., for B. to demand that C. withdraw his patronage from A. under the penalty of losing B.'s services or patronage to which he has no contract right. That there are many cases sustaining the affirmative of this proposition is true. So are there many to the contrary.

Upon a consideration of the authorities I think the sounder rule is that one who is under no contract relation to another may freely and without question withdraw from business relations with that other. This includes the right to cease to deal, not only with one person but with others; not only with the individual who may be pursuing a course deemed detrimental to another who opposes it, but with all who by their patronage aid in the maintenance of the objectionable policies.

The terms "intimidation" and "coercion," so frequently used in the discussion of this question, seem to me to have no application to such acts as were here committed. One cannot be said to be "intimidated" or "coerced" in the sense of unlawful compulsion by being induced to forego business relations with A., rather than lose the benefit of more profitable relations with B. It is equally beside the question to speak of "threats" where that which is threatened is only what the party has a legal right to do. It may be that the combination of great numbers of men, as of great amounts of capital, has placed in the hands of a few persons an immense power, and one which, in the interest of the general welfare, ought to be limited and controlled. But if there be, in such combinations, evils which should be redressed, the remedy is to be sought, as to some extent it has been sought, by legislation. If the conditions require new laws, those laws should be made by the lawmaking power, not by the courts.

From the reading of the many cases that deal with various phases of the boycott it would seem clear that the legal attitude toward it is experiencing much the same change as has occurred with the strike. Conspiracy was the determining factor in early strikes. Though it has been recognized in our courts from the beginning that a man might stop work whenever he thought that by doing so he could improve his condition, yet to act in combination with others was conspiracy. Moreover to quit work in such a way as to harm the employer was readily interpreted as having for its purpose the injury of the employer, and that meant a malicious motive. Combination and motive were the two facts of importance where early courts inflicted punishment upon strikers. But conspiracy has been modified in its application to strikers, and some courts have held that the motive for stopping work is wholly immaterial. The parallel in the case of the boycott is evident, although the development in case of the strike is farther advanced. No court would deny to a laborer the general right to spend his money or refuse to spend it, as he chose, as any other individual may. But a combination to spend or to refuse to spend may be conspiracy, if the motive is to do damage. In but few cases has it been held that the motive is not material.

By bringing the two lines of reasoning together, we may see the fundamental difference between them. Illegality, as a conclusion, is reached very logically from the principles adopted. It is lawful for one to enter into such business relations as are found mutually agreeable to the parties concerned. The purpose of such relations is mutual benefit. Freedom to enter into them implies likewise freedom to refrain. Refraining is assumed to be primarily for the benefit of the one who refuses the relations, and the fact that another may be deprived of an advantage that would have resulted from such relations can not be regarded as a loss to him. But when many combine and by a concerted action refuse business relations, the case is not parallel with individual action. Combination colors the act. The outcome is that the superior right of the combination forces an agreement that would not otherwise have been made. This is coercion and therefore unlawful. The lawful act entered into by many and sought to be accomplished by unlawful means brings it within the meaning of conspiracy. The very name then serves to characterize the act; it is unlawful.

Legality, on the other hand, as a conclusion, is also reached by steps that are logical. The starting point is the same individual right to enter or to refrain from entering into business relations. That right is fundamental, however, and is not affected by the fact that others join in doing the same. If it is to the interest of one to refrain, it may be to the interest of a hundred or a thousand similarly placed to refrain. If they recognize this interest by consultation, come to the conclusion by agreement and unite in common action, no one of the group has done what as an individual he has not a legal right to do. Moreover, if their interests lie to them in refraining from assuming the business relation, they are simply furthering their own welfare, and this is, of course, a worthy motive. That they refrain from the relation cannot be interpreted as a loss to the other party to the relation. It is true that such relations are entered into for mutual gain. If one desires the relation for his gain and the other refrains because he does not see it to his interest to assume the relation, it does not mean that there is a loss. It is true that an opportunity for gain can not be taken advantage of, but that is not a loss. One cannot be said to have suffered a loss of a thousand dollars because he has never found a thousand dollars.

But further, so long as buying and selling are but two views of the same act, an act of voluntary business relation, and so long as the relation must be one of mutual agreement, it is difficult to see where the property right enters in. One's business is of course his property. So in a sense may one's labor be called his property.[1] When one offers for sale and another refuses to buy, there is simply a refusal to exchange property for property. When one points out to another or to many others that it is to his interest not to buy, there is again simply the refusal to exchange. When many meet and decide together or agree not to buy there is concerted refusal to exchange. To interpret this as a malicious destruction of one's business, which is property, and even to interpret it as an infringement of a property right is a manifestation of solicitude for one form of property (a business) at the expense of another form (labor) that it is not easy to justify. The man who goes into business assumes the risk of failure together with the chances of success. If failure comes, it is his risk, so long as it comes from the refusal of others to buy, and is his loss, but it is not a loss for which those who refuse to be purchasers can be held responsible. Clearly the essential difference is in combination and in motive. But it is at just these two points that the opinions show a tendency toward a change of view. Combination and conspiracy are not nearly so synonymous as they have been. Motive is not so material as it has been. Plenty of *obiter* uterances may be found to show this change. With the further modification of these older views will come a further modification of the court's attitude toward the boycott.

Read in the light of modern conditions the changing attitude seems necessary. The courts themselves are beginning to recognize, though somewhat tardily, that combination is a fact of modern industry that may be controlled but not eliminated. Combinations are for the purpose of doing things, and they cannot be expected to be inactive. These

[1] The author objects to speaking of "labor" as "property." The expression is so common, however, among judges in their opinions that it is used here as a brief formula for setting forth the contrast desired.

combinations exist in the fields of both capital and labor. The recognition of this fact however is but the beginning not the end of the difficulty. What may the combinations do within the law, is a question the answer to which must be worked out by the slow process of development.

"The times in which we live seem to require a more extended examination of the subject," wrote Judge Carpenter of Connecticut in 1887. "We are not unmindful of the difficulty often presented to the courts to determine what constitutes an unlawful boycott," added Chief Justice Grant of Michigan in 1898.

The elaborate boycotts that have been organized, and the heartless manner in which they have been conducted, after all, leave much ground for the opinion that they should be controlled. Some of them, beyond a doubt, adopt means that are clearly unlawful. Not even in the most favorable opinions of courts is there basis for hope that these means will be permitted. When, however, the labor organization leaders themselves come to realize this, and learn to keep the boycott within reasonable limits, even to lose a fight if necessary rather than to go to extremes, there is basis for belief that boycotts, without the tyrannical domineering that sometimes accompanies them, may in time be regarded by the courts as legal.

The tendency toward a recognition of the boycott as legal follows from the view accepted by some of the courts in regard to the strike. The right to stop work is not affected by the motive or intent. Chief Justice Beatty, in his opinion in the Parkinson case, very clearly applies this principle to the boycott. Referring to the Cumming case (N. Y. court of appeals) he points out that in Justice Parker's view, supported by three others of that court, every man may stop work with or without reason (where there is no contract relation involved) and whatever his reason may be he is not obliged to give it as a justification of his quitting unless he elects to do so. This proposition, asserts Chief Justice Beatty, is found also in other cases. In a case decided by his own court it took the form, "an act which does not amount to a legal injury cannot be actionable because it is done with a bad intent." In the English case it was stated (Allen *v.* Flood), "An act lawful in itself is not converted by a malicious or bad motive into an unlawful act so as to make the doer of the act liable to a civil action." The Chief Justice then concludes:

The rule of law, therefore, as firmly established in England, in this state, and in most of the United States, supports the conclusion of Chief Justice Parker and the majority of the court of appeals of New York . . . so far as it rests upon the doctrine, "that an act lawful in itself is not converted by a malicious or bad motive into an unlawful act so as to make the doer of the act liable to a civil action."

CHAPTER VI

The Picket

It would hardly be possible for workingmen to carry through a strike without picketing. Picketing has thus often been passed upon by the courts. While coming in incidentally as a rule, it has also been brought forward as the main question in some instances. Even when the right to strike is conceded, it is not clear what may be done by the strikers. Picketing is usually considered as part of the question: What may strikers do?

The definition in Black's *Law Dictionary* is generally accepted by the courts.

> Picketing, by members of a trade union on strike, consists in posting members at all the approaches to the works struck against, for the purpose of observing and reporting the workmen going to or coming from the works, and of using such influence as may be in their power to prevent the workmen from accepting work there.

Chief Justice Grant, of Michigan (Beck *v.* Railway Teamsters), prefers the more drastic definition of the *Century Dictionary:* " A body of men belonging to a trades union sent to watch and annoy men working in a shop not belonging to the union, or against which a strike is in progress." " The word originally had no such meaning," he adds. " This definition is the result of what has been done under it, and the common application that has been made of it." Vice Chancellor Reed, of New Jersey (Cumberland Glass

Co. *v.* Glass Bottle Blowers), uses the word in the sense of "relays of guards in front of a factory or the place of business of the employer, for the purpose of watching who should enter or leave the same." District Judge Tayler (Pope Motor Car Co. *v.* Keegan), adopts as its meaning a

detachment of men in suitable places for the purpose of coming into personal relations with the new workmen, in order, if possible, to induce them, by means of peaceful argument, to leave the places which they have taken, for such natural and proper reasons as may appeal to men in such circumstances.

From these definitions it will appear that there is very general agreement as to the meaning of the term, and yet one very important difference emerges as soon as a further analysis is made. The border line between picketing and intimidation is not easy to establish. It is difficult to classify the opinions with reference to legality and illegality, for all of them are at some pains to emphasize that, whatever may be their decision in the case at court, picketing may easily become intimidation.

That the picket may be legal, or that picketing is in itself legal, is expressed in several opinions. Judge Holmes, speaking from the Massachusetts bench, in his dissenting opinion (Vegelahn *v.* Guntner), says:

It appears to me that the opinion of the majority turns in part on the assumption that the patrol necessarily carries with it a threat of bodily harm. That assumption I think unwarranted. . . . It cannot be said, I think, that two men, walking together up and down a sidewalk, and speaking to those who enter a certain shop, do necessarily and always thereby convey a threat of force. I do not think it possible to discriminate, and to say that two workmen, or even two representatives of an organization of workmen, do. . . . I may add that I think the more intelligent workingmen believe as fully as I do that they no more can be permitted to usurp the state's prerogative of force than can their opponents in their controversies. [Although the doing of damage by combined persuasion is actionable] nevertheless, in numberless instances the law warrants the intentional infliction of temporal damage, because it regards it as justified. It is on the question of what shall amount to a justification, and more especially on the nature of the considerations which really determine or ought to determine the answer to that question, that judicial reasoning seems to me often to be inadequate. . . .

The policy of allowing free competition justifies the intentional inflicting of temporal damage, including the damage of interference with a man's business by some means, when the damage is done, not for its own sake, but as an instrumentality in reaching the end of victory in the battle of trade. In such a case it cannot matter whether the plaintiff is the only rival of the defendant, and so is aimed at specially, or is one of a class all of whom are hit. The only debatable ground is the nature of the means by which such damage may be inflicted. We all agree that it cannot be done by force or threats of force. We all agree, I presume, that it may be done by persuasion to leave a rival's shop, and come to the defendant's. It may be done by the refusal or withdrawal of various pecuniary advantages, which, apart from this consequence, are within the defendant's lawful control. It may be done by the withdrawal of, or threat to withdraw, such advantages from third persons who have a right to deal or not to deal with the plaintiff, as a means of inducing them not to deal with him either as customers or servants.

Several other opinions express views not altogether unfavorable to the picket. Among these may be noted the following expressed by Vice Chancellor Reed, of New Jersey:

I cannot say that the law is so settled that a preliminary injunction can go upon the notion that picketing, without some other act evidential of coercion, is in itself evidence of intimidation. The decision of the question, I think, must depend upon the circumstances surrounding each case. There must be taken into account the size of the guard, the extent of their occupation of the street, and what they say and do. Taking every circumstance into account, if it appears that the purpose of the picketing is to interfere with those passing into or out of the works, or those wishing to pass into the works, by other than persuasive means, it is illegal. If the design of the picketing is to see who can be the subject of persuasive inducements, such picketing is legal. (Cumberland Glass Co. *v.* Glass Bottle Blowers.)

Vice Chancellor Stevenson, of the same court, writes:

The counsel for complainant practically confined his argument to the proposition that a preliminary injunction should go in the case to restrain picketing, without reference to the object of the picketing or its effect. If this view is correct, it follows that workmen maintaining a strike have no right to station pickets merely for the purpose of giving them such information in regard to their late employers' operations as may be discovered by ordinary observation. It seems to me that this claim is not well founded; that it is contrary to the great weight of reason as well as authority.

Picketing may be lawful; picketing may be unlawful. Whether picketing is lawful or unlawful depends wholly upon the purpose with which it is carried on, or perhaps, it would be more accurate to say, the effect which is produced by it. If the purpose and effect are to intimidate, to interfere with the liberty of workmen in seeking employment, to interfere with what in another case I called the employer's right to have labor flow freely to him so that a reasonably courageous person would be restrained from offering his labor to such employer, then picketing is unlawful, and, where the other necessary conditions for the interference of a court of equity exist, will be prohibited by an injunction.

If, however, the picketing is carried on for the mere purpose of obtaining information, or for the purpose of conveying information to persons seeking or willing to receive the same, or even, in some cases, for the purpose of bringing orderly and peaceable persuasions to bear upon the minds of men who desire to listen to the same, the object of such persuasions not including in any way the disruption of an existing contract for labor, then there may be no unlawful element in the picketing, and carrying it on may found no action even at law, and certainly may not call for any interference on the part of a court of equity. (Fletcher Co. *v.* International Machinists.)

District Judge Tayler, writing from the circuit court, expresses himself at some length:

Much has been said by the courts, and by others, as to the peace-disturbing quality of picketing, and it is claimed by many that picketing, though intended to be peaceable, and engaged in by no more than two or three at each station, necessarily results in violence or intimidation, and is itself intimidating. A learned judge, in 1867, said that, in his opinion, "it was impossible to have an effectual system of picketing without being guilty of that alarm, intimidation, and obstruction which is a breach of the law." Possibly that may still be true, but it cannot now be said without qualification, as it then could. In knowledge of their rights, in law-abiding spirit, in general intelligence, there has been a great advance, especially among skilled artisans. In this country, at least, they make up a large part of our intelligent and law-abiding citizens.

If we can apprehend anything, we must observe that a better practice is prevailing, due, doubtless, to the increasing intelligence and good sense of those involved, and also to the fact that courts have come to be recognized as ready to protect persons in their rights, and to punish those who unlawfully interfere with them. Undoubtedly violence and intimidation have, to some extent, been associated with picketing in this case; not always, though perhaps generally, at the hands of the strikers themselves. The idle, the dissolute, and the lawless are likely to take advantage of such a situation as this to commit unlawful acts, and the state of mind into which striking mechanics are likely to come, in such a case as we have here, is more or less likely either to make them indifferent to these acts when committed by others, or, in some instances, to encourage them. Nevertheless, I cannot believe that, under proper circumstances, and with such a sense of self-restraint as men can exercise, picketing may not be properly conducted. (Pope Co. *v.* Keegan.)

At this point the opinion includes a quotation concerning which it adds: " With the rule laid down in this case I am in full accord." The quotation is from Judge Hadley of Indiana and reads:

So, in a contest between capital and labor, on the one hand to secure higher wages, and on the other to resist it, argument and persuasion to win support and co-operation from others are proper to either side, provided they are of a character to leave the persons solicited feeling at liberty to comply or not, as they please. Likewise, a union may appoint pickets or a committee to visit the vicinity of factories for the purpose of taking note of the persons employed, and to secure, if it can be done by lawful means, the names and places of residence for the purpose of peaceful visitation. (Karges Furniture Co. *v.* Woodworkers Union.)

Presiding Justice Evans, of Georgia, in an opinion not at all favorable to the picket, as it was shown to have been used in the case before him, admits that

the law does not forbid employees who have quit their employer from using legitimate argument to induce others to refrain from taking their places. The current of authority is that a court of equity will not enjoin employees who have quit the service of their employer from attempting to persuade, by proper argument, others from taking their places, so long as they do not resort to intimidation or obstruct the public thoroughfares. . . . As we have pointed out, it was not unlawful for the strikers to use legitimate argument and moral suasion in presenting their case to those who offered to take their places, so long as it is neither coercive and intimidating in character. (Jones *v.* Van Winkle.)

These opinions express a view very favorable to the picket. Not all courts are ready to admit that it is so easy to separate the act of picketing from acts of intimidation. There are many cases where evidence of this may be found. One of these is Beck *v.* Railway Teamsters, in which Chief Justice Grant says:

To picket complainants' premises in order to intercept their teamsters or persons going there to trade is unlawful. It itself is an act of intimidation, and an unwarrantable interference with the right of free trade. The highways and public streets must be free to all for the purposes of trade, commerce, and labor. The law protects the buyer, the seller, the merchant, the manufacturer, and the laborer in the right to walk and use the streets unmolested. It is no respecter of persons; and it makes no difference, in effect, whether the picketing is done 10 or 1,000 feet away.

It will not do to say that these pickets are thrown out for the purpose of peaceable argument and persuasion. They are intended to intimidate and coerce.

Another expression is by Judge Mitchell:

An attempt is made to argue that the strikers only congregated at the place of arrival of the new men, in accordance with the custom at boat and train arrivals in small towns. But this disguise is too flimsy to hide the real purpose. If they desired in good faith to meet peaceably and lawfully for their own business, they should have selected another place, sufficiently remote to be free from the excitement and crowds which, their own testimony admits, attended the arrival of the new men, and also far enough away to avoid the intimidating effect of a hostile crowd on the newcomers. But, in truth, they did not desire to avoid that effect. On the contrary, that was what they were there for, and their presence indicates their real intentions too plainly for any verbal denials on their part to offset.

It is further urged that the strikers, through their committees, only exercised ("insisted on" is the phrase their counsel use in the court) their right to talk to the new men to persuade them not to go to work. There was no such right. These men were there presumably under contract with the plaintiff, and certainly in search of work, if not yet actually under pay. They were not at leisure, and their time, whether their own or their employer's, could not lawfully be taken up, and their progress interfered with, by these or any other outsiders, on any pretense or under any claim of right to argue or persuade them to break their contracts. Even, therefore, if the arguments and persuasion had been confined to lawful means, they were exerted at an improper time, and were an interference with the plaintiff's rights which made the perpetrators liable for any damages the plaintiff suffered in consequence. (O'Neil *v.* Behanna.)

District Judge Beatty says:

The law does give the right of peaceable persuasion. It is the abuse of this right which leads to all the trouble. In their desire to succeed they too often go in great numbers. Among them are generally some who are lawless and reckless of rights or consequences. They do that which the conservative and better classes do not approve of, and the general result is that the conscious power of great numbers leads along from one act to another, to the usual end that violence and abuse are resorted to when advice and persuasion fail.

But it must be understood that when any assemble in numbers for some object they must be held responsible for what their associates do, whether they approve of or advise it or not. (Gulf Bag Co. *v.* Suttner.)

Presiding Judge Evans, of Georgia, states further in his opinion already quoted:

When strikers patrol the streets and approaches of the premises where the strike is in progress, and their number is so great, or their conduct is such, as to intimidate and coerce the employees into quitting their employment, or others from seeking employment, they are guilty of unlawful acts, and will be enjoined from a continuance of them. Sometimes the number of strikers engaged on the patrol may be so great that those intended to be affected by the demonstration will be intimidated by the number of the strikers or their sympathizers without special overt acts. The courts have repeatedly held that the assembling of strikers around the establishment of the employer in such numbers as will serve as a menace to those employed, or the keeping of patrols in front of or about the premises of the employer, accompanied by violence or any manner of coercion to prevent others from entering into or remaining in his service, will be enjoined. . . .

The very word "picket" is borrowed from the nomenclature of warfare, and is strongly suggestive of a hostile attitude towards the individual or corporation against whom the labor union has a grievance. To quote Mr. Eddy: "It is conceivable, however, that a picket entirely lawful might be established about a factory, but such a picket would go no further than interviews and lawful persuasion and inducement. The slightest evidence of threats, violence, or intimidation of any character ought to be sufficient to convince court and jury of the unlawful character of the picket, since the picket under the most favorable considerations means an interference between the employer seeking employees and men seeking employment." (Jones *v.* Van Winkle.)

Such views are not always so judiciously expressed. Extreme statements, like the following, are also found:

> There is and can be no such thing as peaceful picketing, any more than there can be chaste vulgarity, or peaceful mobbing, or lawful lynching. When men want to converse or persuade, they do not organize a picket line. When they only want to see who are at work, they go and see, and then leave, and disturb no one physically or mentally. . . . The argument seems to be that anything short of physical violence is lawful. One man can be intimidated only when knocked down. But the peaceful, law-abiding man can be and is intimidated by gesticulations, by menaces, by being called harsh names, and by being followed, or compelled to pass by men known to be unfriendly. Perhaps such a man may not be a bully, but is frail in size and strength, or he may be a timid man, but such a man is just as much entitled to go and come in quiet, without even mental disturbance, as is the man afraid of no one and able with or without weapons to cope with all comers. The frail man, or the man who shuns disturbances, or the timid man, must be protected, and the company has the right to employ such. (District Judge McPherson, Atchinson T. & S. F. Ry. Co. *v.* Gee.)

District Judge Sanborn, in Allis Chalmers Co. *v.* Iron Moulders Union, declares that,

> while "peaceful picketing" is very much of an illusion, yet it is at least theoretically possible, and entirely lawful. . . . Where peaceful picketing develops, as it generally does in a strike, into "strong, persistent, and organized persuasion," and social pressure of every description, making the condition of workmen disagreeable and intolerable, followed by hints of injury, veiled threats, offensive or abusive language, and occasional instances of assault and personal violence . . . the condition has passed from that of the peaceful purpose of promoting the economic ends of the union men, and has entered

the unlawful stage of malicious injury, without just cause or excuse, to rights just as important, and as fully protected by the Constitution, as those on whose behalf these acts are committed.

The foregoing extracts indicate how hard it is to distinguish between the legal picket and the illegal in any practical way. This difficulty does not pass unrecognized by the judges, and in some opinions it is openly expressed. Presiding Judge Evans, whose opinion has been referred to, points out that

the lawfulness or unlawfulness of "picketing" has been the subject-matter of discussion in a large number of cases in this country. . . . In many cases it may be difficult to draw the line of demarcation between intimidation and inoffensive persuasion. In a New York case it was said: "It may be impossible to lay down a general rule as to what surrounding circumstances will characterize persuasion and entreaty as intimidation. Each case must probably depend upon its own surroundings. But, where evidence presents such a case as to convince the court that the employees are being induced to leave the employer by operating upon their fears rather than upon their judgments or their sympathy, the court will be quick to lend its strong arm to his protection."

That general principles alone apart from the circumstances of the case are not sufficient basis for judgment is pointed out by Judge Holmes in the following terms:

The true grounds of decision are considerations of policy and of social advantage, and it is vain to suppose that solutions can be attained merely by logic and general propositions of law which nobody disputes. Propositions as to public policy rarely are unanimously accepted, and still more rarely, if ever, are capable of unanswerable proof.

Such are the types of opinion as expressed in the leading cases. The authorities seem to agree that picketing, in its limited sense, is not unlawful. Following the favorable interpretations of common law, and for the purpose of annulling those interpretations that are not favorable, the English Parliament has legalized the picket by special legislative enactment. This course has been followed in several states of the Union. Where such laws have not been enacted, the same effect has been secured by court interpretation of common law. Stimson concludes that the law has

> pretty well settled down to the view that picketing, for the purpose of mere persuasion of workmen not to take employment, and not attended with any disorder or physical or moral intimidation, is now held legal; at least when conducted in a reasonable manner and with not too great a crowd.[1]

Even Cogley agrees that picketing is legal, though he does so reluctantly. "Ordinarily," he says, "picketing is a part of boycotting," but legislatures

> have so far yielded to the encroachments of mobs as to legalize acts and conduct that at first were crimes. It may now be stated as to the rule both in England and the United States that if picketing is peacefully conducted and the acts of the pickets confined to watching, observation and persuasion, it is not a criminal offense.[2]

The lawfulness of the picket, then, seems established. Yet one cannot read the opinions without feeling that many judges admit the legality with reluctance. The very fact that the matter is involved in a disturbance that is serious enough to be brought into court is sufficient to create an atmosphere that is hostile to favorable consideration. The

[1] *Handbook*, p. 290.

[2] *Law of Strikes*, p. 290.

predilection of judges for fair play and their thorough schooling in the rights of individuals make it easy for the implications of the charge to have considerable weight. Then recognition of the broad and not very clearly defined meaning of the term "intimidation," as including the mental and moral as well as the physical, makes it easy to find that picketing is intimidating in its effects. It is of interest to note that some of the broadest and most unequivocal statements of the legality of the picket in itself are in connection with cases where the violence and intimidation have been most flagrant. The riotous conditions make it easy to find grounds for legal condemnation. Where the acts are less flagrant, and where the picket has been conducted in a more orderly and peaceful manner, these general statements of the lawfulness of the picket in itself give way to finer-spun definitions of intimidation, to the drawing of the line so that the boundaries of lawful picketing are considerably narrowed. The conclusion suggested by the opinions is that judges do not look with favor upon the picket but that they are led to admit its legality within very narrow limits by the force of logical inference flowing from well-known and generally-accepted legal principles. The courts always stand ready to defend personal liberty, and they are willing to leave room for the legal picket rather than yield so much of the principles of personal liberty as would be necessary to condemn it in law. It is doubtful, however, if one can expect much progress toward a recognition of a broader right to picket through judicial decisions. The strike has come into full legal recognition. The boycott also, but to a less extent. There is not the same hope for the picket. Views of motive and of action in combination appear to change more readily than views of coercion and intimidation.

CHAPTER VII

THE BLACKLIST

DISCUSSIONS of blacklisting are not such as to contribute much to the purpose of this work. Cases which deal with it are involved in details and special circumstances and the discussion of these occupies by far the larger portion of the opinions.

In 1892 a case came before the supreme court of Massachusetts. Some weavers had struck for higher wages. Their employer sent their names to other mills on a blacklist. The weavers were unable to find work. The matter was brought to court on a charge of conspiracy against the employers. Chief Justice Field, of Massachusetts, who wrote the opinion, was particularly guarded in expressing the view of the court.

> If the petition sets forth such a conspiracy as constitutes a misdemeanor at common law—on which we express no opinion—the remedy is by indictment. If the injury which had been received by the petitioners at the time the petition was filed constitutes a cause of action—on which we express no opinion—the remedy is by an action of tort, to be brought by each petitioner separately. The only grievance alleged which is continuing in its nature is the conspiracy not to employ the petitioners, and there are no approved precedents in equity for enjoining the defendants from continuing such a conspiracy, or for compelling the defendants either to employ the petitioners or to procure employment for them with other persons. (Worthington *v.* Waring.)

In Hundley *v.* L. and N. Railroad Co., the defendant complained that he had been blacklisted by railroads and was unable to secure employment. Damages were asked in the sum of five thousand dollars. Judge Paynter of Kentucky, in writing the opinion, states the familiar principles of law that express in general terms the rights of both employers and employees. The opinion is then brought to its conclusion in the following sentences:

The petition does not state a cause of action against the defendant. The averments that he had been deprived of the "right" to again engage in the employment of other railroad companies, and that the alleged wrongful act had made it impossible for him to ever again get employment with other railroad companies, are mere conclusions of the pleader from the facts alleged. It should have been averred that he had sought, and been refused, employment by reason of the alleged wrongful act. An agreement made with other railroad companies not to employ defendant's discharged employees does not injure the plaintiff unless carried out. An averment that the defendant conspired and combined with other railroad companies to do an act, if unlawful, would not obviate the necessity of making the averment that he had sought and been refused employment by reason of the alleged wrongful act. Injury is the gist of the action. The liability is damages for doing, not for conspiracy. The charge of conspiracy does not change the nature of the act. In an action for damages, there must be some overt act, consequent upon the agreement to do a wrong, to give the plaintiff a standing in a court of law.

The blacklist was involved in the case of the alleged attempt of the Western Union to break up the Commercial Telegraphers' Union. The opinion in that case was written by District Judge Rogers from the bench of the circuit court.

But it is said that defendant maintains a blacklist containing a list of names of such persons as may have incurred its displeasure and have been discharged from its service, and that, by methods not known to them, it prevents such discharged persons from getting employment as telegraph operators; that they have blacklisted people solely because they belong to the union, and that they intend to blacklist others for the same thing, etc. We have seen it is not unlawful to discharge plaintiffs because they belong to the union. Is it unlawful for defendant to keep a book showing that they were discharged because they belonged to the union? The union presumably, and especially in view of the allegations in the bill, is an honorable, reputable, and useful organization, intended to better the conditions and elevate the character of its members. Is it illegal for defendant to keep a book showing that it had discharged members of such a union solely because they belong to it? That seems to be the real essence of the bill. Is it illegal to notify others that it keeps such a book and that they can inspect it, or to inform others what such a book shows? That seems to be the ground of complaint. There can be no question about it; the positive, direct, and unequivocal allegation is that defendant keeps such a book; that plaintiffs are placed on it solely because they belong to the union, and have been discharged solely because they did belong to the union. Can a court of equity grant relief to a man who says for his cause of action that he belongs to a reputable organization, and that he has been discharged solely because he did belong to it; that his employer who discharged him keeps a book on which is placed his name, and has set opposite thereto the fact that he discharged him solely because he belonged to such organization; and that he gives that information to other persons, who refuse to employ him on that account? Suppose a man should file a bill alleging that he belonged to the Honorable and Ancient Order of Freemasons, or to the Presbyterian Church, or to the Grand Army of the Republic; that his employer had discharged him solely on that account; that he had discharged others of his employees, and intended to discharge all of them, for the same reason; that he kept a book which contained all the names of such discharged persons, and set opposite the name of each discharged person the fact that he had been discharged solely on the ground that he belonged to such organization; and that he had given such information to others, who refused to employ such persons on that account. Is it possible a court of equity could grant relief? If so, pray, on what ground? And yet that is a perfectly parallel case to this as made by the bill. (Boyer *v.* Western Union.)

One of the most recent reported cases in which the principle of the blacklist is dealt with occurred in 1909. In this opinion Judge Henry, of Maryland, wrote:

It may be well to announce as a principle of law that any malicious interference with the business or occupation of another, if followed by damage, is an actionable wrong. Such interference may be by a single individual, or by a number of individuals conspiring together, but it is the damage which constitutes the gist of the action, and not the conspiracy; the latter being a matter of aggravation, if proven, as affecting the means and manner of redress. We find no Maryland case that goes to the extent of sustaining the position contended for by the appellant to the effect that the "blacklisting" of discharged employees by a combination of employers is in itself actionable, without proof of damage. . . . An employer, where no right of contract is involved, may lawfully discharge an employee at what time he pleases, and for what cause he chooses, while, on the other hand, an employee may sell his labor to whomsoever he desires, at such wages as he is willing to accept, and may quit such employment at his pleasure, yet neither has the right to interfere, without cause, with the business or occupation of the other. While the law does not furnish a shield against the effects of fair and honest competition, yet injury to the business of another, if accomplished by threats or coercion, constitutes a ground of action for damages on the part of the person so injured. In furtherance of their common welfare and in settlement of their ofttimes conflicting interests, both employers and employees stand upon a plane of perfect equality before the law, enjoying the same freedom and amenable to the same restrictions. Both may combine in unions or associations, but such associations, like individuals, must employ lawful methods for the attainment of lawful purposes. This was not always so. . . . It is now clearly settled that the same law which permits the organization of employers, and interposes to protect manufacturers and merchants from the violence of "strikes," or the "intimidation of boycotts," is also vigilant to see that the right and opportunity to work, which is the most valuable asset of the laboring man, as well as the privilege of organization, shall not be unjustifiably interfered with by employers, acting either as individuals or in combinations. (Willner *v.* Silverman.)

In Minnesota the question came up on the interpretation of a statute, entitled, "An act to prohibit the practice of black-listing and the coercing and influencing of employees by their employers." The contention was that the law infringed the right of the employer, a "natural right, under the constitution, state and federal, to give such advice and information as he desires with respect to his employees, whether they have been discharged for cause or without cause, or whether they have voluntarily left the employment." The opinion does not adopt such a view. An employee who voluntarily leaves his employment, says the opinion,

is entitled to the presumption that his reputation as an employee has been unharmed by the fact of his leaving. The fact that such an employee voluntarily abandons his employment does not give the employer a right to prejudice his employment elsewhere. Under such circumstances a communication designed to prevent such employment is presumably a reflection upon the standing of the employee. . . . The act does not attempt to interfere with the right of an employer to discharge an employee for cause or without cause. It does not seek to prohibit an employer from communicating to other employers the nature and character of his employees, when the facts would be for their interests. While such interference by an employer is not expressly characterized as malicious, that intent is necessarily implied. It is the purpose of this law to protect employees in the enjoyment of those natural rights and privileges guaranteed them by the constitution, viz., the right to sell their labor and acquire property thereby. The act is valid. (State *v.* Justus.)

These views indicate that the question is both new and difficult for the courts so far as it concerns the particular application of general rules. Reasoned on the basis of general rights, the employer may discharge or refuse to employ for any reason or for no reason. The advantage here certainly lies with the employer. The charge of conspiracy cannot be raised with the same degree of success as it has been by employers. The numbers are not so great and conspiracy is more difficult to prove. The employers may act with an understanding much more easily than can the employees and consequently a more elaborate organization is not necessary. Blacklisting is not easy to establish as a legal fact. All of these considerations make it difficult to bring cases before the court and still more difficult to establish to the court's satisfaction that the rights of the employees are being infringed to an unlawful extent.

Legislation to prevent blacklisting has been enacted by several states. The court in the above cited case upheld the principle involved in the legislation. But laws of this kind are difficult to enforce for the reasons already stated. The act which is forbidden is not easy to detect nor to prove to the satisfaction of a court of law.

CHAPTER VIII

UNIONISM

IN the preceding chapters the more characteristic methods of labor organizations have been treated. While the strike and the boycott are among the most generally known activities of these associations, they do not complete the list. There remains a large field within which their activities are of industrial importance. These activities are with increasing frequency brought before the courts. The result is that the number of opinions is large, the variety of problems dealt with complex and the conclusions reached not altogether in agreement. These varied problems may all be gathered together under the general heading, Unionism, though they include a great variety of topics.

First there is the fact of the union, the organization of laborers associated together for a common purpose and under definite rules and regulations. What is the attitude of courts toward unionism itself? The answer may be considered with reference to two quite distinct points: (1) the union, the fact of organization or combination; (2) the activities of the union, the policies it adopts and the means it uses to carry them into effect. The second of these two points may be subdivided into a number of special topics. They will be considered in turn in the chapters that follow.

How do courts regard the existence of associations of workmen? In a preceding chapter, the attitude during the first half of the nineteenth century has been described. This period closed with the influential opinion in the case of

Commonwealth *v.* Hunt. From that time to the present there has been a steady expression by various judges of opinions similar to that one in principle. In that early case, as already shown, Chief Justice Shaw made it clear that associations might be formed for purposes that were useful and honorable, as, for example, to afford assistance in sickness, distress or poverty or other praiseworthy objects. There may be some reasonable ground for holding that this view was entertained from the first although not so clearly expressed. Whether this be so or not, the expressions are now so generally scattered throughout the opinions that one cannot doubt that courts accept without question the view that associations of laborers, so far as the mere fact of association apart from their acts is concerned, are lawful. The influence of precedent is of course strong. It appears frequently. It finds a double authority when Judge Browning of Minnesota (Gray *v.* Building Trades Council) quotes from Judge Thayer of the United States circuit court of appeals (Hopkins *v.* Oxley Stave Co.): "The courts have invariably upheld the right of individuals to form labor organizations for the protection of the interests of laboring classes." In Curran *v.* Galen is read the further statement that "In the general consideration of the subject, it must be premised that the organization or the co-operation of workingmen is not against any public policy."

More broadly than these quotations would indicate, courts sometimes view the fact of organization from a different angle. One of these views may be expressed in terms of individualism, the right of individuals to combine. Reasoning from this starting point, courts find another basis for justification. The Wabash Railroad case affords an instance of this. The opinion, after citing several authorities, concludes:

Enough has been said to clearly indicate the general rule, which may be briefly summarized as follows: An employee has an unquestionable right to place a price and impose conditions upon his labor at the outset of his employment, or, unless restrained by contract obligations, upon the continuance of his labor at any time thereafter; and, if the terms and conditions are not complied with by the employer, he has a clear right either not to engage or having engaged in his service to cease from work. What one may do all may do.

They may seek and obtain counsel and advice concerning their rights, duties, and obligations in relation to their employer, and persons interested in their welfare may advise, aid, and assist them in securing such terms and conditions of service as will best subserve their interests, and what they may lawfully do singly or together they may organize and combine to accomplish.

Judge Loring of Massachusetts enters upon an elaborate discussion of these rights in Pickett *v.* Walsh.

The right of laborers to organize unions . . . is an exercise of the common-law right of every citizen to pursue his calling, whether of labor or business, as he in his judgment thinks fit. . . . This common-law right was raised to the dignity of a constitutional right by being incorporated in the constitution of the commonwealth. . . . In Article I. of the Declaration of Rights it is declared that "all men are born free and equal, and have certain natural, essential, and unalienable rights; among which may be reckoned the right of . . . acquiring, possessing, and protecting property; in fine, that of seeking and obtaining their safety and happiness." It is in the exercise of this right that laborers can legally combine together in what are called labor unions. [This right is simply the right of every individual, and] is limited by the existence of the same right in all other citizens. [Quoting from Sir William Earl's *Trade Unions*]: Every person has a right under the law, as between him and his fellow subjects, to full freedom in disposing of his own labor or his own capital according to his own will. It follows that every other person is subject to the correlative duty arising therefrom, and is prohibited from any obstruction to the fullest exercise of this right which can be made compatible with the exercise of similar rights by others.

To this may be added the remarks of Circuit Judge Taft in the Thomas case.

Now, it may be conceded in the outset that the employees of the receiver had the right to organize into or to join a labor union which should take joint action as to their terms of employment. It is of benefit to them and to the public that laborers should unite in their common interest and for lawful purposes. They have labor to sell. If they stand together, they are often able, all of them, to command better prices for their labor than when dealing singly with rich employers, because the necessities of the single employee may compel him to accept any terms offered him. The accumulation of a fund for the support of those who feel that the wages offered are below market prices is one of the legitimate objects of such an organization. They have the right to appoint officers who shall advise them as to the course to be taken by them in their relations with their employer. They may unite with other unions. The officers they appoint, or any other person to whom they choose to listen, may advise them as to the proper course to be taken by them in regard to their employment, or, if they choose to repose such authority in any one, may order them, on pain of expulsion from their union, peaceably to leave the employ of their employer because any of the terms of their employment are unsatisfactory.

Still another of these various views that courts have adopted in justification of unionism may be expressed in terms of association and combination, facts so obvious in modern competitive industry. Thus in Curran *v.* Galen the court says: "It is proper and praiseworthy, and perhaps falls within the general view of human society which perceives an underlying law that men should unite to achieve that which each by himself cannot achieve, or can achieve less readily." This is stated in terms very general. Other expressions come much nearer to practical affairs. The clearest instance of this view is in the dissenting opinion of Mr. Justice Holmes written in 1896.

> It is plain from the slightest consideration of practical affairs, or the most superficial reading of industrial history, that free competition means combination, and that the organization of the world, now going on so fast, means an ever-increasing might and scope of combination. It seems to me futile to set our faces against this tendency. Whether beneficial on the whole, as I think it, or detrimental, it is inevitable, unless the fundamental axioms of society, and even the fundamental conditions of life, are to be changed.
>
> One of the eternal conflicts out of which life is made up is that between the effort of every man to get the most he can for his services, and that of society, disguised under the name of capital, to get his services for the least possible return. Combination on the one side is patent and powerful. Combination on the other is the necessary and desirable counterpart, if the battle is to be carried on in a fair and equal way. (Vegelahn *v.* Guntner.)

Other quotations might be added to show the acceptance by judges of the view that combination is one of the great facts of our industry and that combinations of labor are but one phase of the general movement.

Judge Sheldon, in the Willcut case, writes:

> Gloomy vaticinations of injurious results to be apprehended from the excessive power which labor unions may acquire by their combination of many individuals into one body do not greatly impress us. The power of capital hitherto has not been found insufficient to prevent other than proper advan-

tages from being gained by the representatives of labor, nor does it seem to us likely to be insufficient in the future. If it shall appear that there is such a danger, yet we cannot alter the law by denying to labor unions the rights and powers which the law gives to all lawful associations.

This statement was made in a dissenting opinion. The prevailing opinion in the same case, however, recognizes the same, in the following words: " A combination among persons merely to regulate their own conduct is within allowable competition, and is lawful, although others may be indirectly affected thereby." Both of these statements from the prevailing and the dissenting opinions were later cited and adopted by District Judge Adams in a prevailing opinion in the circuit court (Wabash R. R. Co. *v.* Hannahan). After quoting from these authorities Judge Adams concludes: " I might continue at length in the citation of cases stating or illustrating the foregoing propositions, but enough has been said to clearly indicate the general rule, . . . in like manner as capital is combined for legitimate purposes, so labor may combine for legitimate purposes."

It must not be inferred, from the foregoing statements however, that these judicial views are unqualified. They are modified in very important particulars. The mere fact of organization is of course not of primary importance in itself. Even without going so far as to indicate that the particular means used to accomplish purposes are not to be overlooked, nearly every general statement that endorses the association qualifies the endorsement. In the quotation above cited Judge Taft found the defendant guilty of the charge, though he was a regularly-recognized officer of the union. The purposes of the strike were not lawful and so the actions in seeking to accomplish those purposes were of course not lawful. A few brief statements from the opinions will serve to show the nature of these more general qualifications. Judge Adams limits his statements just quoted.

> In like manner, as capital is combined for legitimate purposes, so labor may combine for legitimate purposes, but this right of combination, and the resulting right to strike or quit their employment, is a weapon for the defense and protection of employees, and not a weapon of attack. They may, by peaceful and lawful combination and concert of action, be able to so control the supply of labor as to compel the employer to come to their terms, but they are not at liberty to make use of this weapon to otherwise interfere with or injure the employer or co-employee. (Wabash Railroad Co. *v.* Hannahan.)

"Confined to proper limits," says Judge Mitchell,

> both as to end and means, they [the unions] are not only lawful, but laudable. Carried beyond those limits, they are liable to become dangerous agencies for wrong and oppression. Beyond what limits these associations or combinations cannot go, without interfering with the legal rights of others, is a problem which, in various phases, the courts will doubtless be frequently called to pass upon. (Bohn Mfg. Co. *v.* Hollis.)

"Organization . . . must be regarded as having the sanction of law when it is for such legitimate purposes as that of obtaining an advance in the rate of wages or compensation, or of maintaining such rate." This statement is followed, in Curran *v.* Galen, by the one quoted above: "It is proper and praiseworthy, and perhaps falls within the general view of human society which perceives an underlying law that men should unite to achieve that which each by himself cannot achieve, or can achieve less rapidly." Then the qualification is made: "But the social principle which justifies such organizations is departed from when they are so extended in their operation as either to intend or to accomplish injury to others." "The law encourages combination for good," says Judge Carpenter of Connecticut, "and combinations by workmen to better their condition by legitimate and fair means are commendable, and should be encouraged. But combinations for evil purposes, whether by one class of men or another, are detrimental to the public weal and cannot be regarded with favor by the courts." (State *v.* Glidden.)

In one instance the judge in writing the opinion goes further in making his qualification than is usual. District Judge Jackson shows very clearly his feeling in the matter, as appears in the following extract from U. S. *v.* Haggerty.

While I recognize the right for all laborers to combine for the purpose of protecting all their lawful rights, I do not recognize the right of laborers to conspire together to compel employees who are not dissatisfied with their work in the mines to lay down their picks and shovels and to quit their work, without a just and proper reason therefor, merely to gratify a professional set of "agitators, organizers, and walking delegates," who roam all over the country as agents for some combination, who are vampires that live and fatten on the honest labor of the coal miners of the country, and who are busybodies creating dissatisfaction amongst a class of people who are quiet, well-disposed, and who do not want to be disturbed by the unceasing agitation of this class of people. In the case we have under consideration these defendants are known as professional agitators, organizers, and walking delegates. They have nothing in common with the people who are employed in the mines of the Clarksburg Fuel Co. . . . Their mission here is to foment trouble, create dissatisfaction among the employees in coal mines, producing strikes, which tend greatly to damage and injure the business of the employers. . . . The right of a citizen to labor for wages that he is satisfied with is a right protected by law, and is entitled to the same protection as free speech and should be better protected than the abuse of free speech, in which the organizers and agitators indulge in trying to produce strikes.

As to the attitude of courts toward organization, so far as the mere existence of the organization is concerned, there can be no doubt. In a legal sense as well as in an industrial sense, it has come to stay. Iis legal rlght to existence is so generally taken for granted that such expressions are becoming less frequent. As Vice Chancellor Green expresses it:

> No unprejudiced person at this day wishes to place any obstacle in the way of labor organizations conducting their operations within lawful limits. . . . Every one must acknowledge that organization has accomplished much in the past for the benefit of the workingman, and recognize its possibilities to secure to them, in the future, the enjoyment of other privileges. (Barr *v.* Essex Trades Council.)

The same attitude is again concisely expressed by Presiding Justice Chipman of California.

> We do not find it necessary to enter upon a discussion of the right of labor to organize for mutual benefit and self-protection. All sane thinking persons concede this right. . . . Nor are we called upon to lay down general rules by which labor organizations should be governed in their relations to the business interests of the country and to society. (Jordahl *v.* Hayda.)

With the right to form associations so generally established, the difficulties are far from settled. In fact it is not until this point is reached that any real obstacle arises. What may these associations do and what may they not do in carrying forward their purposes? The answers to these questions must be considered more in detail. The courts lay down no general propositions that may be taken as a final answer. Each act in furtherance of trade union purposes is taken by itself and is put to the tests that exist in the already established general rules of law. Out of the numerous cases have appeared the general principles in the minds of the several courts toward the various points. It is these cases that must be examined and the opinions expressed in connection with them that must be studied in order to reach any general answer to the question that has been stated.

CHAPTER IX

Unionism—Legislation

Among the numerous plans devised by labor leaders to secure advantage to their organizations one that seemed at first most promising was legislation. Through their regularly-organized means of appealing to state legislatures, laws were secured in several states intended to help the union man against the employer and the non-unionist. The legislation thus secured was substantially uniform. It made it a misdemeanor for an employer to discharge an employee because he was, or was about to become, a member of a labor union. In one instance a law was passed forbidding an employer to compel an employee to agree not to join a union as a condition of employment. These laws were soon brought before the courts of the several states and the United States supreme court for adjudication. There is no difference in the conclusions reached by the courts in reference to this issue. Some dissenting opinions were written, however, and the views expressed in these are both interesting and important.

The line of argument adopted in the majority opinions is in the main the same, though some are much more fully elaborated. Its most concise and direct expression is perhaps that written by Judge Magruder of Illinois.

One citizen cannot be compelled to give employment to another citizen, nor can any one be compelled to be employed against his will. The act of 1893, now under consideration, deprives the employer of the right to terminate his contract with his employee. The right to terminate such a contract is guaranteed by the organic law of the state. The legislature is forbidden to deprive the employer or employee of the exercise of that right. The legislature has no authority to pronounce the performance of an innocent act criminal, when the public health, safety, comfort, or welfare is not interfered with. The statute in question says that, if a man exercises his constitutional right to terminate a contract with his employee, he shall, without a hearing, be punished as for the commission of a crime. . . . Liberty includes not only the right to labor, but to refuse to labor, and consequently the right to contract to labor or for labor, and to terminate such contracts, and to refuse to make such contracts. (Gillespie *v.* People.)

That such legislation as this is in violation of the right of contract, and that the right of contract is a constitutional right, is forcibly set forth by Judge Sherwood of Missouri. This opinion was the earliest of the important ones, being handed down in 1895.

These terms, "life," "liberty," and "property," are representative terms, and cover every right to which a member of the body politic is entitled under the law. Within their comprehensive scope are embraced . . . the right to buy and sell as others may—all our liberties, personal, civil and political —in short, all that makes life worth living; and of none of these liberties can any one be deprived except by due process of law. Now, as before stated, each of these rights heretofore mentioned carries with it, as its natural and necessary coincident, all that effectuates and renders complete the full, unrestrained enjoyment of that right. Take, for instance, that of property. Necessarily blended with that right are those of acquiring property by labor, by contract, and also of terminating that contract at pleasure, being liable, however, civilly for any unwarranted termination. . . .

Here, the law under review declares that to be a crime which consists alone in the exercise of a constitutional right, to wit, that of terminating a contract—one of the essential attributes of property, indeed property itself, under preceding definitions. Brought to the bar of a court on such a charge, the accused would have been prejudged in so far as the criminality of the act charged is concerned. No question could there be made or admitted as to the quality of the act. That would have been settled by the previous legislative declaration, and it would only remain to find the fact as charged in order to declare the guilt as charged. But the fact as charged, as already seen, is not a crime, and will not be a crime so long as constitutional guaranties and constitutional prohibitions are respected and enforced. If an owner, etc., obeys the law on which this prosecution rests, he is thereby deprived of a right and a liberty to contract or terminate a contract, as all others may; if he disobeys it, then he is punished for the performance of an act wholly innocent, unless, indeed, the doing of such act, guaranteed by the organic law—the exercise of a right of which the legislature is forbidden to deprive him—can by that body be conclusively pronounced criminal. We deny the power of the legislature to do this, to brand as an offense that which the constitution designates and declares to be a right, and therefore an innocent act; and consequently we hold that the statute which professes to exert such a power is nothing more nor less than a "legislative judgment," and an attempt to deprive all who are included within its terms of a constitutional right without due process of law. (State *v.* Julow.)

The most elaborate opinion of this series comes from the Wisconsin court. It was written by Judge Dodge. Of this opinion as a whole it has been said from the United States circuit court (Union Pacific *v.* Ruef):

As to what the rights of property mean, and of what liberty of contract consists, of all that has been written upon these all-important and most vital questions there is no paper of greater ability, evidencing more learning, than the very recent opinion of the supreme court of Wisconsin in the case of State *v.* Kreutzberg.

The case cannot be here quoted in full, but extensive citations from it should be made:

However well established that the words "liberty" and "pursuit of happiness" include the right of private contract, so that a deprivation of the latter is a deprivation of each of the former, yet the far more difficult question remains whether any given statute constitutes a forbidden deprivation. . . .

Free will in making private contracts, and even in greater degree in refusing to make them, is one of the most important and sacred of the individual rights intended to be protected. That the present act curtails it directly, seriously, and prejudicially, cannot be doubted. The success in life of the employer depends on the efficiency, fidelity, and loyalty of his employees. Without enlarging upon or debating the relative advantages or disadvantages of the labor union, either to its members or to the community at large, it is axiomatic that an employer cannot have undivided fidelity, loyalty, and devotion to his interests from an employee who has given to an association right to control his conduct. He may by its decisions be required to limit the amount of his daily product. He may be restrained from teaching his art to others. He may be forbidden to work in association with other men whose service the employer desires. He may not be at liberty to work with such machines or upon such materials or products as the employer deems essential to his success. In all these respects he may be disabled from the full degree of usefulness attributable to the same abilities in another who had not yielded up to an association any right to restrain his freedom of will and exertion in his employer's behalf according to the latter's wishes. Such considerations an employer has a right to deem valid reasons for preferring not to jeopardize his success by employing members of organizations. A man who has by agreement or otherwise shackled any of his faculties—even his freedom of will—may well be considered less useful or less desirable by some employers than if free and untrammeled. Whether the workman can find in his membership in such organizations advantages and compensations to offset his lessened desirability in the industrial market is a question each must decide for himself. His right to freedom in so doing is of the same grade and sacredness as that of the employer to consent or refuse to employ him according to the decision he makes. We must not forget that our government is founded on the idea of equality of all individuals before the law. Such restraints as may be placed on one may be placed on another. If the liberty of the employer to contract or refuse to contract may be denied, so may that of the employee. In answering the question now before us, we may not forget the possibility of being called on to answer whether the legislature may make a criminal of the employee who quits, for example, because his employer joins a blacklisting association; because non-union men or members of some other union are employed, or non-union or forbidden machines or materials are used; because of an obnoxious foreman; because excessive hours of work are required; because compelled to trade at employer's store or board at his boarding house; or because of any other fact or conduct now considered entirely adequate reason for refusing or leaving a particular service. It must not be forgotten, if, as counsel for the state argues, the laborer is too weak to meet the employer on equal terms in the field of contract, that he will be far more subject to the latter's control and oppression in the field of politics, and that laws of the above character will surely come, if within the proper province of the legislature, unless, as we have faith to believe, the character and the individuality of the wage earners of the country are sufficient to maintain their independence—both contractual and political—in a field of equal rights under the law, and of full liberty to each to sell and buy labor to and from whom he will. . . .

In considering our own statute under which relator is committed, it must first be noted that we are concerned only with that portion added to pre-existing statutes (section 4466b, Rev. St., 1898) by the act of 1890: " No person or corporation shall discharge an employee because he is a member of any labor organization," for the relator is not charged with breach of any other of the provisions of that act. Confining ourselves, then, to the act so charged, and the statutory prohibition involved, is it within the legislative power to make criminal the refusal to contract with another for his labor for any reason which the employer deems cogent? We speak of refusal to contract, for, while the act mentions only discharge, it is in no wise limited to situations where there is any contract or other right to continuance of employment, and is obviously intended by the framers to apply generally to the relation of employer and employee, where, as common knowledge assures us, there is usually no term of employment, and each day constitutes a new contract. As each morning comes, the employee is free to decide not to work, the employer to decide not to receive him, but for this statute. That the act in question invades the liberty of the employer in an extreme degree, and in a respect entitled to be held sacred, except for the most cogent and urgent countervailing considerations, we have pointed out. Hardly any of the personal civil rights is higher than that of free will in forming and continuing the relation of master and servant. If that may be denied by law, the result is legalized thralldom, not liberty—certainly not to the laboring men of the country. This aspect of the subject is too clear to warrant further discussion.

The most authoritative opinion is that of the United States supreme court written in 1908 by Justice Harlan (Adair *v.* U. S.). The case dealt specifically with a federal law making it unlawful for an officer of an interstate carrier to discharge an employee because of his membership in a labor union. Though dealing with interstate commerce primarily, the opinion deals in such a way with the principles involved as to make it of wide importance. After having studied the question "with care and deliberation," as "admittedly one of importance," the court "reached a conclusion which, in its judgment, is consistent with both the words and spirit of the Constitution, and is sustained as well by sound reason." The section is "in our opinion an invasion of the personal liberty, as well as of the right of property guaranteed by the (Fifth) Amendment."

It is sufficient in this case to say that, as agent of the railroad company, and, as such, responsible for the conduct of the business of one of its departments, it was the defendant Adair's right—and that right inhered in his personal liberty, and was also a right of property—to serve his employer as best he could, so long as he did nothing that was reasonably forbidden by law as injurious to the public interests. It was the right of the defendant to prescribe the terms upon which the services of Coppage would be accepted, and it was the right of Coppage to become or not, as he chose, an employee of the railroad company upon the terms offered to him. Mr. Cooley, in his treatise on *Torts,* p. 278, well says: "It is a part of every man's civil rights that he be left at liberty to refuse business relations with any person whomsoever, whether the refusal rests upon reason, or is the result of whim, caprice, prejudice or malice. With his reasons neither the public nor third persons have any legal concern. It is also his right to have business relations with anyone with whom he can make contracts, and, if he is wrongfully deprived of this right by others, he is entitled to redress." . . .

While, as already suggested, the right of liberty and property guaranteed by the Constitution against deprivation without due process of law is subject to such reasonable restraints as the common good or the general welfare may require, it is not within the functions of government—at least, in the absence of contract between the parties—to compel any person, in the course of his business and against his will, to accept or retain the personal services of another, or to compel any person, against his will, to perform personal services for another. The right of a person to sell his labor upon such terms as he deems proper is, in its essence, the same as the right of the purchaser of labor to prescribe the conditions upon which he will accept such labor from the person offering to sell it. So the right of the employee to quit the service of the employer, for whatever reason, is the same as the right of the employer, for whatever reason, to dispense with the services of such employee. It was the legal right of the defendant, Adair—however unwise such a course might have been—to discharge Coppage because of his being a member of a labor organization, as it was the legal right of Coppage, if he saw fit to do so—however unwise such a course on his part might have been—to quit the service in which he was engaged, because the defendant employed some persons who were not members of a labor organization. In all such particulars the employer and employee have equality of right, and any legislation that disturbs that equality is an arbitrary interference with the liberty of contract which no government can legally justify in a free land. . . . In the absence, however, of a valid contract between the parties controlling their conduct towards each other and fixing a period of service, it cannot be, we repeat, that an employer is under any legal obligation, against his will, to retain an employee in his personal service any more than an employee can be compelled, against his will, to remain in the personal service of another. So far as this record discloses the facts the defendant, who seemed to have authority in the premises, did not agree to keep Coppage in service for any particular time, nor did Coppage agree to remain in such service a moment longer than he chose. The latter was at liberty to quit the service without assigning any reason for his leaving. And the defendant was at liberty, in his discretion, to discharge Coppage from service without giving any reason for so doing.

As the relations and the conduct of the parties towards each other were not controlled by any contract other than a general employment on one side to accept the services of the employee and a general agreement on the other side to render services to the employer—no term being fixed for the continuance of the employment—Congress could not, consistently with the Fifth Amendment, make it a crime against the United States to discharge the employee because of his being a member of a labor organization. . . .

If such a power exists in Congress it is difficult to perceive why it might not, by absolute regulation, require interstate carriers, under penalties, to employ, in the conduct of its interstate business, *only* members of labor organizations, or *only* those who are *not* members of such organizations—a power which could not be recognized as existing under the Constitution of the United States.

In the case of the enactment of a law forbidding an employer to compel an employee to agree not to join a union as a condition of employment, the line of reasoning was much the same. The case came before the New York court of appeals as People *v.* Marcus. The conclusion was that "the freedom of contract which entitles an employer to make by agreement his place of business wholly within the control of a labor union entitles him, if he so desires, to require of his employees that they be wholly independent of any labor union."

These opinions leave no doubt as to the views of the great majority of those judges who have been called upon to render decisions. The restriction which the legislation under consideration seeks to place upon the employer in favor of the union workman is opposed to individual liberty and also to property rights. In consequence of these rights everyone enjoys freedom to contract with any one who is willing to enter into the contract relation. Nor can the restriction be justified as an excercise of the police power.

There is no reason in public policy that will justify such legislation.

The prevalence of this view is indicated by the fact that courts that have heard these cases have been made up of at least thirty-two judges and that only three of these have recorded dissenting opinions. The importance of these dissents may be measured by noticing the cases. One was before the New York court of appeals and dealt with the statute forbidding an employer to require, as a condition of employment, that a workman shall agree not to join a union. Justice Bartlett wrote the dissenting opinion in this case. The other was the case before the United States supreme court to which reference has already been made. Justices McKenna and Holmes wrote two dissenting opinions, which because of their position as federal supreme court justices are of considerable weight. That the case dealt specifically with interstate commerce detracts but little from its importance. The leading principles were raised and fully discussed, as has already been shown.

Justice Bartlett's view may be summed up in the following extract taken from his dissenting opinion:

The freedom of contract should be untrammeled. A person desiring employment ought not to be required to abstain from joining any labor organization, nor should he be compelled to join a labor organization. The statute should have covered both cases. I regard this legislation as a step in the right direction, although it was evidently drawn in the interest of labor organizations and without regard to securing absolute freedom of contract. The employer is to be protected and the employed as well. I trust the day is not far distant when to every workingman will be open all the avenues of employment, whether he belongs to labor unions or other organizations, or stands alone upon his individual right to work for such a wage as seems to him just. This statute is not, in my opinion, unconstitutional, but is to be regarded as a step in the direction dictated by every consideration of public policy.

Justice McKenna, in his opinion enters into a careful analysis of the provisions of the entire law of which the contested section was a part and insists that the section must be considered with reference to the other sections. The purpose of the statute as a whole is to prevent or settle disputes between carriers and their employees. In the light of this purpose the section in question gets its justification. Liberty is not entirely free from restraints, even under the Fifth Amendment. Some restrictions are justifiable. The question then is whether the section in dispute

has relation to the purpose which induced the act, and which it was enacted to accomplish, and whether such purpose is in aid of interstate commerce, and not a mere restriction upon the liberty of carriers to employ whom they please or to have business relations with whom they please.

The purpose of the act is to be approved, and in its efforts to attain this purpose "the congressional judgment of means should not be brought under a rigid limitation." If labor associations are to be commended, Congress certainly may recognize their existence and their power "as conditions to be counted with in framing its legislation." The justification of Congress in its efforts to accomplish its purpose is evident in the events of 1894. The law of 1888

did not recognize labor associations or distinguish between the members of such associations and the other employees of carriers. It failed in its purpose, whether from defect in its provisions or other cause, we may only conjecture. At any rate it did not avert the strike of 1894. Investigation followed, and, as a result of it, the act of 1898 was finally passed. Presumably its provisions and remedy were addressed to the mischief which the act of 1888 failed to reach or avert. It was the judgment of Congress that the scheme of arbitration might be helped by engaging in it the labor associations.

The final conclusion of the opinion is that if the disputed section is to be stricken from the law, the law is made ineffective in accomplishing its purpose.

Justice Holmes bases his dissent upon the following considerations:

As we all know, there are special labor unions of men engaged in the service of carriers. These unions exercise a direct influence upon the employment of labor in that business, upon the terms of such employment, and upon the business itself. Their very existence is directed specifically to the business, and their connection with it is, at least, as intimate and important as that of safety couplers, and, I should think, as the liability of master to servant—matters which, it is admitted, Congress might regulate, so far as they concern commerce among the states. I suppose that it hardly would be denied that some of the relations of railroads with unions of railroad employees are closely enough connected with commerce to justify legislation by Congress. If so, legislation to prevent the exclusion of such unions from employment is sufficiently near.

The ground on which this particular law is held bad is not so much that it deals with matters remote from commerce among the states, as that it interferes with the paramount individual rights secured by the Fifth Amendment. The section is, in substance, a very limited interference with freedom of contract, no more. It does not require the carriers to employ anyone. It does not forbid them to refuse to employ anyone, for any reason they deem good, even where the notion of a choice of persons is a fiction and wholesale employment is necessary upon general principles that it might be proper to control. The section simply prohibits the more powerful party to exact certain undertakings, or to threaten dismissal or unjustly discriminate on certain grounds against those already employed. I hardly can suppose that the grounds on which a contract lawfully may be made to end are less open to regulation than other terms. So I turn to the general question whether the employment can be regulated at all. I confess that I think that the right to make contracts at will that has been derived from the word "liberty" in the Amendments has been stretched to its extreme by the decisions; but they agree that sometimes the right may be restrained. Where there is, or generally is believed to be, an important ground of public policy for restraint, the Constitution does not forbid it, whether this court agrees or disagrees with the policy pursued. It cannot be doubted that to prevent strikes, and, so far as possible, to foster its scheme of arbitration, might be deemed by Congress an important point of policy, and I think it impossible to say that Congress might not reasonably think that the provision in question would help a good deal to carry its policy along. But suppose the only effect really were to tend to bring about the complete unionizing of such railroad laborers as Congress can deal with, I think that object alone would justify the act. I quite agree that the question what and how much good labor unions do, is one on which intelligent people may differ; I think that laboring men sometimes attribute to them advantages, as many attribute to combinations of capital disadvantages, that really are due to economic conditions of a far wider and deeper kind; but I could not pronounce it unwarranted if Congress should decide that to foster a strong union was for the best interest, not only of the men, but of the railroads and the country at large.

While the unconstitutionality of laws to prevent the discharge of men because of their membership in unions cannot be doubted, yet the principles underlying the dissenting opinions are of interest. They suggest the question, whether in spite of the almost unanimous agreement there are not signs of the beginning of a modification, if not a change, in the view. The majority opinion is based on the long-established and widely-accepted understanding of freedom of contract. This is inherited from an earlier individualist period. Is that understanding formed in that earlier period to pass unmodified into our modern view of socialized industry? The extracts above quoted reveal clearly the origin of the view held by the majority of the judges. Do the dissenting opinions show the entrance of a new view?

Mr. Justice Knowlton, of the Massachusetts court, in a prevailing opinion, held such a law to be as unreasonable as would be a law which would prohibit the coercion of a person into joining a labor organization as a condition of employment, the two alike being a violation of freedom of contract. (Berry *v.* Donovan.) Mr. Justice Bartlett, of the New York court, in his dissenting opinion, at the outset declares positively in favor of freedom of contract. He then maintains that "a person desiring employment ought not to be required to abstain from joining any labor organization, nor should he be compelled to join a labor organization. The statute should have covered both cases." Yet he declares that he regards the legislation "as a step in the right direction" and concludes that the statute is not unconstitutional "but is to be regarded as a step in the direction dictated by every consideration of public policy."

Both are thus insistent upon freedom of contract. In the one case it is to be preserved through non-interference. Legislation forbidding an employer to require an employee either to join or not to join a union is an infringement of contractual freedom. This is the older view. It is also one that considers principally the position of the employer and his right to contract with whomever he may choose. In the other case freedom of contract is to be preserved, but by a different method—that of legal enactment. Legislation declaring that an employer shall not discharge an employee because of either membership or non-membership in a union should be held as no infringement upon contractual freedom but rather as a protection to such freedom. This is the newer view. It is also one that considers the position of the employee and his right to contract with an employer for employment without regard to his relation with organized labor. The difference is a significant one. The position of the employee becomes one equal in importance to that of the employer.

These are the two views as revealed in the prevailing and dissenting opinions. If real equality before the law and real freedom of contract, applied equally to both parties, lies in either one of these two views and not in the other, it is important that it be known which is the one to be chosen. If it be true that actual equality lies in the minority view, that view must ultimately express itself in the majority opinions. If labor unions are to continue to be recognized as legal in themselves, it is not easy to see why the employer should be left undisturbed in his position of bargaining advantage to dictate whether his employees should be members of unions or not. Clearly when one side has a decided advantage in making a bargain as the employer generally has, it is not an exaggeration of terms to use the word " dictate."

There are principles in Mr. Justice Holmes's dissenting opinion that are also significant. First is the fact of railroads as common carriers. Legislatures always exercise a positive control over public-service corporations. The public interest is especially concerned. If unions are inseparably connected with the activity of these public-service corporations, should not the government recognize it? Safety couplers, liability of master to servant, are simply instances of a large number of cases where legislatures now interfere. It seems to the mind of the justice that labor unions may reasonably be included in the list.

But the second point is of greater import. Individual rights as secured in the Fifth Amendment are at stake. But who are the individuals concerned? and what are the rights? The individuals are employees as well as employers. "The section simply prohibits the more powerful party to exact certain undertakings or to threaten dismissal or unjustly discriminate on certain grounds against those already employed." The notion of a choice of persons, or of individual bargaining, is referred to as a "fiction," both the fact and the necessity in actual industry being "wholesale employment." "This it might be proper to control." This is the practical view of employment as it exists. It throws altogether a new light upon the older view of individual rights in freedom of contract. What are the rights? The rights of these individuals are not passed without comment. The right to make contracts at will, derived from the word "liberty" in the Amendments, has, in the opinion of the justice, been "stretched to its extreme" by the decisions. Even these decisions, however, agree that sometimes the right may be restrained. The necessity arising out of public policy justifies the restriction and it is not for the court to determine the necessity. This is the newer view again as applied to unions and common carriers. If it is to have any influence, it will be in the direction of bringing the majority opinions of the future more fully into line with the changed conditions of industry.

CHAPTER X

Unionism—Closed Shop Contracts

Failing in their efforts to secure legislation that would assist in strengthening the position of organized labor, the leaders have entered upon other lines of activity with a view to accomplishing the same ends. The courts had insisted strongly that freedom of contract should be left undisturbed. With the right to contract so jealously guarded this seemed to suggest a way out. Contracts could be entered into with employers in which the employers, for various considerations, would agree to employ only union men. That such contracts have been made frequently is a matter of common knowledge. In connection with some of them troubles have arisen and the courts have been appealed to. Their opinions in such cases are on some points very clear and uniform. This uniformity does not, however, extend to all cases nor include all judges.

A case of this kind came before the Massachusetts court for full consideration in Berry *v.* Donovan, the opinion being written by Chief Justice Knowlton. The agreement had been made in rather elaborate form. The second clause was as follows:

In consideration of the foregoing valuable privileges, the employer agrees to hire, as shoe workers, only members of the Boot and Shoe Workers' Union in good standing, and further agrees not to retain any shoe worker in his employment after receiving notice from the union that such shoe worker is objectionable to the union, either on account of being in arrears for dues, or disobedience of union rules or laws, or from any other cause.

In accordance with this agreement the plaintiff had been discharged after having worked for nearly four years. He brought suit for damages. The court recognizes that the plaintiff was employed under a contract that was terminable at will. Yet the agreement with the employer, thought the court, authorized the union "to interfere and deprive any workman of his employment for no reason whatever, in the arbitrary exercise of its power." These two points are reconciled in the following manner: "Whatever the contracting parties may do if no one but themselves is concerned, it is evident that, as against the workman, a contract of this kind does not of itself justify interference with his employment by a third person who made the contract with his employer." The interference, even though made in accordance with a contract, is held by the court to be from a motive to injure. This consideration was decisive and damages were awarded. The fact that the workman had been for some time in the employ of Goodrich and Company is the point upon which the opinion is made to turn. "The fact that the plaintiff's contract was terminable at will, instead of ending at a stated time, does not affect his right to recover. It only affects the amount that he is to receive as damages." That the views expressed in the opinion may not be interpreted too broadly the concluding statement places a limitation.

We hold that the defendant was not justified by the contract with Goodrich & Co., or by his relations to the plaintiff, in interfering with the plaintiff's employment under his contract. How far the principles which we adopt would apply, under different conceivable forms of contract, to an interference with a workman not engaged, but seeking employment, or to different methods of boycotting, we have no occasion in this case to decide.

The first case of importance in New York state was Curran *v.* Galen. The parties had agreed that no employee should be allowed to work for longer than four weeks without becoming a member of the union. The opinion first deals in a more general way with the principles involved.

Public policy and the interests of society favor the utmost freedom in the citizen to pursue his lawful trade or calling, and if the purpose of an organization or combination of workingmen be to hamper or to restrict that freedom, and, through contracts or arrangements with employers, to coerce other workingmen to become members of the organization and to come under its rules and conditions, under the penalty of the loss of their positions and of deprivation of employment, then that purpose seems clearly unlawful, and militates against the spirit of our government and the nature of our institutions. The effectuation of such a purpose would conflict with that principle of public policy which prohibits monopolies and exclusive privileges. It would tend to deprive the public of the services of men in useful employments and capacities. It would, to use the language of Mr. Justice Barrett, " impoverish and crush a citizen for no reason connected in the slightest degree with the advancement of wages or the maintenance of the rate."

Following this, and bearing more directly upon the facts of the case, it is stated that:

While it may be true, as argued, that the contract was entered into, on the part of the [employers], with the object of avoiding disputes and conflicts with the workingmen's organization, that feature and such an intention cannot aid the defense, nor legalize a plan of compelling workingmen not in affiliation with the organization to join it, at the peril of being deprived of their employment and of the means of making a livelihood.

Before the next important case came to the New York court, that court handed down its important decision and opinion in National Protective Association *v.* Cumming. This has by some been held to be a reversal of the view announced in Curran *v.* Galen. Others regard these two cases as not at all at variance. The minority opinion in the more recent case referred for its authority to the Curran case. This was the condition when Jacobs *v.* Cohen came before the court for a verdict on a closed shop contract. The opinion was influenced by that written in the Cumming case. The line of argument in this last opinion is not elaborate. It may be summed-up in the following extract from Judge Gray's opinion:

> Within even the view expressed by the minority of the judges of this court in the Cumming case, the contract in the present case was not unlawful which the employer made with his workingmen. . . . This contract was voluntarily entered into by Cohens, and, if it provided for the performance of the firm's work by those only who were accredited members in good standing of an organization of a class of workingmen whom they employed, were they not free to do so? If they regarded it as beneficial for them to do so (and such is a recital of the contract), does it lie in their mouths now to urge its illegality? That, incidentally, it might result in the discharge of some of those employed, for failure to come into affiliation with their fellow workmen's organization, or that it might prevent others from being engaged upon the work, is neither something of which the employers may complain, nor something with which public policy is concerned.

That the view expressed was not unanimously adopted is evident from the dissenting opinion written by Judge

Vann. He expressed his views so vigorously and the views themselves are so unusual that an extended extract is inserted.

The business affected did not belong to the union, or its members, but to the defendants, who agreed, voluntarily, of course, to employ and discharge workmen at the dictation of the union. The labor department of the industry was under the control of the union, for both employer and employed, abrogating their own rights, placed themselves under its command in that respect. This was a form of slavery, even if voluntarily submitted to; for whoever controls the means by which a man lives controls the man himself. Both the proprietors and the workmen seem to have walked under the yoke of the union without a protest. The employers could employ no one who was not a member of the union, and not even then unless he bore its pass card. They could have no apprentices. Even in an emergency and with the consent of their workmen, they could not exceed the hours of labor prescribed by the union. A baster, however willing, could not sew on a button, and a presser, even if he wanted to, could not make a buttonhole. . . . Thus master and men bound themselves by these remarkable stipulations made with a voluntary association, which had no pecuniary interest in the business or in the labor of those employed. The labor of the employees belonged to themselves, and they had a right to sell it to whom they chose and on such conditions as were mutually satisfactory. The business belonged to the defendants, and they had the right to employ any man who was willing to work for them; but by this agreement an outsider intervened, and compelled those who owned the business and those who did the work to submit to its direction. As was said by the court below, the will of the employer "was subjected by executory contract to an arbitrary domination, which not only deprived" him "of all freedom of action, but also crushed the rights and interests of all independent competition in the field of labor." The manifest purpose of the contract was to prevent competition and create a monopoly of labor. A combination of capital, or labor, or as in this case of both, to prevent the free pursuit of any lawful business, trade, or occupation, is forbidden both by statute and the common law.

When read by the side of the prevailing opinion the protest seems ineffective indeed. There seems to be in the mind of the writer of this dissent a vague feeling that a closed shop is an injustice to the non-union workmen and to the employer as well, but the reasoning by which the view is supported certainly is not strong.

These are the leading cases that discuss the question squarely on its merits. Two others have resulted in long opinions, but they deal primarily with the right of unionists to strike for the purpose of securing a closed shop agreement. In O'Brien *v.* People, the company had refused to sign such a contract. The unionists had stopped work for the purpose of inducing thereby the employer to accept the agreement. This act is interpreted by the court as coercion.

There can be no doubt that any attempt to coerce [the employer] into signing said agreement by threats to order a strike was unlawful. It was violative of the clear legal right of the company, and was unjust and oppressive as to those who did not belong to the labor organizations.

By the strike and its accompanying acts the unionists "sought by threats, intimidation, and violence to prevent men and women from taking the places of the strikers." Further evidence of lawlessness led the court to view the entire matter as one of unlawful coercion.

The last case to be considered under this topic was also a strike, in this instance against an open shop policy that the employer proposed to adopt. (Reynolds *v.* Davis.) Two opinions were written, both reaching the same conclusion but by different courses of reasoning. Judge Loring's argument has to do largely with the rights of unions as against non-union men. This general subject is treated elsewhere. Chief Justice Knowlton bases his conclusions on the ground that

> the strike was for a closed shop in the sense that the shop should be closed arbitrarily to all workmen not members of the union, not because such workmen were personally objectionable in any particular, nor because there was not work enough for all the members of the union if non-union men were employed, but to compel all workmen to join the union for the purpose of creating a monopoly in the labor market, whereby to be able to contend successfully with employers whenever a controversy should arise. . . . A strike to compel a closed shop, merely to accomplish such a purpose, would not be justifiable on principles of competition, either as against non-union workmen or as against the employer, but would be unlawful.

The judical attitude, then, is not settled into agreement. Of course violence or intimidation will, if used by one party to secure agreement, free the other from the binding force of the contract. There is uniformity on that point worked out through other channels and applicable in all cases. Coercion aside, there remains the uncertainty as to how the courts will view a contract of this kind. It may come within the right of the contracting parties so long as the agreement is entered upon voluntarily. It may, on the other hand, be viewed as a monopoly against which even the freedom of contract will not stand.

CHAPTER XI

Unionism—Rights of Unions

In the foregoing pages have been considered the strike, the boycott, the picket and the blacklist, also the right of organization and certain policies directly connected with such right, as legislation and contracts intended to secure to the associations a more certain existence. There remain yet for consideration a variety of topics growing naturally out of these leading points of policy and very directly connected with them. Though the legal views on the points already considered may not seem so clear and unanimous as one might desire, yet compared with those that are to follow they are far more satisfactory.

The complex interrelations between the employer, the non-union employee, the unionist and the consumer, and the relation of the unionist to his employer and to his union offer a situation that has not yet been fully analyzed by our courts. Indeed many of the problems are so new that judges have expressed themselves with unusual caution.

The extracts that follow necessarily lack somewhat in consecutiveness, as each deals with a particular set of facts. Yet a reading of them will serve to reveal the attitude of the judges better than any attempted summary could do.

The problems that arise and concerning which the authorities are not in agreement are summed up by Judge Goode of Missouri as three in number.

The principal discrepancies among the authorities in cases like this are: (a) As to what means may lawfully be used by a collection or order of workmen to cause the discharge of other workmen; but most courts hold the means must not pass beyond persuasion, and take on a coercive, violent, or punitive character. (b) Whether means which would be lawful if used by an individual become unlawful and amount to a conspiracy when used in combination. (c) Whether acts which might lawfully be done simply to further the welfare of those who participate in them become unlawful when inspired by a malevolent design to injure obnoxious workmen. (Carter *v.* Oster.)

Judge Halloway of Montana (Lindsay *v.* Montana F. of L.) declares that "great diversity of opinion among the courts has arisen over a consideration of the question: what means may trade unions employ to further the objects of their organizations?"

Again the difficulty is dwelt upon by District Judge Sanborn, writing from the circuit court.

The right to strike being clear, the first question which comes up is, how far may the union and its members go to make the strike effective by preventing the employer from engaging other workmen, so that he will eventually be compelled to yield to the demands of the strikers? This is usually the pinch of the situation.

Finally, Judge Loring of Massachusetts, writing in 1906, admits his perplexity as follows:

In other words, we have to deal with one of the great and pressing questions growing out of the powerful combinations, sometimes of capital and sometimes of labor, which have been instituted in recent years where their actions come into conflict with the interests of individuals. The combination in the case at bar is a combination of workmen, and the conflict is between a labor union on the one hand and several unorganized laborers on the other hand.

It is only in recent years that these great and powerful combinations have made their appearance, and the limits to which they may go in enforcing their demands are far from being settled. (Picket *v.* Walsh.)

But statements setting forth the newness of the problems involved and the difficulty of settling them do not help the court materially, for a decision must be made and one that the court is willing to stand for. This has kept the courts within very narrow limits so far as expression of principles is concerned and has at the same time forced them back to fundamental propositions. Much depends, as will readily be seen, upon what principles are adopted as fundamental and what ones are deemed secondary. The views may be classed roughly as those favorable to the unions and those unfavorable. Of the first class are the following. Judge Sanborn, after making the statement that has just been quoted, declares the difficulty of the problem.

Here is the point where two equally clear and valuable constitutional rights come into opposition—the right of the workmen to get as much as possible for himself on the best terms, and the right of the employer to use his capital and ability as he pleases to secure whatever profit his investment and skill may bring. The legal right involved is single, but asserted by two independent and conflicting interests, and the question is, which one must yield his right to that of the other, so far as they conflict.

The general answer to this question is that neither must be permitted to maliciously injure the other without just cause or excuse. A more special answer is that so long as each, in the conflict between them, pursues only his own fair interest or advantage, and not the injury of the other, he is not liable for any injury which is merely incidental. . . . In other words, indirect interference by a labor union with the employer's business, not amounting to coercion, by preventing him from getting workmen to carry on his shop, is not unlawful so long as the combination is merely taking measures to secure its own legitimate advantage or economic advancement, although harm may incidentally result to the employer. So long as the betterment of labor conditions is the main object sought, even though the strikers may succeed in persuading all the available laborers to join their union, and support the strike, and, having thus secured a monopoly of the labor market, compel the employer, after long struggle and great loss of profit, to yield to the demands or go out of business, yet such injuries cannot be regarded as malicious, or such acts as criminal or unlawful, either at the common law or under section 4466a of the Wisconsin Revised Statutes of 1898.

The opinions that expressly favor the union man in his rivalry with the non-union workman are not numerous. State *v.* Kreutzberg has several times been referred to and quoted. It argues directly against laws that forbid the discharge of men because of their membership in unions. In that opinion views were expressed in favor of the freedom of the laborer which, as principles, are quite as much on the side of the union laborer as on that of his non-union rival. Of particular interest are the extracts from other opinions that are cited and adopted.

A man's right not to work or not to pursue a particular trade or calling, or to determine when or where or with whom he will work, is in law a right of precisely the same nature, and entitled to just the same protection, as a man's right to trade or work. (Herschell, J., Allen *v.* Flood.) It is, in my opinion, the absolute right of every workman to exercise his own option with regard to the persons in whose society he will agree or continue to work. (Lord Watson, Allen *v.* Flood.) Every man has a right under the law, as between himself and others, to full freedom in disposing of his own labor or capital according to his own will. (Doremus *v.* Hennessy.) It is a part of every man's civil rights that he be left at liberty to refuse business relations with any person whomsoever, whether the refusal rests upon reason, or is the result of whim, caprice, prejudice, or malice. (Judge Cooley.) Every man has a natural right to hire his services to any one he pleases, or refrain from such hiring; and so, likewise, it is the right of every one to determine whose services he will hire. . . . Governments, therefore, cannot exert any restraint upon the actions of the parties. (Tiedeman.)

Judge Goode of Missouri says:

Many decisions, and perhaps the weight of authority, uphold the right of employees, either individually or in combination, to quit working because some fellow servant is obnoxious to them when they are not governed by a contract of service of definite duration. This is on the principle that employees may choose both their employer and their working associates; and it may well be that, if not under contract, they may leave an employment when they please for any purpose they conceive to be for their welfare, or likely to aid in the amelioration of the lot of the laboring classes, if their conduct is dominated by such a motive rather than by a malicious desire to injure some one else. In recognition of this principle, the right of artisans to strike for an increase of wages or for shorter hours, or because a co-employee is obnoxious to them, has been often adjudged, though perhaps it cannot be said that the current of authority is unbroken in favor of the right to strike when the immediate purpose is to cause the discharge of an obnoxious fellow servant, even though the ultimate purpose may be the attainment of better economic and social conditions. (Carter *v.* Oster.)

In Wabash Railroad *v.* Hannahan there is brought out another phase of the argument. To set it forth in Judge Adams's own words:

It is contended that the threatened strike was resorted to by the defendants, not in good faith to redress grievances or secure desired concessions, but as a result of a combination and conspiracy to accomplish the ulterior purpose of securing recognition of their unions or brotherhoods, as authoritative agents or representatives of its members, in all their dealings with the company, and also to unionize the roads of the company, and that the defendants did not honestly and fairly secure the two-thirds vote of the brotherhood employees in favor of the strike, but did secure the same by coercion, misrepresentation, and fraud.

An interesting and able argument in support of this contention is drawn from the provisions of the constitution and general rules of the two brotherhoods involved in this litigation, whereby it is made to appear that a strike may be declared which will have the effect of forcing the minority of the brotherhood members who vote against it and also all nonunion employees in service upon the road of the employer out of work without their consent and even against their wishes. Attention is particularly called to the situation disclosed by the proof in this cause, that a large majority of complainant's employees working on roads east of the Mississippi river, for whose special benefit largely the threatened strike was intended, voted against it; and it is argued that these and other like considerations disclose that the necessary operative results of the system and methods of the brotherhoods in question are subversive alike of the fundamental rights of the employer to manage his own business, and of the employees to bestow their labor as they will.

This kind of argument enters deeply into the domain of political science, and might well be addressed to a body of constructive statesmen or men originally contemplating a labor organization. It is an argument that would be pertinent against the organization of society into government. The will of the individual must consent to yield to the will of the majority, or no organization either of society into government, capital into combination, or labor into coalition can ever be effected. The individual must yield in order that the many may receive a greater benefit. The right of labor to organize for lawful purposes and by organic agreement to subject the individual members to rules, regulations, and conduct prescribed by the majority is no longer an open question in the jurisprudence of this country.

A case that comes close to the border line of what unions may do in rivalry with other workmen is Picket *v.* Walsh. The opinion was written by Judge Loring. Extracts have already been quoted in other connections, but the peculiar interest of the main point in the contention justifies a more careful consideration of its leading principles.

The question at issue, as stated in the opinion, is this:

> Is a union of bricklayers and stone masons justified in striking to force a contractor to employ them by the day to do cleaning and pointing at higher wages than pointers are paid, where the contractors wish to make contracts with the pointers for such work to be done by the piece, because they think they get better work at less cost with no liability for accidents, and where the pointers wish to make contracts for that work with the contractors on terms satisfactory to them?

Before coming to the discussion of the point at issue the opinion reviews the general principles of the rights of working men. These include the right to organize and the general right to strike. This last right, however, in the Commonwealth of Massachusetts is not without limitation. One of the restrictions referred to is that " a labor union could not force other workmen to join it by refusing to work if workmen were employed who were not members of that union." After further consideration of the general principles in which especially the effect of combination is discussed as constituting a limitation upon the rights of workmen, the opinion takes up again the particular case before the court.

The case is a case of competition between the defendant unions and the individual plaintiffs for the work of pointing. The work of pointing for which these two sets of workmen are competing is work which the contractors are obliged to have. One peculiarity of the case therefore is that the fight here is necessarily a triangular one. It necessarily involves the two sets of competing workmen and the contractor, and is not confined to the two parties to the contract, as is the case where workmen strike to get better wages from their employer or other conditions which are better for them. . . .

The right which the defendant unions claim to exercise in carrying their point in the course of this competition is a trade advantage, namely, that they have labor which the contractors want, or, if you please, cannot get elsewhere; and they insist upon using this trade advantage to get additional work, namely, the work of pointing the bricks and stone which they lay. . . . But having regard to the right on which the defendants' organization as a labor union rests, the correlative duty owed by it to others, and the limitation of the defendants' rights coming from the increased power of organization, we are of opinion that it was within the rights of these unions to compete for the work of doing the pointing and, in the exercise of their right of competition, to refuse to lay bricks and set stones unless they were given the work of pointing them when laid. . . .

The result to which that conclusion brings us in the case at bar ought not to be passed by without consideration.

The result is harsh on the contractors, who prefer to give the work to the pointers because (1) the pointers do it by contract (in which case the contractors escape the liability incident to the relation of employer and employee); because (2) the contractors think that the pointers do the work better and if not well done the buildings may be permanently injured by acid; and finally (3) because they get from the pointers better work with less liability at a smaller cost. Again, so far as the pointers (who cannot lay brick or stone) are concerned, the result is disastrous. But all that the labor unions have done is to say you must employ us for all the work or none of it. They have not said that if you employ the pointers you must pay us a fine, as they did in Carew *v.* Rutherford. They have not undertaken to forbid the contractors employing pointers, as they did in Plant *v.* Woods. So far as the labor unions are concerned the contractors can employ pointers if they choose, but if the contractors choose to give the work of pointing the bricks and stones to others, the unions take the stand that the contractors will have to get some one else to lay them. The effect of this in the case at bar appears to be that the contractors are forced against their will to give the work of pointing to the masons and bricklayers. But the fact that the contractors are forced to do what they do not want to do is not decisive of the legality of the labor union's acts. That is true wherever a strike is successful. The contractors doubtless would have liked it better if there had been no competition between the bricklayers and masons on the one hand and the individual pointers on the other hand. But there is competition. There being competition, they prefer the course they have taken. They prefer to give all the work to the unions rather than get nonunion men to lay bricks and stone to be pointed by the plaintiffs.

Further, the effect of complying with the labor unions' demands apparently will be the destruction of the plaintiff's business. But the fact that the business of the plaintiff is destroyed by the acts of the defendants done in pursuance of their right of competition is not decisive of the illegality of them. It is well said by Hammond, J., in Martell *v.* White, 69 N. E., 1085, in regard to the right of a citizen to pursue his business without interference by a combination to destroy it: "Speaking generally, however, competition in business is permitted, although frequently disastrous to those engaged in it. It is always selfish, often sharp, and sometimes deadly."

Justice Holmes has more then once given expression to

a dissenting opinion. The views usually expressed in these opinions take advanced ground. It is doubtful whether the majority of the courts will accept them for some time. The two following extracts are from dissenting opinions written while he was a member of the Massachusetts court.

Although this is not the place for extended economic discussion, and although the law may not always reach ultimate economic conceptions, I think it well to add that I cherish no illusions as to the meaning and effect of strikes. While I think the strike a lawful instrument in the universal struggle of life, I think it pure phantasy to suppose that there is a body of capital of which labor, as a whole, secures a larger share by its means.

The annual product, subject to an infinitesimal deduction for the luxuries of the few, is directed to consumption by the multitude, and is consumed by the multitude always. Organization and strikes may get a larger share for the members of an organization, but, if they do, they get it at the expense of the less organized and less powerful portion of the laboring mass. They do not create something out of nothing.

It is only by divesting our minds of questions of ownership and other machinery of distribution, and by looking solely at the question of consumption,—asking ourselves what is the annual product, who consumes it, and what changes would or could we make,—that we can keep in the world of realities.

But, subject to the qualifications which I have expressed, I think it lawful for a body of workmen to try by combination to get more than they now are getting, although they do it at the expense of their fellows, and to that end to strengthen their union by the boycott and the strike. (Plant *v.* Woods.)

I feel pretty confident that they equally will abandon the idea that an organized refusal by workmen of social intercourse with a man who shall enter their antagonist's employ is lawful, if it is dissociated from any threat of violence, and is made for the sole object of prevailing, if possible, in a contest with their employer about the rate of wages. The fact that the immediate object of the act by which the benefit to themselves is to be gained is to injure their antagonist does not necessarily make it unlawful, any more than when a great house lowers the price of goods for the purpose and with the effect of driving a smaller antagonist from the business. (Vegelahn *v.* Guntner.)

Turning to the other side of the case, there are to be found in abundance expressions of opinion against the lawfulness of efforts of union men to displace their rivals. Separated from the context, many of these expressions sound very similar to those that uphold union rights. The point is stated in its most general terms by Circuit Judge Drummond (Secor *v.* Railway) as early as 1877 before much of the complexity had developed.

We all acknowledge the rights of labor. It is simply the right of the man who performs labor to obtain the price he can from his employer, and not to dictate terms to the employer. The rights of labor result from an agreement made among men, not by an order, or a dictation from one man to another. . . . But when it is claimed that the right of labor consists in not only refusing to labor, but in interfering with the labor of others, we, of course, can have no feeling of respect for any such right as that. . . . What I wish to impress particularly upon them is, that it is incomprehensible to every man of any intelligence, any man who can sympathize even with what are sometimes called the wrongs of labor, that there can be any pretense of right in preventing other men from labor. As I said before, it is an absurdity to say that you can protect the rights of labor by trampling upon the rights of labor.

Twenty years later in the New York court it was said:

The sympathies or the fellow feeling which, as a social

principle, underlies the association of workingmen for their common benefit, are not consistent with a purpose to oppress the individual who prefers by single effort to gain his livelihood. If organization of workingmen is in line with good government, it is because it is intended as a legitimate instrumentality to promote the common good of its members. If it militates against the general public interest, if its powers are directed towards the repression of individual freedom, upon what principle shall it be justified? (Curran *v.* Galen.)

Taking the point of view of the employer's right Judge Brown of Pennsylvania asserts:

The appellee had an unquestioned right, in the conduct of his business, to employ workmen who were independent of any labor union, and he had the further right to adopt a system of apprenticeship which excluded his apprentices from membership in such a union. He was responsible to no one for his reasons in adopting such a system, and no one had a right to interfere with it to his prejudice or injury. Such an interference with it was an interference with his business, and, if unlawful, cannot be permitted. (Flaccus *v.* Smith.)

From the same bench two years later Judge Dean took the right of non-union laborers as a starting point and asserted:

Trades unions may cease to work, for reasons satisfactory to their members; but if they combine to prevent others from obtaining work by threats of a strike, or combine to prevent an employer from employing others by threats of a strike, they combine to accomplish an unlawful purpose—a purpose as unlawful now as it ever was, though not punishable by indictment. Such combination is a despotic and tyrannical violation of the indefeasible right of labor to acquire property, which courts are bound to restrain. It is utterly subversive of the letter and spirit of the Declaration of Rights. If such combination be in accord with the law of the trades union, then that law and the organic law of the people of a free commonwealth cannot stand together. One or the other must go down. (Erdman *v.* Mitchell.)

Judge Wiswell of Maine viewed the matter from the point of view of the threat involved in the acts of the union.

Our conclusion is that wherever a person, by means of fraud or intimidation, procures either the breach of a contract, or the discharge of a plaintiff from an employment, which, but for such wrongful interference, would have continued, he is liable in damages for such injuries as naturally result therefrom; and that the rule is the same whether by these wrongful means a contract of employment definite as to time is broken, or an employer is induced, solely by reason of such procurement, to discharge an employee whom he would otherwise have retained. . . . We think that the important question in an act of this kind is as to the nature of the defendant's act, and the means adopted by him to accomplish his purpose. Merely to induce another to leave an employment, or to discharge an employee, by persuasion or argument, however whimsical, unreasonable, or absurd, is not, in and of itself, unlawful, and we do not decide that such interference may become unlawful by reason of the defendant's malicious motives, but simply that to intimidate an employer by threats, if the threats are of such a character as to produce this result, and thereby cause him to discharge an employee whom he desired to retain, and would have retained, except for such unlawful threats, is an actionable wrong. (Perkins *v.* Pendleton.)

Circuit Judge Brown says:

Associations have no more right to inflict injury upon others than individuals have. All combinations and associations designed to coerce workmen to become members, or to interfere with, obstruct, vex, or annoy them in working, or in obtaining work, because they are not members, or in order to induce them to become members; or designed to prevent employers from making a just discrimination in the rate of wages paid to the skillful and to the unskillful; to the diligent and to the lazy; to the efficient and to the inefficient; and all associations designed to interfere with the perfect freedom of employers in the proper management and control of their lawful business, or to dictate in any particular the terms upon which their business shall be conducted, by means of threats of injury or loss, by interference with their property or traffic, or with their lawful employment of other persons, or designed to abridge any of these rights,—are *pro tanto* illegal combinations or associations; and all acts done in furtherance of such intentions by such means and accompanied by damage, are actionable. (Old Dominion Steamship Co. *v.* McKenna.)

Judge Hammond of Massachusetts in his opinion in Plant *v.* Woods seeks to eliminate the element of unionism and to settle the question on the principle of the rights of laborers.

It is to be observed that this is not a case between the employer and employed, or, to use a hackneyed expression, between capital and labor, but between laborers all of the same craft, and each having the same right as any one of the others to pursue his calling. In this as in every other case of equal rights the right of each individual is to be exercised with due regard to the similar right of all others, and the right of one be said to end where that of another begins. The right involved is the right to dispose of one's labor with full freedom. This is a legal right, and it is entitled to legal protection. Sir William Erle, in his book on Trades Unions (page 12), has stated this in the following language, which has been several times quoted with approval by judges in England: "Every person has a right, under the law, as between himself and his fellow subjects, to full freedom in disposing of his own labor or his own capital according to his own will. It follows that every other person is subject to the correlative duty arising therefrom, and is prohibited from any obstruction to the fullest exercise of this right which can be made compatible with the exercise of similar rights by others. Every act causing an obstruction to another in the exercise of the right comprised within this description, done not in the exercise of the actor's own right, but for the purpose of obstruction, would, if damage should be caused thereby to the party obstructed, be a violation of this prohibition." The same rule is stated with care and discrimination by Wells, J., in Walker *v.* Cronin: "Every one has a right to enjoy the fruits and advantages of his own enterprise, industry, skill, and credit. He has no right to be protected against competition, but he has a right to be free from malicious and wanton interference, disturbance, or annoyance. If disturbance or loss come as the result of competition, or the exercise of like rights by others, it is damnum absque injuria, unless some superior right by contract, or otherwise, is interfered with. But if it come from the merely wanton or malicious acts of others, without the justification of competition, or the service of any interest or lawful purpose, it then stands upon a different footing." In this case the acts complained of were calculated to cause damage to the plaintiffs, and did actually cause such damage; and they were intentionally done for that purpose. Unless, therefore, there was justifiable cause, the acts were malicious and unlawful.

Some judges are impressed by the fact of organization and the influence that such organization has in controlling the acts of its members. To some even this control appears to be coercion. Quotations previously made indicate the view of some courts favorable to such organization. The following extracts indicate an impression in the minds of judges decidedly unfavorable to the unions. In Booth *v.* Burgess the court was dealing with a strike called to compel an employer to cease to deal with another employer whose workmen had a grievance; a sympathetic strike. The court, speaking through Vice Chancellor Stevenson, says:

These workmen are to be forced to strike against their will whenever the defendants shall say the word. The coercion consists in the fact that if any workman refuses to strike he is liable to a fine, and also to expulsion from his union. Expulsion from the union subjects the victim not only to obloquy but also to pecuniary loss, and makes it more difficult for him to get employment and make his living, as is amply illustrated in this case.

Barr *v.* Essex Trades Council dealt with an extensively organized boycott against a paper that refused to unionize its press and type rooms. The Trades Council took up the prosecution of the boycott and pushed it through the various labor organizations of the community. Vice Chancellor Green wrote the opinion of the court, in which is found the following:

It is said that it was only the exercise by each person of his right to spend his money as his own will dictated. The fallacy of this is apparent. It loses sight of the combination, the whole strength of which lies in the fact that each individual has surrendered his own discretion and will to the direction of the accredited representative of all the organizations. He no longer uses his own judgment, but by entering into the combination agrees to be bound by its decree. As is said in Temperton *v.* Russell: "Those men had bound themselves to obey, and they knew they had done so, and that, if they did not obey, they would be fined or expelled from the union to which they belonged." It is common knowledge, if, indeed, it does not amply so appear by the papers in this case, that a member of a labor organization who does not submit to the edict of his union asserts his independence of judgment and action at the risk, if not the absolute sacrifice, of all association with his fellow members. They will not eat, drink, live, or work, in his company. Branded by the peculiarly offensive epithets adopted, he must exist ostracized, socially and industrially, so far as his former associates are concerned. Freedom of will, under such circumstances, cannot be expected.

In Berry *v.* Donovan the question of competition was raised as between the union and non-union workmen. Chief Justice Knowlton in writing the opinion of the court dealt with that phase of the question fully, in the following:

The only argument that we have heard in support of interference by labor unions in cases of this kind is that it is justifiable as a kind of competition. It is true that fair competition in business brings persons into rivalry, and often justifies action for one's self which interferes with proper action of another. Such action on both sides is the exercise by competing persons of equal conflicting rights. The principle appealed to would justify a member of the union, who was seeking employment for himself, in making an offer to serve on such terms as would result, and as he knew would result, in the discharge of the plaintiff by his employer, to make a place for the new comer. Such an offer, for such a purpose, would be unobjectionable. It would be merely the exercise of a personal right, equal in importance to the plaintiff's right. But an interference by a combination of persons to obtain the discharge of a workman because he refuses to comply with their wishes, for their advantage, in some matter in which he has a right to act independently, is not competition. In such a case the action taken by the combination is not in the regular course of their business as employees, either in the service in which they are engaged or in an effort to obtain employment in other service. The result which they seek to obtain cannot come directly from anything that they do within the regular line of their business as workers competing in the labor market. It can only come from action outside of the province of workingmen, intended directly to injure another, for the purpose of compelling him to submit to their dictation. It is difficult to see how the object to be gained can come within the field of fair competition. If we consider it in reference to the right of employees to compete with one another, inducing a person to join a union has no tendency to aid them in such competition. Indeed, the object of organizations of this kind is not to make competition of employees with one another more easy or successful. It is rather, by association, to prevent such competition, to bring all to equality and to make them act together in a common interest. Plainly, then, interference with one working under a contract, with a view to compel him to join a union, cannot be justified as a part of the competition of workmen with one another.

We understand that the attempted justification rests entirely upon another kind of so-called competition, namely, competition between employers and the employed, in the attempt of each class to obtain as large a share as possible of the income from their combined efforts in the industrial field. In a strict sense this is hardly competition. It is a struggle or contention of interests of different kinds, which are in opposition, so far as the division of profits is concerned. In a broad sense, perhaps, the contending forces may be called competitors. At all events, we may assume that, as between themselves, the principle which warrants competition permits also reasonable efforts, of a proper kind, which have a direct tendency to benefit one party in his business at the expense of the other. It is no legal objection to action whose direct effect is helpful to one of the parties in the struggle that it is also directly detrimental to the other. But when action is directed against the other primarily for the purpose of doing him harm, and thus compelling him to yield to the demand of the actor, and this action does not directly affect the property or business or status of the actor, the case is different, even if the actor expects to derive a remote or indirect benefit from the act. The gain which a labor union may expect to derive from inducing others to join it is not an improvement to be obtained directly in the conditions under which the men are working, but only added strength for such contests with employers as may arise in the future. An object of this kind is too remote to be considered a benefit in business, such as to justify the infliction of intentional injury upon a third person for the purpose of obtaining it. If such an object were treated as legitimate, and allowed to be pursued to its complete accomplishment, every employee would be forced into membership in a union, and the unions, by a combination of those in different trades and occupations, would have complete and absolute control of all the industries of the country. Employers would be forced to yield to all their demands or give up business. The attainment of such an object in the struggle with employers would not be competition, but monopoly. A monopoly, controlling anything which the world must have, is fatal to prosperity and progress. In matters of this kind the law does not tolerate monopolies. The attempt to force all laborers to combine in unions is against the policy of the law, because it aims at monopoly. It therefore does not justify causing the discharge, by his employer, of an individual laborer working under a contract. It is easy to see that for different reasons an act which might be done in legitimate competition by one or two or three persons, each proceeding independently, might take on an entirely different character, both in its nature and its purpose, if done by hundreds in combination.

We have no desire to put obstacles in the way of employees who are seeking by combination to obtain better conditions for themselves and their families. We have no doubt that laboring men have derived and may hereafter derive advantages from organization. We only say that under correct rules of law, and with a proper regard for the rights of individuals, labor unions cannot be permitted to drive men out of employment because they choose to work independently. If disagreements between those who furnish the capital and those who perform the labor employed in industrial enterprises are to be settled only by industrial wars, it would give a great advantage to combinations of employees, if they could be permitted by force to obtain a monopoly of the labor market. But we are hopeful that this kind of warfare will soon give way to industrial peace, and that rational methods of settling such controversies will be adopted universally.

In Reynolds *v.* Davis the supreme court of Massachusetts recorded an opinion that entered upon the consideration of the rights of unions over their own members. The union had undertaken to maintain practically a closed shop, by refusing to work for an employer who had announced that open-shop rules were to prevail. The court were in agreement that a strike for such a purpose was not lawful. A concurring opinion was written in which the strike was condemned but not for the same reasons. The opinion of the majority reveals its view of the menace of the union in the following extract:

By the working and trade rules of this council every grievance which a member of a local union affiliated with the council has against his employer is to be investigated by the executive board of the council, and if the employer does not comply with the decision of the executive board he is reported to the council as "unfair," and upon being declared "unfair" by the council the executive board is "to again interview" the employer, and if the employer continues in his refusal to comply with the demands of the council the board "shall at once remove all union men" from his employ, and "no union man shall be allowed to go to work" for him until he is "again placed upon the fair list by the . . . council."

In other words, the members of the defendant unions, by the terms of their own rules undertook to decide each case of an individual grievance between a single employee and his employer, to decree what should be done by the employer as well as by the employee and to enforce compliance with its decision by threatening and instituting a strike in which all members were bound to join. What we mean by an individual grievance is (for example) the discharge by his employer of a member of the union for drunkenness or inefficiency.

This statement of the make-up of the defendant unions and the trades council with which they are affiliated makes plain what the plaintiffs were aiming at in the open shop rules. And it also makes plain what was the main or one of the main purposes for which the strike in question was instituted by the individual defendants.

The strike in question was a combination for the purpose of making the trades council, composed of delegates from the unions of which the individual defendants are members, the arbiter of all questions between individual employees and their employers.

It purports to include questions arising under contracts still in existence between the two. To force the employer to submit to a delegate body of employees his rights under an existing contract by a combination for that purpose is not a justifiable interference with their employer's business.

And in cases arising outside existing contracts it is an attempt to force compliance on the part of employers with the decision of this delegate body of employees as to whether a single employee is or is not to work for the employer, which decision is to be enforced by a strike. Such a strike would be a strike in the nature of a sympathetic strike, that is to say, it is a strike not to forward the common interests of the strikers but to forward the interests of an individual employee in respect to a grievance between him and his employer where no contract of employment exists.

We do not mean to say that a labor union cannot combine to support a committee to take up individual grievances in behalf of the several members. What we now decide to be illegal is a combination that such grievances (that is to say, grievances between an individual member of a union and his employer which are not common to the union members as a class) shall be decided by the employees and that decision enforced by a strike on the part of all.

Chief Justice Knowlton, after stating that the opinion reached by the majority seemed to him "erroneous in the grounds on which it purports to rest" and declaring that "with the final disposition of the case I am satisfied," states the grounds that seem to him more satisfactory. These have been referred to more fully in connection with the closed shop discussion. Of the views expressed by the majority he writes:

It is right that all the members of such a union should unite for the protection of the interests of every individual member. If the feeblest of its members has a just grievance as an employee against their common employer, it is proper that the whole combination should act together to obtain redress of the wrong. The most effectual way of enforcing the right of every member to just treatment from his employer, in reference to wages, hours of labor and other things affecting his interests, is by withholding the labor of the union until justice is done. To make this a potent inducement the union must be able to act as one body, and to hold every member to the performance of his duties to his fellow members, so that all may be a united force. Of course there must be a method of determining what action, if any, shall be taken by the union in any case of an alleged grievance. Such a determination cannot properly be made without an investigation of the facts. Such an investigation ordinarily would involve conferences with the employer, and negotiations to see whether he would consent to an improvement of the conditions, if they should appear to be unjust to the employee. Such conferences and negotiations, without which ordinarily no labor union would be justified in striking, call for a representative or representatives of the union to present its side of the controversy to the employer, and to act for the union in the maintenance of its interests against the opposite party. In such cases the employer and employee often come together as adverse parties, each contending for that which seems for his advantage. The final determination of the position to be taken by the union may be by a vote of its members. It may be by the action of a board of officers to whom the union intrusts this duty. In favor of the latter method is the fact that, in times of excitement, assemblies of men and women often act hastily under a misapprehension of the facts, and under an impulse of passion aroused by inflammatory appeals to their feelings. But, in one way or another, such determinations must be made, and must be treated as finally settling the position which the union is to take for itself, as a party dealing with an adverse party in reference to its supposed rights. Of course, if the employer takes a different view, neither is bound by the action of the other, and each may make any lawful effort to prevail in the contest with the other.

In the opinion the present strike is condemned because of the rules which govern the union. Under these, every grievance is to be investigated by the executive board of the council. Surely this is right and proper. If the employer refuses to do that which the executive board thinks he ought to do, the facts are reported by the board to the next meeting of the Building Trades Council, with a recommendation that he be declared unfair. If he is then declared unfair by the Building Trades Council, that is equivalent to a decision that he is in the wrong. It is then the duty of the executive board to again interview the employer, and if he fails to comply with the conditions that the Building Trades Council deems just, a strike is to be declared and maintained by the union until he complies with these conditions.

It is to be noticed that this course of proceeding is entirely for the guidance of the members of the union. The employer takes such measures and acts upon such principles as he chooses for his own guidance. If the result is a failure to agree, then each stands upon his rights, and it is a question which can force the other to yield, or how they can afterwards reach a compromise. The trades council is no more the arbiter of questions between individual employees and their employers than the employer is. The trades council, as a representative official board, decides for one party and determines its action, and the employer decides for the other party and determines his action. Neither assumes to determine anything for the other, but the action of each is governed by its own determination.

I do not see how any rule can be more just and proper for the guidance of a labor union when a dispute arises between its members, or any one of its members, and the employer. Suppose the case is the reduction of wages by the employer which the members of the union deem unjust. What more fair or equitable method of dealing with such a supposed injustice could be devised? To say that a strike founded on such a reduction is illegal because of a rule providing this method of dealing with the grievance, is, in my judgment, equivalent to saying that no labor union shall be permitted to do anything to promote the proper objects of its organization.

It is objected that the rule does not exclude questions arising under contracts subsisting between the employer and individual members of the union. Why should it exclude any question which arises under a complaint of an alleged grievance? Every member of the union is entitled to the support of his fellow members in regard to any question directly affecting his rights as an employee, if he is in the right and his employer is in the wrong. How can the union ascertain whether action should be taken in his behalf without an investigation? If the investigation should show that the aid which he seeks is to enable him to break a contract with his employer, it is to be assumed that the council would immediately decline to help him. If a strike should be ordered to compel an employer to submit to a breach of contract by one of his employees, such a strike would be illegal because it would be for an illegal object, not because of the method prescribed by the rules of the union for investigating the matter, or for declaring a strike. It must be assumed that these rules were adopted to be properly applied in proper cases. They do not purport to authorize the trades council to declare a strike for an illegal object. It is to be presumed that the council would refuse to declare a strike in any case in which the investigation showed that the desired object was illegal. In the present case there is no testimony nor suggestion that one of the purposes of the strike was to compel submission by an employer to a breach of his contract with an employee.

In framing rules for a labor union, it would be unreasonable and impracticable to mention expressly all possible cases in which a strike ought not to be ordered, and, in terms, to forbid action in all such cases.

I find nothing in this part of the rules and by-laws except that which I should expect to find in those of any well-organized labor union. I discover nothing in the master's report or the evidence to indicate that these rules were intended to be used for the unlawful promotion of a purely sympathetic strike, or that they ever were so used. I have endeavored to show that if any member of a union should have a grievance as an employee against his employer, even if it was not common to members of the union as a class, it would be the duty of his fellow members, in accordance with fundamental principles of labor unionism, to unite for the redress of the grievance, even by striking, if that should be necessary.

So far as appears, the posting and publication of the open shop rules, and the employment or attempt at employment of nonunion men, which were the only matters complained of by the defendants, had a relation to members of each of the local unions before the court, as direct as it had to any other union men. Members of these unions were employed in the shops of the plaintiff. If the ground of complaint had been a proper subject for adverse action by an individual workman, it would have been a proper subject for investigation and action by the union of which he was a member.

Because the opinion in this case makes the decision turn upon the rules and by-laws to which I have referred, I do not agree with it.

There is yet one case coming under this general topic that must not be passed over. It came before the Massachusetts supreme court and the opinion was handed down in 1908 (Willcutt *v.* Bricklayers Union). The prevailing opinion written by Judge Hammond sets forth fully one view and the dissenting opinion by Judge Sheldon expresses in detail the opposite. The point of interest in the case is the control of a union over its members by use of fines. The strike itself was for a lawful purpose and justifiable. The means used in carrying on the strike were in question. In the words of the trial judge:

In case of a justifiable strike, has the contractor the right to invoke the aid of the court to prevent the labor union from imposing a fine (which the court has found to be coercive in its nature) or taking action to impose one upon one or more of its members under its rules to induce them to leave the contractor's employ to his injury?

It is of more than incidental interest that the question of the imposition of fines by an organization upon its members had been before the court in an earlier case, where the organizations were not labor unions (Martell *v.* White). Certain granite manufacturers had formed an association, a by-law of which provided that any member having business transactions with any other such manufacturer of the city in relation to granite should, for each such transaction, contribute to the expenses of the association from $1.00 to $500.00, the amount to be determined by the association. By means of fines varying from $10.00 to $100.00 the plaintiff's business had been ruined. The court in that case had adjudged that the coercion of members by fines into refusing to trade with plaintiff was not consistent with competition. Of this case the court says:

The case was carefully presented by counsel, the questions involved were regarded as important, and there was a difference of opinion among the judges who sat in it. It was therefore considered at great length; and the conclusion was reached after a most exhaustive discussion and the most careful deliberation. It stands as a solemn adjudication by this court after such discussion and deliberation.

The case had been referred to frequently and always with satisfaction. The court felt the controlling influence of the former opinion and rendered its decision on the basis of the precedent. Apparently feeling that further justification was necessary an extended discussion of the principles is entered upon in the opinion. This is because of the dissenting view of the minority who think that the principle laid down in the former case was not correct, or if correct, was not applicable to the case at bar. "We are also somewhat influenced [to add more] by reason of the importance of the question and its relation to a part of the law still in the nebulous but clearing stage." The essential point in the case is declared to be that the contention is not between the party imposing and the party compelled to pay the fine. It is between the part imposing the fine and a third party asserting himself to be damaged by its imposition.

Shortly stated the case is this: The plaintiff's men are being coerced by threats of a fine to leave its employ, greatly to its injury, the fines to be levied in accordance with the by-laws of a voluntary association of which the proposed victims are members. This injury to the plaintiff is intended by the defendants. Has the plaintiff any standing in equity to an injunction against the infliction of such injury?

The opinion then contains a statement in general terms of the rights of the parties. The employer has a right to employ whom he chooses, the right to a free labor market.

The workmen also have rights. They may labor, sell their labor, organize to improve their conditions, make appropriate by-laws to strengthen their organization. The court concludes after elaborating them at some length.

> But not much progress is made by this general statement of the rights of the respective parties. We are still only on the skirmish line. . . . In the case before us neither the right of the plaintiff to a free labor market nor the right of the union to impose a fine upon its members is absolute. Neither is to be considered apart from the other, or without reference to any other conflicting right, whether public or private; but each must be regarded as having in the rules of human conduct its own place beyond the limits of which it must not go.

So far as the application of these principles to the employer and employee is concerned, the court is of the opinion that the parties must adjust them by their own efforts, keeping within the limits established by law and applicable impartially to both.

> So long as the by-laws of a union relate to matters in which no one is interested except the association and its members, and violate no right of a third party or no rule of public policy, they are valid. . . . It cannot be successfully contended, however, that as against the right of some party other than the association and its members an act, otherwise a violation of the third party's rights, is any less a violation because done by some member in obedience to a by-law.
>
> The principle at the bottom of such a decision is this, namely: An interference with the right of a third party cannot be justified upon the ground that the intruder is acting in accordance with an agreement between him and some other person. In a word, so long as a fine is imposed for the guidance of members in matters in which outside parties have no interest, or in which there is no violation of a right of an outside party, then no such party can complain. But when

the right of such a party is invaded, it is no defense, either to the person fined or to those who have imposed the fine, that the invasive act was done in accordance with the by-laws of an association.

[In the law of the commonwealth it is settled] that the flow of labor to the employer cannot be obstructed by intimidation or coercion produced by means of injury to person or property, or by threats of such injury . . . even though the ultimate object of the strike be legal. There can be no doubt that fining is one method of injuring a man in his estate, and that a threat to fine is a threat of such an injury.

The next step in the argument deals with the effect of organization; "when the intimidation is exerted by a union upon its members in accordance with its by-laws." On this point it is asserted that

it can make no difference to the public or to the employer (who in this case is the other party) that the person intimidated is or is not a member of the society intimidating. In either case the injury is the same and is from the same cause, namely intimidation. The workman is no longer free.

To show that the member of the union is not free, the following view is expressed:

If it be said that the member fined may take his choice either to leave the organization or abide by its rules to which he has before assented, and that where there is a choice there can be no coercion, the answer is that in almost every conceivable case of coercion short of an actual overpowering of the physical forces of the victim there is a choice. The highwayman, who presents his cocked pistol to the traveler and demands his purse under pain of instant death in case of refusal, offers his victim a choice. He may either give up his purse and live, or refuse and die. In Carew *v.* Rutherford the victim had a choice either to pay a fine or take the consequences of a refusal. And so the member of a labor union has the choice either to pay the fine or leave the union. Is it difficult to realize what that choice is in these days of organized labor? Is it too much to say that many times it is very difficult, indeed practically impossible, for a workman to get bread for himself and his family by working at his trade unless he is a member of a union? It is true he has a choice between paying his fine and not paying it, but is it not frequently a hard one? May not the coercion upon him sometimes be most severe and effective? Such is not a free choice. And a market filled with such men is not a reasonably free market. In this connection the language of Boutwell *v.* Marr seems significant and appropriate: "The law cannot be compelled by any initial agreement of an associate member to treat him as one having no choice but that of the majority, nor as a willing participant in whatever action may be taken. The voluntary acceptance of by-laws providing for the imposition of coercive fines does not make them legal and collectable. . . . The law sees in the member of an association of this character both the authors of its coercive system and the victims of this unlawful pressure. If this were not so, men could deprive their fellows of established rights, and evade the duty of compensation simply by working through an association."

In considering this question we cannot lose sight of the great power of organization. It should be taken into account when one is considering where the line should be drawn between the right of the employer to a free market and the right of workmen to interfere with that market by coercion through the rules of a labor union. It is not universally true that what one man may do any number of men by concerted action may do. . . .

This organization of labor to better the condition of the laborer is natural and proper. There can be no doubt that it is the most effective way, perhaps the only effective way, in which as against the organization of capital the rights of the laborer can be adequately protected. In many ways the labor unions have succeeded in bettering the condition of the laborer, and so far as their ultimate intentions and the means used in accomplishing them are legal they are entitled to protection to the extreme limit of the law.

But their powers must not be so far extended as to encroach upon the rights of others. It is clear that if the power to intimidate by fine be regarded as one of the powers which labor unions may rightfully exercise, then the right to a free market for labor—nay, even the right of the laborer to be free—is seriously interfered with, to the injury both of the public and the employer as well as the laborer.

Finally the opinion is summed up in the following conclusion.

A majority of the court are of opinion that the overwhelming sense of the thing is that the principle that the right of the employer is not subject to coercion or intimidation by injury or threats of injury to the persons or property of laborers standing in the market to meet him, should apply to the coercion and intimidation exerted by labor unions upon their members by fines or threats of fines. Any other conclusion is inconsistent with the existence of a reasonably free labor market to which both the employer and the employee are entitled.

To this line of argument and conclusion two members of the court did not agree. Chief Justice Knowlton and Justice Sheldon presented a dissenting opinion written by the latter.

They point out first that the strike is conceded to be a lawful one. That being admitted, it follows that the defendants have the right to seek to make the strike successful " by the use of whatever rightful means were available to them." As to the rights of the two parties the general conception is the same. The opinion holds that, when a conflict arises:

the plaintiff's right to a free labor market is not only not a paramount right, but it is and must be subject to the higher right of the defendants to combine and to carry on a strike by the use of whatever lawful means may be in their power; and we cannot see how this right can be further limited than by restricting it to acts which are not forbidden by law, either as being unlawful in themselves or at variance with a sound public policy. Accordingly, the question now to be decided is whether we can say that the members of a labor union have no right, acting in conformity with rules previously established, to impose a fine upon one of their own members if he goes to work or continues to work for an employer against whom a justifiable strike has been declared in accordance with those rules, where there is no contractual right or duty on either side for the performance of such work.

If we are right in what thus far has been said, the answer to this question must depend upon whether the imposition of such a fine is either forbidden by some rule of law or is found to be inconsistent with some rule of public policy. But in our opinion neither of these affirmations can be made.

The right of all voluntary associations to establish appropriate by-laws, " not only for their own internal management but also to regulate the conduct of their members towards each other and in matters affecting the general interests of the body," is next asserted. This implies the generally recognized right to enforce obedience to said by-laws. That these general rules are applicable to labor unions, as voluntary associations, is not only beyond question but that there is a special significance in their applicability to such unions, is also clear.

The very purpose for which they are created makes it highly important that their members should be held together by the strongest possible bonds, so as to work with absolute unanimity, especially in the time of a trade dispute or strike.

Pledges and promises binding all the members are desirable. Voluntary agreements to abide in such matters by the will of a majority of the members under a coercive pecuniary influence, or even under pain of expulsion, cannot be objectionable. Indeed, the right of labor unions to enforce, under penalty of fine or expulsion, compliance by all their members with rules and regulations which have been adopted because deemed by a sufficient majority to be for the common good and which are not in themselves inappropriate or unlawful, is necessary to their continued existence. It is to the united action of all their members that such organizations owe their strength and their ability to accomplish the results at which they aim. Doubtless persons who do not agree in the desirability of those results or in the wisdom or efficiency of the means adopted to secure them, cannot be required to continue as members against their will, any more than they could have been compelled to become members in the first instance.

It is of the very essence of a voluntary organization that membership in it is and must continue to be itself voluntary, and this must be so on both sides as long as property rights do not come in question. (Cases cited.) So long, however, as such membership continues and the organization still serves the purpose for which it was created, "the will of the individual must," as was said by the court in Wabash R. R. *v.* Hannahan, "consent to yield to the will of the majority, or no organization, whether of society into government, capital into combination, or labor into coalition, can ever be effectual. The individual must yield in order that the many may receive a greater benefit. The right of labor to organize for lawful purposes and by organic agreement to subject the individual members to rules, regulations and conduct prescribed by the majority, is no longer an open question in the jurisprudence of this country." . . . Indeed, we do not understand it to be denied that those members of the unions who declined to join in the strike which was ordered were liable to expulsion by the unions acting in good faith, and as it has been found that the defendants are pecuniarily irresponsible, payment of the fines threatened could have been enforced only by expulsion. And the member of a union upon whom such a fine has been lawfully imposed in accordance with by-laws to which he has himself previously assented, is in no respect in the predicament of a highwayman's victim who has the bare option of parting with his money to save his life or of losing his life without thereby saving his money. The situation of one who finds himself compelled to choose between two alternatives, however distasteful, which he has brought upon himself and neither of which is unlawful, is in no way comparable to that of one who is compelled by wrongful force to elect between submitting to one of two alternative injuries, both of which are unlawful. An argument which rests upon such a comparison is without foundation.

Nor can we say that the imposition of fines, not in themselves unlawful and not injurious to the plaintiff except as they restrict an inferior right by the lawful exercise of a higher right, is to be regarded as contrary to a sound public policy. Gloomy vaticinations of injurious results to be apprehended from the excessive power which labor unions may acquire by their combination of many individuals into one body do not greatly impress us. The power of capital hitherto has not been found insufficient to prevent other than proper advantages from being gained by the representatives of labor, nor does it seem to us likely to be insufficient in the future. If it shall appear that there is such a danger, yet we cannot alter the law by denying to labor unions the rights and powers which the law gives to all lawful associations.

The law does not do so vain a thing as to allow the formation of labor unions and to declare their right to initiate and by lawful means to carry on a justifiable strike, and then refuse them the use of the only practical means by which their acknowledged rights can be secured. . . . The books are full of cases recognizing the right of labor unions to enforce their rules upon their members in a reasonable way. There are but few cases that discuss by-laws authorizing the imposition of fines for a violation of rules; for their validity is almost universally conceded. It is believed that most of the many thousand labor unions in this country and Great Britain have such a rule or by-law, under which they are acting to-day without complaint from any one. In such action they are in our judgment simply adopting a principle which is of general application for similar purposes.

It is true of course that no man lawfully can be compelled at the mere dictation of other men to abstain from working for such prices and during such periods of labor as he may be willing to accept; but it is no less true that when one chooses voluntarily to unite with others of the same craft in forming an organization for the purpose of bringing about by the united action of all its members more favorable conditions of employment, he is bound, so long as he desires to remain a member of that organization, to submit within certain limits his own freedom alike of judgment and of action to the judgment of his associates, and to conform his conduct to that standard which they shall have agreed to be for the best interest of all and of each. Unity of action would be impossible upon any such terms. Accordingly, all the members of such a body have a right to expect, and by reasonable rules and appropriate penalties to provide for, the observance of such terms. Those who desire to employ the members of such organizations must expect this to be the case, and have no right to complain of the requirements of such rules, and of their reasonable enforcement upon each other by the members of such organizations. To this extent, the employer's relative right to a free labor market must yield to the higher right of the laborers to combine and to act in unison for the purpose of obtaining better terms from their employer. In other words, the general right of an employer to go into the market to hire laborers does not deprive a union, in carrying on a lawful strike, of the right to use upon its individual members, for the purpose of keeping them up to the performance of their duty as such members, all the influences that any other organization properly could use, including the imposition of fines. The right to use such influences is an independent and paramount right. The interests of the employer are subordinate to this right, and must yield to it.

Coming more directly to the point of difference, the dissenting opinion then asserts:

Doubtless this power of discipline by fines or by the ultimate penalty of expulsion cannot properly be resorted to for the purpose of requiring conduct intrinsically unlawful, or for the purpose of compelling a minority member to join in action the ultimate object of which is to damage a third person. Just as the rules of an association cannot protect its members who have done actionable injury to a third person, so a plaintiff who has suffered injury by the enforcement of its rules and penalties upon its own members for a wrongful purpose may properly be allowed a remedy. If a strike should be declared for an unlawful object, it would be illegal because of its object; and all the members trying to maintain it by direct or indirect action against the employer might be liable in damages and subject to injunction. They would be so liable just as much without a by-law authorizing the imposition of fines as with one. . . . But if the object of a strike is legal and commendable, an effort to keep the members together by the imposition of fines, if need be, under a by-law previously adopted, is also legal and commendable.

Summing up the argument, the opinion concludes:

What seems to us the fallacy of the majority opinion is its failure to act upon the fact that the strike in this case was upon justifiable grounds, and of course was lawful. It follows that the action of each member of the union in trying to maintain the strike, without force, or wrongful coercion or intimidation exercised upon any one, was justifiable and lawful. It was not an interference with the rights of the plaintiff, because, as we have seen, the right of an employer to conduct his business without interference in the labor market is subordinate to the right of his employees to strike and to maintain the strike in a lawful manner. As against this right of the employees the employer has no right to have their labor flow to him uninfluenced or undiverted.

Justice Loring also wrote an opinion. He agreed with the decision made by the majority of the court. But his reasons for doing so were solely in the fact that the previous decision had been made on that principle and that such decision should be binding. The court should not reverse itself unless for reasons more weighty than any that had been offered in the dissenting opinion. He asserts that no harm can result if the decision made is confined to the points decided and is not extended to broader propositions. These broader propositions that he has in mind are three in number and are stated as follows:

First, that employees have a right to combine to better their condition and to do all acts (not unlawful) necessary to make the combination an efficient one; secondly, that they have a right to strike to gain that end if their demands therefor are not granted by their employer, and to do all acts (not unlawful) necessary to make the strike successful; and, third, that these rights of the employees are superior to the right of the employer to have a free flow of labor in his business.

There is nothing in the decision in Martell *v.* White, or in the decision in the case at bar, which calls in question these propositions or any one of them. . . .

In my opinion the case at bar is covered by the decision in Martell *v.* White, that decision ought not to be overruled in this case, and the plaintiff is entitled to the decree stated in the opinion of a majority of the court.

PROBABLE EXPECTANCY

The relations of workingmen to each other and to employers were stated in somewhat new terms by Vice Chancellor Stevenson of New Jersey. The term used by the Justice in his opinion is "probable expectancy." The idea is expanded in an opinion of considerable length. The important parts are inserted in the Justice's own words.

The underlying right in this particular case under consideration, which seems to be coming into general recognition as the subject of protection by courts of equity through the instrumentality of an injunction, appears to be the right to enjoy a certain free and natural condition of the labor market, which in a recent case in the house of lords was referred to, in the language of Lord Ellenborough, as a "probable expectancy." This underlying right has otherwise been broadly defined or described as the right which every man has to earn his living, or to pursue his trade or business, without undue interference, and might otherwise be described as the right which every man has, whether employer or employee, of absolute freedom to employ or to be employed. The peculiar element of this perhaps newly recognized right is that it is an interest which one man has in the freedom of another. In the case before this court, the Jersey City Printing Company claims the right not only to be free in employing labor, but also the right that labor shall be free to be employed by it, the Jersey City Printing Company. A large part of what is most valuable in modern life seems to depend more or less directly upon "probable expectancies." When they fail, civilization as at present organized may go down. As social and industrial life developes and grows more complex, these "probable expectancies" are bound to increase. It would seem to be inevitable that courts of law, as our system of jurisprudence is evolved to meet the growing wants of an increasingly complex social order, will discover, define, and protect from undue interference more of these "probable expectancies." In undertaking to ascertain and define the rights and remedies of employers and employees in respect of their "probable expectancies" in relation to the labor market, it is well not to lose sight altogether of any other analogous rights and remedies which are based upon similar "probable expectancies." It will probably be found in the end, I think, that the natural expectancy of employers in relation to the labor market, and the natural expectancies of merchants in respect to the merchandise market, must be recognized to the same extent by courts of law and courts of equity, and protected by substantially the same rules. It is freedom in the market, freedom in the purchase and sale of all things, including both goods and labor, that our modern law is endeavoring to insure to every dealer on either side of the market. The valuable thing to merchant and to customer, to employer and to employee, manifestly, is freedom on both sides of the market. . . . It is, however, the right of the employer and employee to a free labor market that is the particular thing under consideration in this case. . . . Our law in its recent development undertakes to insure to him (an employer), not only that he may employ whom he pleases, but that all who wish to be employed by him may enter into and remain in such employment freely, without threats of harm, without unreasonable molestation and annoyance from the words, actions, or other conduct of any other persons acting in combination. What is the measure or test by which the conduct of a combination of persons must be judged in order to determine whether or not it is an unlawful interference with freedom of employment in the labor market, and as such injurious to an employer of labor in respect of his "probable expectancies," has not as yet been clearly defined. Perhaps no better definition could be suggested than that which may be framed by conveniently using that important legal fictitious person who has taken such a large part in the development of our law during the last 50 years, the reasonably prudent, reasonably courageous, and not unreasonably sensitive man. . . . A man may not be liable to an action for slander for calling a workman a "scab" in the street, but if 100 men combine to have this workman denounced as a "scab" in the street, or followed in the streets to and from his home, so as to attract public attention to him, and place him in an annoyingly conspicuous position, such conduct—the result of such combination—is held to be an invasion of the "probable expectancy" of his employer or contemplated employer, an invasion of this employer's right to have labor flow freely to him. Without any regard to the rights and remedies which the molested workman may have, the injunction goes, at the suit of the employer, to protect his "probable expectancy,"—to secure freedom in the labor market to employ and to be employed, upon which the continuance of his entire industry may depend.

I think it is safe to say that, all through this development of strike law during the last decade, no principle becomes established which does not operate equally upon both employer and employee. The rights of both classes are absolutely equal in respect of all these "probable expectancies." An operator upon printing machines has a right to offer his labor freely to any of the printing shops in Jersey City. These shops may all combine to refuse to employ him on account of his race, or membership in a labor union, or for any other reason, or for no reason, precisely as 20 employees in one printing shop may combine, and arbitrarily refuse to be further employed unless the business is conducted in accordance with their views. But, in the case of the operative seeking employment, he has a right to have the action of the masters of the printing shops in reference to employing him left absolutely free. If, after obtaining or seeking to obtain employment in a shop, the master of that shop should be subjected to annoyances and molestation instigated by the proprietors of other printing shops, who combine to compel, by such molestation and annoyance, this one master printer, against his will and wish, to exclude the operative from employment, this operative, in my judgment, would have a right to an action at law for damages, and would have a right to an injunction if his case presented the other ordinary conditions upon which injunctions issue. But the common-law courts have not had time to speak distinctly on this subject as yet, and it is necessary to be cautious in dealing with a subject in which both courts of law and courts of equity as yet are feeling their way. I think that the leading principle enforced in the restraining order in this case is not inconsistent with any authorities which control this court. This principle is that a combination of employers or a combination of employees, the object of which is to interfere with the freedom of the employer to employ, or of the employee to be employed (in either of which cases there is an interference with the enjoyment of a "probable expectancy," which the law recognizes as something in the nature of property), by means of such molestation or personal annoyance as would be liable to coerce the person upon whom it was inflicted, assuming that he is reasonably courageous and not unreasonably sensitive, to refrain from employing or being employed, is illegal, and founds an action for damages on the part of any person knowingly injured in respect of his "probable expectancy" by such interference, and also, when the other necessary conditions exist, affords the basis of an injunction from a court of equity.

Four years later in Booth *v.* Burgess, Vice Chancellor Stevenson refers to this opinion, saying: "My opinion in that case, though hurriedly formulated, was the result of a very careful examination and consideration of the authorities." The right to a free market is characterized as a primary legal right belonging to the complainant, and is one of three rights in the case. The three rights are (1) "the right in a contract," (2) "the right to contract," (3) "the righ to a free market," that is "the right of every dealer, in the full enjoyment of his right to contract, to have all other possible dealers with him left free to deal or not as they may voluntarily elect. Thus recognition is accorded to the 'interest which one man has in the freedom of another.'"

The idea is referred to by Judge Hammond in the Willcutt case, already fully reviewed. That the opinion is influenced by the statement of Vice Chancellor Stevenson appears in the reference made to the rights of the plaintiff. Says Judge Hammond:

It is to be premised, that the right which the plaintiff seeks to have protected against the acts of the defendants arises from no contract or statute, but out of the nature of things. It is one of the large body of rights which have their foundation in the fitting necessities of civilized society. It is the common law right to a reasonably free labor market. Vice Chancellor Stevenson, in speaking of it, says it has been called a "probable expectancy" and describes it as "the right which every man has to earn his living or pursue his trade without undue interference."

What is to be the future of this idea, it is of course not possible to state. The references to it since its first appearance eight years ago have been very few, the ones just referred to being the leading ones. Yet it is of significance in its possibilities. Its importance will depend upon the particular direction that is given to its development in its practical applications.

CHAPTER XII

Special Topics

In addition to the foregoing general topics there are others that are of no small importance, though they come in for discussion in the opinions only incidentally.

I

INTIMIDATION

What constitutes intimidation is always a perplexing question for the court to answer. Much depends upon the point of view taken by the judge and much also upon his individuality. This latter difference is emphasized in the opinion in State *v.* Van Pelt.

To a timid, conservative judicial mind trained to regard even the slightest disturbance of such forces as portending danger to the peace of the state, "intimidation would doubtless include many acts that would not come within its meaning" to a different type of judicial mind believing that the safety and highest interest of the state are promoted by the freest possible play of mind and action in trade competition.

Some instances cited from various opinions will illustrate the different views. Justice Brewer in United States *v.* Kane said:

I have no doubt that some men, who are excessively bold, might have laughed at [the demonstration] and waited, believing that no personal violence would be used; but men are not all equally bold and courageous; the average man has a feeling that it is his duty to regard his personal safety; we all know that, and we act upon that presumption. . . . Every man knows that ordinarily prudent men are not going to risk their personal safety when there is nothing to be gained by it. . . . Everyone understands that these men felt overawed, intimidated, and quit work, not because they wanted to,—some of them, at least,—but because they felt that their personal safety, personal prudence, required them to do it. It would be, as it seems to me, blinding my eyes to obvious facts to say that there was not intimidation.

Vice Chancellor Green of New Jersey (Barr *v.* Trades Council) admitted that in the case before him there was

no public disturbance, no physical injury, no direct threats of personal violence, or of actual attack on or destruction of tangible property, as a means of intimidation or coercion. But, I do not understand that intimidation . . . necessarily presupposes personal injury or the fear thereof. The clear weight of authority undoubtedly is that a man may be intimidated into doing, or refraining from doing, by fear of loss of business, property, or reputation, as well as by dread of loss of life, or injury to health or limb; and the extent of this fear need not be abject, but only such as to overcome his judgment, or induce him not to do or to do that which otherwise he would have done or have left undone.

Judge McPherson, United States District Judge, writing the opinion in Atchison Railway Co. *v.* Gee, insists upon the following interpretation.

The argument seems to be that anything short of physical violence is lawful. One man can be intimidated only when knocked down. But the peaceful, law-abiding man can be and is intimidated by gesticulations, by menaces, by being called harsh names, and by being followed, or compelled to pass by men known to be unfriendly. Perhaps such a man may not be a bully, but is frail in size and strength, or he may be a timid man; but such a man is just as much entitled to go and come in quiet, without even mental disturbance, as is the man afraid of no one and able with or without weapons to cope with all comers. The frail man, or the man who shuns disturbances, or the timid man, must be protected, and the company has the right to employ such.

United States District Judge Sanborn draws the following distinction:

I understand the word intimidation to denote two kinds of coercion: (1) A threat by word or act of an individual, or by a combination of persons, to do something unlawful, reasonably calculated to compel the person threatened to do or not to do something; and (2) request or persuasion by or on behalf of a combination of persons to do or not to do something, resulting in coercion of the will from the mere force of numbers. In the first case the nature of the act, and the coercion, determine liability; in the second the conspiracy or concerted act and the coercion determine it. A. threatens B. with assault unless he quits work, and thus coerces him. A number of men, representing themselves and a large number, request B. to quit work, and by the force of numbers coerce him to do so. Civil liability follows in both cases—in the first, from the nature of the act threatened; in the second from the coercion by force of numbers. (Allis Chalmers Case.)

A modified view is expressed by Justice Holmes in writing a dissenting opinion while on the Massachusetts bench in Vegelahn *v.* Guntner.

I pause here to remark that the word "threats" often is used as if, when it appeared that threats had been made, it appeared that unlawful conduct had begun. But it depends on what you threaten. As a general rule, even if subject to some exceptions, what you may do in a certain event you may threaten to do—that is, give warning of your intention to do

—in that event, and thus allow the other person the chance of avoiding the consequence. So, as to "compulsion," it depends on how you "compel." So as to "annoyance" or "intimidation."

Chief Justice Parker enters into the elaboration of this point at some length in the Cumming Case. He thinks that much more importance had been attached to the acts than would have been "had not the draftsman characterized the notice given to the employers by the associations of their intention to strike as 'threats.'" The case was one, as the opinion goes on to state, in which certain men wanted to place their associates in positions held by non-union men.

They set about doing it in a perfectly lawful way. They determined that if it were necessary they would bear the burden and expense of a strike to accomplish that result, and in so determining they were clearly within their rights, as all agree. . . . Instead of taking that course, they chose to inform the contractors of their determination, and the reason for it. It is the giving of this information—a simple notification of their determination, which it was right and proper and reasonable to give—that has been characterized as "threats" by the special term, and which has led to no inconsiderable amount of misunderstanding since. But the sense in which the word was employed by the court is of no consequence, for the defendant associations had the absolute right to threaten to do that which they had the right to do. Having the right to insist that plaintiff's men be discharged, and defendants' men put in their place, if the services of the other members of the organization were to be retained, they also had the right to threaten that none of their men would stay unless their members could have all the work there was to do.

Against this view may be stated the opinion of Judge Wiswell of Maine (Perkins *v.* Pendleton).

We think that the important question in an act of this kind [securing the discharge of an employee] is as to the nature of the defendant's act, and the means adopted by him to accomplish his purpose. Merely to induce another to leave an employment, or to discharge an employee, by persuasion or argument, however whimsical, unreasonable, or absurd, is not, in and of itself, unlawful, and we do not decide that such interference may become unlawful by reason of the defendant's malicious motives, but simply that to intimidate an employer by threats, if the threats are of such a character as to produce this result, and thereby cause him to discharge an employee whom he desired to retain, and would have retained, except for such unlawful threats, is an actionable wrong.

II

ABSOLUTE AND RELATIVE RIGHTS

In many cases that come before the courts the essential point lies in the determination of the relation that shall exist between "rights." When a workman is acting clearly within his "right," there is no problem in the case. When an employer is so acting there is again no problem. When, however, each claims to be within his "right" and in acting accordingly a deadlock is brought about in the industrial field, then there is a problem and a very important one. The effort to adjust the "right" of the workman to the "right" of the employer has led to the recognition of some "rights" as of more importance than others. Thus there appear in the opinions such expressions as "absolute rights" or "primary rights" and "relative rights" or "secondary rights." The chief difficulty does not arise in adopting such a schedule of classification. It comes in classifying rights as "absolute" or "relative," "primary" or "secondary," after such a schedule has been adopted. It is comparatively easy to agree that some "rights" are more important than others, and to adopt some expression that will indicate this relation. But it is not so easy to agree upon the question as between the employer and his striking employees whether the "rights" of the strikers are superior or inferior to those against whom the strike has been called. Some of the judges have adopted quite positive views, as is shown in the opinions, while others seem not so certain. A further difficulty arises when it is found that the more positive judges are not in agreement among themselves.

The opinion of Vice Chancellor Stevenson in the Jersey City Printing Case has been elsewhere referred to and quoted. This opinion places emphasis upon the right to a free market. It is there spoken of as the right that every man has "of absolute freedom" to employ or to be employed. In a later opinion this judge referred to this as a "primary legal right," using the expression: "The primary legal right which it seems to me should be recognized as belonging to the complainant in this case may be defined or described as the right to a free market."

In the same opinion (Booth *v.* Burgess) the idea of absolute rights is expressed more at length as follows.

> We must bear in mind at every stage two principles which I think at the present day are established beyond question. The first of these principles is the absolute right of all men to contract or refrain from contracting, which is one of the rights hereinbefore enumerated. The motives which actuate a man in refraining from making a contract in relation to labor or merchandise or anything else are absolutely beyond all inquiry or challenge. . . . The right to refrain from contracting is an absolute right, which every man can exercise justly or unjustly, for a good purpose or for a bad purpose, "maliciously," in the popular sense of the term, or benevolently. The second principle to keep in view is not at present universally recognized as sound law, viz., that men

have an absolute right to act in voluntary combination with respect to contracting or refraining from contracting. . . . It seems to me that the settled American doctrine, apart from all recent statutes, is that all dealers in the market, whether in merchandise or in labor, on each side of the market, have an absolute right to combine voluntarily to concurrently exercise their several rights to refrain from contracting if they see fit to do so, however immoral their motives may be. If this is not good law, then the right to refrain from contracting is subject to a most extraordinary limitation which leads to absurd results.

Opposed to this view of the absoluteness of the right to a free labor market is the opinion expressed by the judges in the Willcutt Case. Judge Hammond insists that

In the jurisprudence of any civilized country there are but few, if any, absolute rights—rights which bend to nothing and to which everything else must bend. The right to one's life would seem to be quite absolute, but it must yield to the private right of self-defense and to the public right to punish for crime. And so in the case before us, neither the right of the plaintiff to a free labor market nor the right of the union to impose a fine upon its members is absolute.

The right of an employer to free labor is subject to the right of the laborer to hamper him by many expedients short of fraud or intimidation amounting to injury to the person or property of those who desire to enter his employ, or threats of such injury.

Judges Sheldon and Loring, writing opinions in the same case go further and quite distinctly state that the right to the free market is secondary to other rights. Judge Loring says that the right to organize to improve conditions and to strike in furtherance of this object and to do all acts (not unlawful) to make the strike successful—"these rights of the employees are superior to the right of the employer to have a free flow of labor in his business."

Judge Sheldon adds, going into the discussion more at length:

The general right of an employer to go into the market to hire laborers does not deprive a union, in carrying on a lawful strike, of the right to use upon its individual members, for the purpose of keeping them up to the performance of their duty as such members, all the influences that any other organization properly could use, including the imposition of fines. The right to use such influences is an independent and paramount right. The interests of the employer are subordinate to this right, and must yield to it. . . . The right of an employer to conduct his business without interference in the labor market is subordinate to the right of his employees to strike and to maintain the strike in a lawful manner.

The plaintiff in the case before us has indeed, like every other employer of labor, a right to enjoy a free labor market, to have a free flow of labor come to him; that is, he has a right to employ such men as are willing to work for him upon such terms as may be mutually agreed upon between him and them. The strongest statements of this right may perhaps be found in some of the cases cited in the majority opinion. (Cases cited.) But even these decisions follow the now universal current of authority in recognizing the right of the defendants to curtail and restrict this right of the plaintiff, by combining in labor unions to engage in a lawful strike for the improvement of their own conditions, and in endeavoring to render their strike successful by using all rightful means both to secure unanimity of action among their own members and to dissuade other laborers from entering the employ of the plaintiff. That is, the relative right of the plaintiff to enjoy a free labor market is modified and limited by the right of its employees to enter into an agreement or combination to secure higher wages or to improve otherwise the condition of their employment, and for this purpose to engage in a strike and to use all rightful means to insure the success of their strike by checking, and if they can do so without resorting to wrongful means, by wholly stopping, the free flow of labor to the plaintiff. But if this be so, manifestly the plaintiff's right to a free labor market is not only not a paramount right, but it is and must be subject to the higher right of the defendants to combine and to carry on a strike by the use of whatever lawful means may be in their power; and we cannot see how this right can be further limited than by restricting it to acts which are not forbidden by law, either as being unlawful in themselves or at variance with a sound public policy.

In the Tenement House Case Judge Earl's view was apparently influenced by Blackstone's classification of fundamental rights. He quotes Blackstone on this point in his opinion. "The third absolute right inherent in every Englishman is that of property which consists in the free use, enjoyment and disposal of all his acquisitions without any control or diminution, save only by the law of the land."

One right frequently asserted and insisted upon with much positiveness is the right of the employer to carry on his business without the dictation of employees as to who shall be or who shall not be employed. Judge Parker, however, finds a reason for denying that even this right is unrestricted. In his opinion in the Cumming Case he says:

I know it is said in another opinion in this case that "workmen cannot dictate to employers how they shall carry on their business, nor whom they shall or shall not employ;" but I dissent absolutely from that proposition, and assert that, so long as workmen must assume all the risk of injury that may come to them through the carelessness of co-employees, they have the moral and legal right to say that they will not work with certain men, and the employer must accept their dictation or go without their services.

Judge Sanborn, in the Allis Chalmers Case, makes an

effort to adjust the conflict without deciding the relativity of the rights involved.

Here is the point where two equally clear and valuable constitutional rights come into opposition—the right of the workmen to get as much as possible for himself on the best terms, and the right of the employer to use his capital and ability as he pleases to secure whatever profit his investment and skill may bring. The legal right involved is single, but asserted by two independent and conflicting interests, and the question is, which one must yield his right to that of the other, so far as they conflict.

Such statements as these are evidence of very important and farreaching differences of opinion as to which of certain "rights" shall take precedence over others when they come into conflict. The problem is not one of academic interest alone. When each of two contending parties claims to be within his "rights" and the two cannot reach an agreement out of court, the question of relative and absolute "rights" obviously becomes a very practical one. Certain it is that standards heretofore satisfactory because developed from long experience and well adapted to prevailing conditions have been sufficient in the past. It is just as certain that as conditions have changed they must change accordingly. This brings into strong light the necessity of a standard that will always be related to prevailing conditions. Further it may be added that with no generally recognized code much will depend upon the individual judge. At this point it will not be so much the judge's knowledge of the law that will be of prime importance as it will be his standard of ethics. If trained to individualism, his conclusions will flow from that philosophy. If trained to adopt the social point of view, his conclusions must necessarily be somewhat different.

III

MOTIVE AND COMBINATION

The extent to which questions of motive and combination have entered into the discussions of cases justifies a brief consideration of these topics. The courts generally take up these questions only incidentally. Yet in many instances one feels that the view held by the judge enters largely as a factor in determining the decision.

As to motive, the general view may be shown in a few brief extracts.

The rule of law, therefore, as firmly established in England, in this state, and in most of the United States, supports the conclusion [reached in the Cumming Case] so far as it rests upon the doctrine "that an act lawful in itself is not converted by a malicious or bad motive into an unlawful act so as to make the doer of the act liable to a civil action." (Parkinson *v.* Council.)

If an act be lawful—one that the party has a legal right to do—the fact that he may be actuated by an improper motive does not render it unlawful. (Bohn Mfg. Co. *v.* Hollis.)

It is a part of every man's civil rights that he be left at liberty to refuse business relations with any person whomsoever, whether the refusal rests upon reason, or is the result of whim, caprice, prejudice or malice. With his reasons neither the public nor third persons have any legal concern. (Cooley quoted in Adair *v.* U. S.)

The motive, then, is not usually material. In some decisions it is made so, but the expressions in more general form indicate the direction in which opinion is moving. Doubtless motive will have less rather than more influence. Naturally it will be so, since not only is it almost impossible to determine what the motives really are but also because the motives are usually mixed and it is difficult to pick the determining one. Motives of individuals, complex as they are, become even less determinable when groups of individuals act in concert.

Says Judge Parker in the Cumming Case,

> It seems to me illogical, and little short of absurd to say that the everyday acts of the business world, apparently within the domain of competition, may be either lawful or unlawful according to the motive of the actor. If the motive be good, the act is lawful. If it be bad, the act is unlawful. I do not assent to this proposition, although there is authority for it.

The question of the effect of combination on the legality of strikes and other organized labor activities is not quite so one-sided. The superior influence that a combination may exercise above that exerted by a single individual has been a determining factor in the minds of some judges.

> What is lawful for an individual, is not the test of what is lawful for a combination of individuals; or to state it in another way, there are things which it is lawful for an individual to do which it is not lawful for a combination of individuals to do. (Pickett *v.* Walsh.)
>
> If in any case, it is criminal for many to combine to do what any one may lawfully do singly, it would seem that this would be such a case. Numbers can accomplish what one man cannot,—evil as well as good,—and that is the reason of the combination. (State *v.* Glidden.)

The opposite view is expressed in the following extracts:

> What one man may lawfully do singly, two or more may lawfully agree to do jointly. The number who unite to do the act cannot change its character from lawful to unlawful. (Bohn Mfg. Co. *v.* Hollis.)
>
> There can be found running through our legal literature many remarkable statements that an act perfectly lawful when done by one person becomes by some sort of legerdemain crim-

inal when done by two or more persons acting in concert, and this upon the theory that the concerted action amounts to a conspiracy. But with this doctrine we do not agree. If an individual is clothed with a right when acting alone, he does not lose such right merely by acting with others, each of whom is clothed with the same right. If the act done is lawful, the combination of several persons to commit it does not render it unlawful. In other words, the mere combination of action is not an element which gives character to the act.

Each one could have quit without incurring any civil liability to him. What each one could rightfully do, certainly all could do if they so desired, especially when their concerted action was taken peaceably, without any threats, violence, or attempt at intimidation. (Lindsay *v.* Montana F. of L.)

Whatever one man may do alone, he may do in combination with others, provided they have no unlawful object in view. Mere numbers do not ordinarily affect the quality of the act. (Cumming Case.)

A more moderate view of the matter is expressed by Judge Holmes.

There is a notion, which latterly has been insisted on a good deal, that a combination of persons to do what any one of them lawfully might do by himself will make the otherwise lawful conduct unlawful. It would be rash to say that some as yet unformulated truth may not be hidden under this proposition. But in the general form in which it has been presented and accepted by many courts, I think it plainly untrue, both on authority and principle. (Vegelahn *v.* Guntner.)

IV

LIFE, LIBERTY AND PROPERTY

As one would naturally expect, the terms life, liberty and property are frequently used in the opinions. The comprehensiveness of the terms is emphasized by Judge Sherwood of Missouri.

It will be noted that the rights of life, liberty, and property are grouped together in the same sentence; they constitute a trinity of rights, and each, as opposed to unlawful deprivation thereof, is of equal constitutional importance. With each of those rights, under the operation of a familiar principle, every auxiliary right, every attribute necessary to make the principal right effectual and valuable in its most extensive sense, pass as incidents of the original grant. "The rights thus guaranteed are something more than the mere privileges of locomotion; the guaranty is the negation of arbitrary power in every form which results in the deprivation of a right."

These terms, "life," "liberty" and "property," are representative terms, and cover every right to which a member of the body politic is entitled under the law. Within their comprehensive scope are embraced the right of self-defense, freedom of speech, religious and political freedom, exemption from arbitrary arrests, the right to buy and sell as others may, —all our liberties, personal, civil, and political,—in short, all that makes life worth living; and of none of these liberties can any one be deprived except by due process of law. Now, as before stated, each of the rights heretofore mentioned carries with it, as its natural and necessary coincident, all that effectuates and renders complete the full, unrestrained enjoyment of that right. (State *v.* Julow.)

Again Judge Goode of the same state declares:

A man's trade and the contracts by which he is employed to exercise it are in the nature of property. He has the right to use the former and get the benefit of the latter without tortious interference. We see no reason why the rules applicable in actions for injuries to tangible property should not be applied in the case of an active and relentless conspiracy to prevent a mechanic from earning a living. (Carter *v.* Oster.)

Judge Scholfield of Illinois applies the terms as follows:

The privilege of contracting is both a liberty and a property right, and if A. is denied the right to contract and acquire property in a manner which he has hitherto enjoyed under the law, and which B., C., and D. are still allowed by the law to enjoy, it is clear that he is deprived of both liberty and property to the extent that he is thus denied the right to contract. Our constitution guarantees that no person shall be deprived of life, liberty, or property without due process of law. (Frorer *v.* People.)

Dealing with the imputation that courts are inclined to distinguish between the liberty of individuals and the property rights of individuals, Chief Justice Campbell of Colorado declares:

The right to acquire and possess property includes the right to contract for one's labor. The latter is essentially a property right. The arbitrary classification of rights into rights of persons and rights of things, made by Blackstone and other jurists for purposes of convenience in treatment, has been the occasion for hostile criticism by those favoring socialistic or paternal legislation. Employing the argumentum ad hominem, they say that those decisions in which courts have carefully guarded rights of property put property above the man. A moment's calm reflection will show the falsity of this charge. Property, as such, has no claim upon the protection of the law. When a property right is spoken of, the right of some person over or concerning the property is meant. All rights recognized by the law pertain to persons, natural or artificial. The absolute rights are commonly designated as personal rights. They are such as are annexed to the person, like life and reputation, while property rights are those unconnected with the person, but which none the less belong to some person. All rights, both those spoken of as personal and those denominated as property rights, belong to the individual citizen; and, when it is said that property rights must not be infringed, what is meant is merely that the right of some person to or concerning property must not be interfered with. (*Re* Morgan.)

Somewhat opposed to these views, which are generally accepted by the courts, may be cited the following extracts. Dissenting from the prevailing opinion of the United States supreme court in Adair *v.* United States, Justice Holmes writes:

I confess that I think that the right to make contracts at will that has been derived from the word "liberty" in the Amendments has been stretched to its extreme by the decisions; but they agree that sometimes the right may be restrained. Where there is, or generally is believed to be, an important ground of public policy for restraint, the Constitution does not forbid it, whether this court agrees or disagrees with the policy pursued.

Again in Lochner *v.* People the same justice, again dissenting, says,

I think that the word "liberty," in the 14th Amendment, is perverted when it is held to prevent the natural outcome of a dominant opinion, unless it can be said that a rational and fair man necessarily would admit that the statute proposed would infringe fundamental principles as they have been understood by the traditions of our people and our law.

V

CONCLUSIONS PUSHED TO ABSURDITY

Some opinions show a tendency to denounce certain legislation not so much because of its own inherent evil as because of what it may lead to as a precedent. Instances of this are found in the following cases.

Chief Justice Campbell of Colorado, arguing against the eight-hour law for mines and smelters, incorporates the following argument in the opinion:

If the principle of the decision by which the present [law] is saved, in its logical extension, will protect others that every rational mind will declare void, it is well to stop for reflection; for it is a question of power and not discretion, we are now considering.

Then follows the application. If this legislation may be passed to protect the health of workmen and the day limited to eight hours, continues the argument, the legislature

may hereafter, upon the ground that idleness, resulting from short hours of labor, leads to drunkenness and gambling, and industry, promoted by longer hours, to happiness and health, enact that workmen must labor at these occupations fourteen or sixteen hours per day.

By extending the same principle to other occupations, the legislature may say

that a man weighing one hundred and twenty pounds or less shall not work in a stone quarry, because only large and powerful men can safely work therein; that only men free from a tendency to tuberculosis shall work at indoor occupations, because those so afflicted need more pure air and sunshine than they can get if excluded from the open air; that only persons not needing the aid of eye-glasses shall become makers or repairers of watches, because labor, with such mechanical aids, upon delicate mechanisms, tends to destroy vision; or that those suffering from sluggish livers shall not engage in sedentary occupations, because their health demands active, muscular effort. Then it is only one step further to provide by law the style and quality of garments the citizen may wear, the quantity and quality of food he may eat, and the beverage he may drink. And, because one cannot support and properly educate his family for less than a certain amount of money, the legislature may declare that, to promote the general welfare, no employer shall contract to pay, or pay, an employee less than an arbitrary wage, so fixed as to produce the required sum. Such and other illustrations that readily suggest themselves are germane, and each and every supposed act could be sustained upon the same principle that would make the act before us valid.

In the dissenting opinion in Peel Splint Coal Co. *v.* State Justice English finds an objection to the law in that it applies to mines that employ ten or more workmen. This objection he states as follows. The law excludes from its operation any person operating a coal mine in which less than ten miners are employed, which results in this; that an operator only employing nine need not weigh the coal before it is screened, but one employing twelve must. Can any one say why the operator should be allowed to weigh the coal after it is screened for the nine, and that he must weigh it previously for the twelve? Is not the danger of fraud as great to the individual miner in the one instance as the other? and is not one miner as much entitled to the benefit of the law (if it be beneficial) as another? And again, is there any good reason why the small operator should be allowed to obtain from his mine merchantable coal by using the screen before it is weighed, and the large operator be denied the privilege of thus testing the services of his employees, and obtaining merchantable coal for the wages he pays them? and why is it that the police power of the state should be invoked for the protection of the twelve, while the nine are left to work their way with fear and trembling, and protect themselves from the alleged iniquities of the screen?

Justice Peckham, speaking for the United States supreme court in the Bakers' Case, argued that if the principle on which that law was made to rest were admitted as valid it would lead to conclusions that would be regarded as absurd.

It is unfortunately true, that labor, even in any department, may possibly carry with it the seeds of unhealthiness. But are we all, on that account, at the mercy of legislative majorities? A printer, a tinsmith, a locksmith, a carpenter, a cabinetmaker, a dry goods clerk, a bank's, a lawyer's, or a physician's clerk, or a clerk in almost any kind of business, would all come under the power of the legislature, on this assumption. . . In our large cities there are many buildings into which the sun penetrates for but a short time in each day, and these buildings are occupied by people carrying on the business of bankers, brokers, lawyers, real estate, and many other kinds of business, aided by many clerks, messengers, and other employees. Upon the assumption of the validity of this act under review, it is not possible to say that an act, prohibiting lawyers' or bank clerks, or others, from contracting to labor for their employers more than eight hours a day would be invalid. It might be said that it is unhealthy to work more than that number of hours in an apartment lighted by artificial light during the working hours of the day; that the occupation of the bank clerk, the lawyer's clerk, the real estate clerk, or the broker's clerk, in such offices is therefore unhealthy, and the legislature, in its paternal wisdom, must, therefore, have the right to legislate on the subject of, and to limit, the hours for such labor; and, if it exercises that power, and its validity be questioned, it is sufficient to say, it has reference to the public health; it has reference to the health of the employees condemned to labor day after day in buildings where the sun never shines; it is a health law, and therefore it is valid, and cannot be questioned by the courts. . .

[It is not possible to establish a definite connection between the] number of hours a baker may work in the bakery and the healthful quality of the bread made by the workmen. . . . If the man works ten hours a day it is all right, but if ten and a half or eleven his health is in danger and his bread may be unhealthy, and, therefore, he shall not be permitted to do it. This, we think, is unreasonable and entirely arbitrary.

Judge Carpenter, in State *v.* Glidden, saw in a boycott a purpose to deprive the defendant "of its liberty to carry on its business in its own way." It is then found necessary "to announce from the bench" "that every man may carry on his business as he pleases, may do what he will with his own so long as he does nothing unlawful, and acts with due regard to the rights of others." It is noted with some wonder by the Judge that the occasion for such an announcement should be "not an attempt by government to interfere with the rights of the citizen, nor by the rich and powerful to oppress the poor," but "an attempt by a large body of working-men to control, by means little if any better than force, the action of employers." If employees have this right

then all business enterprises are alike subject to their dictation. No one is safe in engaging in business. . . .It must be remembered that the exercise of the power, if conceded, will by no means be confined to the matter of employing help. Upon the same principle, and for the same reasons, the right to determine what business others shall engage in, when and where it shall be carried on, etc., will be demanded, and must be conceded. The principle, if it once obtains a foothold, is aggressive and is not easily checked. It thrives on what it feeds, and is insatiate in its demands. More requires more. If a large body of irresponsible men demand and receive power outside of law, over and above law, it is not to be expected that they will be satisfied with a moderate and reasonable use of it.

VI

LABOR AS A COMMODITY

The general question of the applicability of the Sherman Anti-Trust Law to conspiracies in restraint of trade formed by labor organizations may be regarded as having been settled by the United States supreme court. The Debs Case and the Loewe Case may be cited in evidence of this fact. Yet the question came up before the supreme court of Iowa in 1908 and led to an opinion that is of more than ordinary interest. The law of that state forbade all agreements "to regulate or fix the price of any article of merchandise or commodity, or to fix or limit the amount or quantity of any article, commodity, or merchandise to be manufactured, mined, produced, or sold in this state." The case that came before the court was one in which physicians were indicted for entering into an agreement to establish fees and charges for their personal services. The relation of the opinion to labor appears in the consideration given to the meaning of the two terms "labor" and "commodity."

The essential point in the case, as expressed in the opinion, is emphasized at the outset. After referring to the provisions of the statute as just quoted the question is raised: "Do the acts charged constitute a crime under this section of the code? . . . Are the charges of a physician or surgeon for his medical skill or ability an article of merchandise or commodity to be produced or sold in this state?" It was contended before the court that the word "commodity" "is broad enough to cover the charge made for professional services or skill." To this contention the opinion replies that in attributing meaning to terms in criminal statutes, they are to have a strict construction. Moreover, in construing any statute, all the language shall be considered, and "such interpretation placed upon any word appearing therein as was within the manifest intent of the body which enacted the law." After discussing the derivative and the dictionary meaning of the term in question, it is concluded that a restricted meaning must be the one adopted. The matter appears of such general importance to the court that Judge Deemer, writing the opinion, discusses this point more at length.

Whilst there is a class of political economists, who treat labor as so much merchandise, the wage being regulated simply by supply and demand, there is another class, which, taking account of the personal equation, sees in it something more than a commodity, and refuses to subscribe to the doctrine that supply and demand alone regulate the price. This latter class of economists refuses to accept the doctrine that a man is rich because he has stored away within him many days' work, and are convinced that his necessities, quite as often as the demand for his labor, fixes the stipend which he is to receive. In other words, the laborer, skilled or unskilled, is not regarded as standing on an equality with him who barters in goods and merchandise. It is not, of course, within the province of courts of justice to adopt or promulgate any particular system of political science; but in the interpretation of statutes they must take notice of current political theory and conviction. If we were to adopt the view so strongly presented by appellant's counsel, it would be on the assumption that the associated words "merchandise" and "commodity" include the wages to be paid for labor, because labor is a sort of merchandise, subject to barter and sale as other goods. . .

Used in connection with the term "merchandise," and qualified as it is in the latter part of the section by the words "manufactured, mined, produced, or sold," it is manifest that the statute was not intended to, and did not, include labor either skilled or unskilled. . . . The only ground upon which appellant can stand with any show of plausibility is that labor is a commodity to be bought, sold, or produced, as merchandise. This is a strained and unnatural construction, and gives to the word "commodity" a meaning which is perhaps permissible, but is not the commonly accepted one. Under our statutes, words and phrases are to be construed according to the context and the approved usage of the language. With this in mind we are constrained to hold that labor is not a commodity within the meaning of the act now in question. . . . .

It seems to be the almost universal holding that it is no crime for any number of persons without an unlawful object in view to associate themselves together, and agree that they will not work for or deal with certain classes of men, or work under a certain price or without certain conditions. . . .

The statute in question was aimed at unlawful conspiracies or combinations in restraint of trade, and was manifestly not intended to cover labor unions. It is the right of miners, artisans, laborers, or professional men to unite for their own improvement or advancement or for any other lawful purpose, and it has never been held, so far as we are able to discover, that a union for the purpose of advancing wages is unlawful under any statutes which have been called to our attention. As said by Judge Taft in Phelan case, "Such unions, when rightly conducted, are beneficial in character." And it would be a strained and unnatural conclusion to hold that a statute aimed at pools and trusts should be held to include agreements as to prices for labor because the word "commodity" is used therein. As the right to combine for the purpose of securing higher wages is recognized as lawful at common law, a statute enacted to prohibit pools and trusts should not be held to apply to combinations to fix the wages for labor, unless it clearly appears that such was the legislative intent. Whatever of doubt there may be regarding the power of the legislature to do so, we do not think that the act in question covers combinations to fix the labor price whether that labor be skilled or unskilled.

Finally, referring to the cases cited by the appellant, the Debs and the Loewe cases, the opinion declares that these cases are not in point.

The statute before us has nothing to do with commerce; nor does it have to do with restraint of trade or commerce as does the Sherman Act. It has to do with pools and trusts organized in this state to fix or regulate the price of any article or commodity, or to fix or limit the amount or quality of any article, commodity or merchandise to be produced or sold in the state. Surely it has no reference to the amount or quality of labor to be produced or sold. Such a construction would be ridiculous. And, if it will not bear that interpretation, it follows that the word "commodity," when used with reference to prices, should not be held to include labor.

CHAPTER XIII

CONCLUSIONS

THE field covered by the preceding chapters suggests some considerations of deep importance. The number of cases to which reference has been made and from which extracts have been quoted is not large. They are nevertheless typical of the far greater number that courts have heard and in which they have written opinions. In all of these there is great variety of circumstances, and the conditions of each particular case have had an important influence in shaping the decision. The present study is not directly concerned either with the particulars of the cases or with the effects of such on the decisions reached. In all the elaboration of opinions set forth in justification of the decisions there appear certain points of view, attitudes of mind and statements of general principles that are of absorbing interest as well as of great importance. In the preceding chapters the purpose has been to state these in such variety and with such fullness as to enable the reader to judge for himself how extended and varied these expressions are. Such a reading leads to certain conclusions that should be pointed out in this chapter.

Where the case presents any unusual difficulty the mind of the judge naturally turns to first principles in search of a solution. This method certainly should lead to a satisfactory result. As a matter of fact, it does no such thing. Instead of eliminating the perplexity it increases it and renders a solution more difficult. An employer appears with the charge that his business is being unlawfully interfered with and asks the court to protect him. Possibly there comes immediately to the mind of the judges such well known and generally accepted propositions as these: every man may do what he will with his own so long as he acts with due regard to the rights of others; every man may carry on his business as he pleases. Such expressions are time-honored and have become almost a part of our political consciousness. The decision seems easy and possibly the prayer of the employer is granted. But possibly in reply to these general propositions the employee who is charged with the interference suggests a different group of propositions equally well known and generally accepted: a man may work or not as he pleases; a man may dispose of his labor on such terms and under such conditions as are acceptable to him, so long as he acts with due regard to the rights of others. Obviously this is disturbing. The case would be an easy one to decide on the basis of either set of propositions were it not for the other. Yet a decision must be made and once made an opinion must be written in support of it.

Possibly one set of propositions will be taken as a statement of the legal principle involved, and from them a logical argument built up sustaining the conclusion; a conclusion, it may be, that the legal right is with the employer, or possibly that it is with the employee. But, which set of general propositions will be chosen? It is at this point that the judges' attitude of mind and habit of thought, a result of legal training and legal practice, become of prime importance. Doubtless this is the cause which has led in so many cases to the choice of the first of these two sets of propositions and to the decision in favor of the employer, although that decision is supported by an opinion expressed in terms of general truths that in themselves are beyond question.

With the increasing complexity of such cases the insufficiency of the reasoning has become more and more obvious. The number of supposedly self-evident legal propositions has increased and with the increase their irreconcilability has become more apparent.

In the numerous efforts to reconcile these various sets of propositions, a variety of conclusions have been reached and different lines of argument adopted in establishing them. The citations chosen furnish abundant evidence of this.

The solution adopted by some courts seemed at first a promising one. It was the assumption of an attitude of aloofness; a position in which the general legal principles were laid down as applicable to both parties with the injunction that the contending parties must settle their differences as best they might, both parties keeping within the legal limits established. This method of meeting the difficulty seemed wholly reasonable and fair, and clearly within the province of the court. The rights were equal but conflicting. There were clearly two sides to every question of this sort. The reasonableness of the demands made on each side the court had no means of determining. The difficulties that are raised through this conflict of equal rights must be settled by mutual agreement between the contending parties, they must be adjusted through freedom of private contract between employer and employee. But such an attempt to solve the difficulty can not be of any permanent value either socially or legally. Each party insists that the right in its case is superior to that of the other. And so, if the court will have nothing to do with such difficulties at this point, the stage is soon reached where it must permit itself to be appealed to, this time on the question of what the respective contending parties may do in the efforts to force their contention upon their opponents. This brings the whole matter back into court again. There it will have to remain until by the slow process of the development of judicial opinion some general principles are evolved that will not be in conflict among themselves and that will be applicable to the conditions to which they are to be applied. This process of legal evolution will doubtless be slow and there may be expected to appear much impatience both with legal principles and with courts before it is completed. Meantime the struggle must presumably go on, and there must be for some time to come continued dissatisfaction with the decisions that the courts make. As with trusts so with trade unions the fact of large combination is more evident than is the means of adjusting their activities to those of individuals. " It is only in recent years that these great and powerful combinations have made their appearance, and the limits to which they may go in enforcing their demands are far from being settled."

Returning, as the courts must, to a consideration of these perplexities, it is found that there are at present certain difficulties the solution of which has not yet been discovered. These difficulties take the form of general propositions seemingly sound in themselves but irreconcilible. The choice between them has been accompanied with increasing embarrassment as labor unions have come into a position of recognized legality. In earlier times when so nearly all phases of individual liberty as applied to industrial conditions were interpreted from the point of view of the employer the difficulties were scarcely realized. The workmen were not in a position to enforce acknowledgment of their point of view and what they contended to be the validity of their claims. As they have gained steadily in recognition it has become apparent that the same generalizations, for so long the bulwark of defense of the employers, were capable of such an interpretation as to become a defense for themselves instead of an obstacle.

Out of this slow transition in the practical relation of the two before courts of justice have developed some as yet irreconcilible propositions so far as their application is concerned. These center around the leading question: What are the rights of organized labor in law? That this question has not received its final answer no one who reads the views expressed in the various opinions can doubt. The fact that laborers have a right to organize seems to be generally recognized. Their legal relations to others has not yet been established. This is "a part of the law still in the nebulous but clearing stage." Both the number of cases brought to the courts and their variety are rapidly increasing. They involve all phases of the general question of transactions between employers and employees. The views of the courts "as to the constitutionality of many such laws are in serious conflict." The situation is well summed up by Judge Halloway when he says:

Whatever may have been the attitude of the courts and legislative bodies in this country towards labor organizations in the past, it is sufficient for our purpose to know that the right of workingmen to organize for the improvement of their industrial condition is now generally admitted. The great diversity of opinions among the courts has arisen over a consideration of the question: What means may trade unions employ to further the objects of their organizations?

The legal doubt of the right to organize has given place to a legal uncertainty as to what the organizations may do.

In this situation the union men find themselves in a position of double difficulty. One phase arises from their relations with employers; the other from their relations with workers who do not join the unions. Naturally with the very positive views that organized laborers entertain concerning unionism and union policies, they deem it of utmost importance that employers and non-union laborers be prevented from establishing such relations as to result in the defeat of their purposes. This makes the difficulty one of great perplexity, especially when the propositions to be reconciled are stated in terms of individual rights. Here arise conflicts that have as yet quite completely baffled the courts. Some of them may be stated in form as follows: What effect upon the general rights of individuals follows from the fact that some of those individuals are employers of labor and some moreover belong to associations of employers where the rules of the association contain voluntary agreements to act in concert; that some of the individuals are workingmen who belong to associations of workmen where the rules of the association contain voluntary agreements to act in concert; and that some of the individuals are workingmen who refuse to enter into any association and insist upon being free from any such rules? From this situation there emerges inevitably a contention between the rights of the individual employer as against those of the individual employee, the rights of the individual union employee as against those of the individual non-union employee, the rights of individual employers and individual non-union employees to establish business relations as against the rights of individual union employees to interfere with those relations. To increase the difficulty the fact of organization and its effects upon individual rights enter into the situation, also the fact of competition and its effect upon the same individual rights. Further there is the difficulty in reconciling the recognition of the right to organize with the right of the organization to act; the right to strike and the purposes for which strikes may be entered upon, the relevancy or the irrelevancy of motives in connection either with strikes or other union activities. These conflicting propositions are to be found running through the large variety of opinions written by many different judges. Though expressed in varying forms they are easily recognizable. It must never be lost from view that these interpretations are often, perhaps usually, determined by the circumstances of the case at bar. Yet no one can read these many opinions in full without realizing that the legal principles that are being slowly evolved are determined to no small degree by the attitude and training of the judges.

From such a situation certain conclusions are forced upon one who studies the opinions with a view to ascertaining something more than the bare fact of what the law is. They indicate certain tendencies that are far more important than the decisions themselves can possibly be. The decisions determine the outcome of particular cases and of similar cases for the future. The opinions indicate the effort to solve problems; to reconcile differences; to formulate legal principles that shall determine the actions of industrial parties before they become parties at law; even to guide them so that they may settle their differences without becoming parties at law.

One cannot escape the impression that general statements of individual rights do not go far toward solving the difficulty as it may exist, for example, between an employer and an employee. In a case which argued forcibly against a law forbidding an employer from discharging an employee because he was a member of a labor organization the court inserted in its opinion general statements of individual right.

A man's right not to work or not to pursue a particular trade or calling, or to determine when or where or with whom he will work, is in law a right of precisely the same nature, and entitled to just the same protection, as a man's right to trade or work. . . . It is, in my opinion, the absolute right of every workman to exercise his own option with regard to the persons in whose society he will agree or continue to work. . . .

Every man has a right under the law, as between himself and others to full freedom in disposing of his own labor or capital according to his own will. . . It is a part of every man's civil rights that he be left at liberty to refuse business relations with any person whomsoever, whether the refusal rests upon reason, or is the result of whim, caprice, prejudice or malice. . . . Every man has a natural right to hire his services to any one he pleases, or refrain from such hiring; and so, likewise, it is the right of every one to determine whose services he will hire.

Such statements as these undoubtedly express legal principles of long standing whose roots reach far into the past. They have commanded the respect of American thought for generations and were among those cherished principles that were finally embodied in our constitutions. Yet what is their application to such difficulties as present themselves in our present-day labor controversies? The case from which these statements have been quoted decided that an employer could not be deprived of his constitutional right to discharge an employee whenever it was his pleasure to do so. Cite these same principles in a case where men are striking against an employer and they have been given quite a different interpretation by some courts. Cite them again where union men are refusing to work with non-union men and it is very material whether they be stated for the non-union men or for their union rivals. These differences of conclusion appear in various cases. Obviously such general propositions cannot be of final value. They state rights that belong to both parties as indiyiduals and do not decide the question at issue because the contention arises from the fact that both parties are standing upon this general right. Each is endeavoring to force the other to yield.

The situation then resolves itself into one where each of two parties claims the same right and each is seeking to exercise that right when its exercise will prevent the other party from the same privilege. In such a situation,—one in which each party claims to be acting within its right in preventing the other from exercising the same right,—it certainly cannot be said that the course of development of legal rights has reached its final stage. When such an issue comes before a court, three courses seem to be open. The court may direct the parties to settle their differences among themselves by some sort of compromise, in the meantime keeping within their legal rights in making the adjustment. This might and very frequently does lead to an industrial deadlock. Again, the court may fall back on some former interpretation of the principle and accept it as a precedent for the present case. This might and frequently does lead to a decision favoring one of the parties against the other. Such a course very probably leads to the interpretation in favor of the employer, as has so often happened in the past. Or finally if the judge be one who is inclined to recognize the disadvantage of the employee in his rivalry with the employer, he might favor the employee at the expense of the employer's equal right. Any one of these courses may result in an injustice. The court may recognize this and seek a fourth course. It may endeavor to reduce the right to terms that will allow of a different interpretation, to find some superior right that will change in some way the nature of the contention. While this last would be the one altogether most desirable, it might very probably require a boldness in departing from precedent which most courts would not dare to exercise; a far step in the evolution of legal principles that judges are seldom willing to take. However great the difficulty of this procedure it is certain that along this line alone will real progress be made.

The history of legal adjustment has been that of modifying recognized rights in order to establish new ones better adjusted to new conditions. The right of the more powerful to take what he was able to seize was modified in the recognition of the right of a person to his property without regard to his physical ability to protect it. The right of one party in a contract was modified by the conditions that surrounded the agreement when the contract was made. The right of the slave owner was materially modified when slaves were made free persons. So the employer cannot employ or discharge entirely at will. The laws of Minnesota and Wyoming, for example, declare that, "Employers are forbidden to require as a condition of employment the surrender of any right of citizenship or to discharge candidates because of their nomination for an election, or to interfere in the matter of such nomination." "In nearly all the states it is made penal or criminal for any person, by threatening to discharge an employee or to reduce his wages, or by promising to give him higher wages, or otherwise, to attempt to influence a voter to give or withhold his vote."[1] So, also, a man is not altogether free to work or not to work as he pleases. Vagrancy and "non-support" are certainly very real limitations while there is the sterner economic law that he who will not work may not eat.

Modifications are being made slowly but inevitably. This course must continue. Rights generally regarded as absolute are coming to be regarded after all as only relative. The conflict in rights governing employment of labor must be eliminated. Restrictions must be so placed as to modify the rights to such a degree as may be necessary. Either the courts must evolve these newer principles or they will be established through some other agency They must come in some way. It is the prime duty of the courts to formulate legal principles that will be in accord with prevailing

[1] Stimson, *Handbook*, p. 117.

conditions and that will furnish a guide for parties that have differences to settle, so that settlements may be made without industrial interruption and consequent economic waste.

That legal generalities should be worth repeating at all in opinions is pointed out by Judge Dodge of Wisconsin. He admits that they

do not greatly advance us toward any *a priori* location of a line of demarcation. They amount to little more than a declaration that police power extends to such measure of restraint as is consistent with liberty; and liberty, that measure of freedom consistent with the police power. . . . This impossibility of exact demarcation characterizes all discussion of the subject, yet the careful expressions of these alternative conceptions of properly limited government, on the one hand, and due freedom from restraint, on the other, are useful when we approach a concrete case. Therefore quotations of some such expressions may be helpful.

When one reads these references to the general individual rights as they occur so frequently it is not easy to avoid the impression that though stated by the court as applicable to all alike, the application is made in such a way as to favor one side only. Granting that the employer may hire whom he pleases and for what price he pleases, and also that the workman may work for whom he pleases and at what price he pleases, it is evident that when the two cannot agree no working relation can be established. A compromise must first be reached as to conditions and wages. If one yields more than he may wish, which ever it may be, the process is simply the " higgling of the market " by which all similar industrial relations are adjusted. Yet as a matter of fact, as revealed in the opinions themselves, the right of the employer seems to pass challenge more easily than does the right of the employee.

The matter was stated very recently by Justice Harlan of

the United States supreme court in a way that illustrates this point very well. "It was the right of the defendant [employer]," declares the opinion, "to prescribe the terms upon which the services of Coppage would be accepted, and it was the right of Coppage to become or not, as he chose, an employee of the railroad company upon the terms offered to him." Certainly that is clear. The conditions of labor were prescribed by the employer. The employee could accept them or let them alone. He had nothing further to do or say. But why so? Why not, so far as the court was concerned, say that it was the right of the employee to prescribe the terms upon which his services would be given and the right of the railroad to become or not, as it chose, an employer of Coppage upon the terms offered. And further, as the railroad was an association of stockholders who had delegated their authority to a board who in turn had authorized its manager to act for it, so the employees might be an association of laborers who had delegated their authority to a group of officers who in turn had authorized an agent to act. The court supported its view with the general proposition that

> it is a part of every man's civil rights that he be left at liberty to refuse business relations with any person whomsoever, whether the refusal rests upon reason, or is the result of whim, caprice, prejudice or malice. With his reasons neither the public nor third persons have any legal concern. It is also his right to have business relations with anyone with whom he can make contracts, and, if he is wrongfully deprived of this right by others, he is entitled to redress.

Suppose this general proposition to be stated in support of the employee. The difference that would result from the reversal of the case would be that instead of the workman going without work the railroad would be unable to operate unless it met the terms prescribed.[1] A question was raised in an early case (1836) that is still very pertinent. When there is failure to reach an agreement and industry is halted, "upon whom should the blame rest—upon him who refused to pay or him who refused to work until he was paid?" The courts seem to have quite fully fallen into the habit of taking it for granted that the blame is with the workmen, that it is for the employer to fix the conditions and for the laborer to accept or reject them assuming the responsibility for industrial disturbance if he rejects. There is clearly, in all reality, an equal obligation and an equal responsibility, if both parties to the agreement are to enjoy real liberty. Unless either may assume the aggressive in the bargaining for wages and conditions of labor the liberty and equality are not real. Bargaining implies that each seeks to secure concessions from the other. If the employee has only the alternative of accepting or rejecting the conditions offered by the employer, the bargaining is seriously limited.

Another difficulty is that arising from the simple fact of organization. The right to organize is granted as has been shown. What the organization may do and what its authority is over its members are questions of practical perplexity. This comes from the uncertainty in the minds of judges as to what the unions may do. The rightful purposes of organized labor could hardly be accomplished without running counter to the interests at some point of both employers and non-union men. Here arises the essential point; is the activity of the organization for the pur-

[1] It may be urged that the case here referred to is not a case in point, as it was a decision against a law which forbade an employer from discharging an employee because he was a member of a union. That is true so far as the technical decision is concerned. Taking the opinion, however, as it is written, the attitude assumed is not changed by this technical fact.

pose of harming others or for reaping an advantage? Strange as it may seem, this difference is insisted upon and judges seriously undertake to decide whether a strike and its prosecution by organized means has for its object the damage of others or the benefit of the strikers. Some denounce the prosecution of the strike on the ground that it is intended deliberately to do harm to the business of the employer. One would have difficulty in finding discussions so serious and so involved aiming to split such a hair outside of labor-case opinions. The strike, it is reasoned, is being organized to do a damage to the employer's business in order that to avoid the damage the employer may yield to the demands of the strikers. Or, the strike is organized to do a damage to other workmen by refusing to work with them and thus bring about their discharge. Certainly if labor unions had no other objects than those expressed in such statements there would have been small chance of their coming to the position of importance and legal recognition that they now occupy. That the real motive lying behind these results is self-improvement seems not to appear to the minds of some judges. They are quite ready to act as interpreter of purposes and thus to characterize acts as lawful or unlawful according to what the motive appears to the court to be. To many judges this matter may really appear important. In many of the opinions however it appears almost impossible for the members of the court to concede any actions by these organizations as legal though practically obliged by precedent to admit the legality of the organization itself. Instances have been cited where, if the view of the court is to be accepted as a final one, there remains nothing for the organization to do but maintain a mere passive existence. To some judges it seems that even the majority view of the members of a union if imposed on the minority is an infringement upon their personal liberty in spite of the fact that the association is a voluntary one and that rules and by-laws regularly established by majority vote must be enforceable upon all if the association is to exist at all. So also fines on members for failure to obey rules appear to some as an invasion of personal liberty. The delegation of power by an association is not recognized as valid by some while others admit the right as a general proposition but are not able to recognize it in a particular instance. In these and other similar matters many courts seem to have set themselves steadily against the attainment of any real efficiency in organization among unions. Concessions are made generally with reluctance if made at all.

In one place the court recognizes the rights of a union so far as to admit that it may seek counsel and advice, and persons interested in its welfare may aid in securing terms of employment that are most satisfactory. The members have the right to appoint officers and to authorize them to order members to leave their positions. One of the judges who expresses his recognition of such rights as these says in another case: "Though we cannot enjoin the engineers from unlawfully quitting, it does not follow that we may not enjoin Arthur from ordering them to do so." This seems very much like admitting that while the court could not enjoin the engineers from unlawfully quitting it could enjoin them from deciding through a representative chosen for the purpose to do so.

A man may say, "I will stop work," and be entirely within his right. If he says, "I will stop work in company with all my associates unless you make the change in conditions that we all desire," he is guilty of a "threat" and may be charged with an intent to damage his employer's business. When an organization is too weak to be of any service one judge, as Judge Burch of Kansas, declares that the wage earners' liberty of choice in making a bargain is "a myth or rather . . . a heartless mockery." When the organization becomes strong enough to be of some consequence a judge becomes concerned about the employer, as in time of a strike by workingmen in insisting upon their demands Chief Justice Beasley of New Jersey declared that "In such a condition of affairs [concerted action by a number of employees] it is idle to suggest that the manufacturer is free to reject the terms which the confederates offer."

The various differences of view may be finally summed up in the expressions chosen from two opinions. "The legality of a strike," says Judge Loring, "depends upon the purpose for which the employees strike." For, as Judge Vann insists, the purpose of a strike must be "not to gratify malice or inflict injury on others but to secure better terms of employment for themselves; not to harm others but to improve their own condition." In opposition to this view Judge Parker declares "the right of one man to refuse to work for another on any ground that he may regard as sufficient and the employer has no right to demand a reason for it." The reasons for undertaking the strike, he continues,

> may seem inadequate to others, but, if it seems to be in their interest as members of an organization to refuse longer to work, it is their legal right to stop. The reason may no more be demanded, as a right, of the organization than of an individual; but if they elect to state the reason, their right to stop work is not cut off because the reason seems inadequate or selfish to the employer or to organized society.

The essence of the difference here is in the importance of the purpose of a strike in determining its legality. In one view the legality depends directly upon the purpose. In the other the purpose is not material since the strikers need not state it unless they choose. If they do state it, it is of no consequence. Court opinion cannot be said to have settled into its final form so long as judges continue to choose between these two views, following in some cases the one and in some the other. Either the purpose is material or it is not. To determine which it is becomes of great importance.

If the whole matter of purpose is to be set aside, as Judge Parker sets it aside, the courts must abandon very much of the control that they have in the past assumed to exercise over various trade-union activities. This would seem to many judges a dangerous course. It would give the union man a decided advantage over his non-union rival. It would enable him by a threat to strike to put powerful pressure upon the employer to cause the discharge of non-union men. Such latitude judges seem unable to grant to organizations of laborers. The restraints upon the actions of union men, such as those against lawlessness in its various forms, seem to many judicial minds wholy inadequate as a means of control.

On the other hand if purpose is to be a criterion for judging of the legality of these several classes of acts the matter seems under much more effective control and doubtless to the judges seems under much safer control. If the purpose seems a worthy one, the courts may hold the actions legal. If the purpose seems unworthy then by very fact of its unworthiness the acts may be declared illegal.

Two objections stand against this latter course, however, each one of which is of practical importance. If the courts are to pass upon the legality of the purposes, that must mean in practice that the judges are to do so. The judges do not look at these matters all from the same angle. Their views of life are various, their training different and their notions of labor unions formed through channels other than a direct study of their activities. The judicial view as to the worthiness of a purpose would be inevitably, almost, that which the judge read into the case as a result of training and former experiences. Another result of such a course would be the setting-up of almost as many standards as there are individual judges or separate courts. It is unfortunate now that acts done within some jurisdictions are found to be illegal when these same acts are in other jurisdictions legal.

A second objection, and a more serious one, lies in the extreme difficulty of determining what the purpose in fact is. The acts may be clear. Their effects may be evident. But the purposes that prompt them are by no means so obvious. Thus the court would be in a constant perplexity in an endeavor to distinguish motives. The Massachusetts court in Willcutt *v.* Bricklayers had to consider a strike that had four objects. One was an increase of wages. Another was for a shorter day. A third was that all foremen should be members of the union. A fourth, that the business agent of the unions should be allowed to visit the buildings under construction. The employer returned a blanket refusal to all the demands. That was interpreted by the court as a refusal to the demand for a better wage and shorter day. The strike was then regarded by the court as a strike for that purpose and therefore lawful. Suppose a different view had been taken by the court. Suppose they had regarded the employer's blanket refusal as a refusal to employ union foremen and to allow business agents to visit the work. That might have changed the purpose from a lawful one to an unlawful one and thus characterized the strike itself as unlawful.

The employees of a street railway company in an eastern city struck because the company employed some non-union men. After the strike had been called the officers of the union went to an attorney to secure his legal services. When he learned that the strike was one for a closed shop on the road he refused to act as counsel unless the strikers included in their demands an advance in wages. His suggestion was acted upon and the strike was fought to the end on the demand for an increase in wages and for the discharge of certain non-union men. This extension could be made at any time and in connection with any strike. As soon as it became known what purposes certain courts would endorse those assumed purposes could be coupled with the real objects and so long as a general refusal was made to all the demands, according to the precedent of the Massachusetts court, the legality would be established.

Extracts have been cited in preceding chapters that indicate very clearly how difficult it is to state the real purpose of any given strike. A strike is announced as having for its object the driving out of non-union men so as to make places for unionists. In such a case one view may be that the purpose is primarily to injure the non-union men. The other view may be that it is primarily to benefit the members of the union. This is expressed by Judge Goode in an effort to emphasize immediate purpose as against ultimate purpose. He refers to a case where "the immediate purpose is to cause the discharge of an obnoxious fellow servant, even though the ultimate purpose may be the attainment of better economic and social conditions." This does not seem to aid much in the adjustment. The outcome of efforts to base legality of actions on purposes seems not likely to lead to very satisfactory results.

No statement could be made more sweeping than the frequently cited words of Judge Cooley in his treatise on *Torts.*

It is a part of every man's civil rights, that he be left at liberty to refuse business relations with any other person whomsoever, whether the refusal rests upon reason, or is the result of whim, caprice, prejudice or malice. With his reasons neither the public nor third persons have any legal concern.

It is also his right to have business relations with anyone with whom he can make contracts, and, if he is wrongfully deprived of this right by others, he is entitled to redress.

Taking the meaning of these words apart from any context they may be made to support the contention of the employer in discharging his workmen, the non-union man who is being interfered with by union men, and the union men themselves in their efforts to drive out non-union rivals. If the principle involved in the statement be accepted as the final word, especially in that part that insists that refusal to work may rest upon reason or upon whim, caprice, prejudice or malice, and that the refusal cannot be called in question by either the public or third persons, then purpose as a criterion must pass and some other means of regulating the whole situation be adopted.

The conclusions drawn from all these opinions and their various ramifications must be that courts have not yet developed legal principles which will stand the test of consistency and practicality in defining the legal limits of trade-union activity. Only the mere outlines of such a body of principles yet appear. A concrete expression of this is found in the words of Judge Reed when discussing a case characterized as coercion. " There is no contrariety of judicial view in respect to the illegality in the use of any act which is calculated to coerce, but in respect to what acts are to be regarded as coercive there is naturally more difference in judicial sentiment." The same is true in respect to the meaning to be attached to intimidation, threat, conspiracy, and other like terms. There is less contrariety of view in respect to the act, but very much more as to what comes within the legal meaning of the term. In many cases a prejudice is created at the very outset by the skilful use of these terms in the indictment Some judges have shown themselves to be on their guard by insisting upon paraphrasing the expressions. The substitution of the word announce in place of the word threat, for example, creates quite a different impression in the charge made in the indictment. Judge Halloway insists that the indictment before it is allowed to stand as influencing the court shall be "stripped of all useless verbiage." The charge in the indictment is then restated by the court after the "stripping" had been done. An especially interesting instance of this is found in Commonwealth *v.* Hunt, the case that came before the Massachusetts court in 1842. The indictment in all of its several counts is reviewed by Chief Justice Shaw and commented on. Much of the indictment he says is "mere recital." "Stripped then of these introductory recitals and alleged injurious consequences, and of the qualifying epithets attached to the facts [such as unlawfully and deceitfully designing and intending unjustly to extort great sums] the averment is this." The whole indictment covering several pages is then stated as follows: "that the defendants and others formed themselves into a society, and agreed not to work for any person, who should employ any journeyman or other person, not a member of such society, after notice given him to discharge such workman."

It is in the working out of modern meanings for these terms that courts have a responsibility. Modern conditions mean new forces, new activities, new methods of rivalry. To keep all these well classified with reference to the old terms is a task which the courts must assume.

It is not an easy task to sum up fully the differences that appear in all these opinions. The circumstances of the case sometimes make it doubtful what the general legal principle is. But among the doubtful points that are of importance are certainly the following.

There is difference of opinion as to what means may lawfully be used by union workingmen in their efforts to secure discharge of other workingmen not members of a union, or in some cases members of a rival union.

There is difference of opinion as to what the effect of combination will be. Some acts are clearly legal if done by a single individual. These same acts if done by concerted action of a combination of individuals may or may not be illegal, they may or may not amount to a conspiracy. What one may do all may do is a rule accepted in some courts but not in others.

There is a difference of opinion as to what will be the effect upon the legality of an act if it can be shown that the act was inspired by a "malevolent design to injure" another workman rather than by a desire to secure his job for union men.

There is a difference of opinion as to what control the union may lawfully exercise over its members, what authority it may delegate to its officers or agents, or what it may do to induce men to join its membership.

Aggravating as many of the decisions may be, it cannot be denied that progress toward a solution of the difficulties is evident. The unions receive fuller recognition in the courts than they did a century ago. The stern logic of circumstances is forcing a recognition of the rights of unions to do something more than merely to exist. But just what they may do is a question not yet fully determined. The recognition of the applicability of general propositions of law to men in unions as well as to men not in unions is the broadest basis of hope. The stern determination, on the other hand, to give new meanings to such terms as coercion, intimidation and threat, is also a sign of progress, though it may lead to a restriction of activities on the part of the unions.

If the courts are to come generally to the view that trade-union activity is after all but a phase of more general industrial competition, the issue between competition and monopoly will become one of prime importance. What the outcome of this issue is to be in the broader field is yet uncertain. This outcome whatever it may be will have a wide influence in finally determining the yet open questions within the field of labor.

The courts have seen fit to recognize as lawful a large degree of organization and co-operation in trade and among capitalists even though the "non-union" trader and capitalist has insisted upon his right to remain independent. A similar course with organized labor would indicate a similar effect upon the non-union laborer. These changes in view are inevitable though they may come slowly. Combination on the side of capital is evident. It has legal recognition. It is inevitable. It has become powerful. Combination on the side of labor is also evident; it also has legal recognition; it is also inevitable. The lesson as Justice Holmes points it out is that "combination on the one side [capital] is patent and powerful. Combination on the other [labor] is the necessary and desirable counterpart, if the battle is to be carried on in a fair and equal way." To treat the employer in a manner that admits of combination and the employee in a manner dictated by individualism is to create a never ending cause of trouble. Ex-Secretary Olney is quoted as saying that "the mass of wage earners can no longer be dealt with by capital as so many isolated units. The time is past when the individual workman is called upon to pit his single feeble strength against the might of organized capital." What is true of capital's dealings with wage earners is also true of the court's dealings with them. Individualism has so dominated the minds of judges that even in the face of their admission of the right to form organizations they insist upon treating the members of these organizations as individuals only. "One fundamental difficulty," says Blackmore "with the position of the majority is that it persists in regarding the members of the union as separate individuals and the act of the union officials as the act of a third party when there are many authorities to the effect that the laborers have a right to combine and be treated as a unit." [1]

Perhaps the most difficult of all the several tasks that fall to the courts from this class of cases is to preserve all that is valuable in individualism in the form of individual rights and at the same time to make room for that organization which in modern industrial society is so necessary and so inevitable in the form of socialization and social rights.

[1] "Intimidation by Fines in Labor Disputes," *Green Bag*, vol. 20, p. 620, Dec., 1908.

PART III

LEGISLATION

CHAPTER XIV

Payment of Wages

One of the questions that has given rise to important differences of opinion is as to the time for the payment of wages. Legislation has been secured requiring payment at regular stated intervals. One week is the period usually adopted. On the constitutionality of such legislation the courts have taken very diverse views. When upheld, it has usually been on the ground of the evident intent of the legislators to improve existing conditions. When declared invalid, on the other hand, it has been on the grounds usually urged against labor legislation.

In State *v.* Brown and Sharpe, Judge Rogers of Rhode Island argued the advantage of the corporation over the individual workman in the adjustment of the conditions of employment. Unless the employees are paid at regular intervals their real wages are less than their nominal wages. This is because they are frequently

> dependent upon their current wages for their daily bread. If they get credit, they must pay for it, as others do, and, in proportion to their inability to pay cash and the risk in trusting them, they have to pay for the time indulgence they obtain. To save labor and expense, many corporate pay rolls were made up but 12 or 13 times a year, and sometimes, when corporate means were cramped, even less often, whereby employees were obliged to wait for their pay, and the longer they had to wait the less it was worth to them.

The counsel for the defense had evidently argued that the

workmen were not obliged to take the work unless they wished; that the agreement was a voluntary contract. The opinion states in reply to this view that " poverty and weakness can wage but an unequal contest with corporate wealth and power," that employees " too often in the sharp and bitter competition for work, have to submit to such terms and conditions as their employers see fit to prescribe." The conclusion reached in the opinion is that the law " was clearly passed in the interest of the employee, and it is not easy to see how it would operate to his disadvantage."

The same question of right to contract was raised by Judge Morrow of California who disposed of the objection in the following words:

> As far as these two sections are concerned, . . . it does not appear in what respects defendant is deprived of any liberty in making contracts by reason of these enactments. They simply constitute an effort to secure the regular payment to the employee of a corporation, by such corporation, of the wages to which he is entitled by virtue of his work performed, and an effort to make his legal remedy for the irregular payment of such wages as little troublesome and as little expensive as possible. The contention of defendant as to the unconstitutionality of the statute must be denied. (Skinner *v.* Garnett Mining Co.)

Representing the opposite line of reasoning opinions have been written by courts of other states upon laws that apply practically the same remedy. Judge Cooper of California found the law invalid and stated as a reason the following:

> The corporation and the laborer are prohibited from making any contract whereby wages are to become due for a longer period than one month as a condition of employment, or by which the laborer is to be paid in anything except money or negotiable checks. The working man of intelligence is treated as an imbecile. Being over 21 years of age, and not a lunatic

or insane, he is deprived of the right to make a contract as to the time when his wages shall become due. Being of sound mind, and knowing the value of a horse, he is not allowed to make an agreement with the corporation that he will work 60 days and take the horse in payment. Business might be such that a corporation could not possibly pay wages without getting laborers who were willing to wait for their wages until the corporation could get money with which to pay them by marketing its products. The laborer might be interested in the corporation, or for some reason willing to wait until the corporation could pay him. Yet the parties, being able to contract and willing to contract, and desiring for the good of each other to contract, are by this statute forbidden to do so. (Johnson *v.* Goodyear Mining Co.)

In Republic Iron and Steel Co. *v.* State the attorney general had emphasized the inequality of bargaining power between employers and employees and had argued that the law was justified on the ground that it tended to equalize the conditions. To this line of argument the court in the opinion opposed the constitution itself, and regarded its provisions as a sufficient obstacle to the acceptance of the law. Chief Justice Hadley of Indiana stated the view in his opinion as follows:

Assuming all these things to be true, they do not of themselves justify the arbitrary invasion of the personal rights and liberty of the citizen. Liberty to contract on one's own terms, to decide for himself his own employment, to buy and sell, to exchange one belonging for another, are among his most valuable and cherished rights. . . . "If there is one thing more than another," says Justice Shiras, "public policy requires, it is that men of full age and competent understanding shall have the utmost liberty of contracting, and that their contracts, when entered into freely and voluntarily, shall be held sacred and shall be enforced by courts of justice."

Is the statute in question a reasonable regulation, and reasonable in its operation upon the persons whom it affects? The contract prohibited affects employer and employee alike. If the master can employ only upon terms of weekly payment, the workman can find employment on no other terms. It will be observed that the statute gives the parties no choice—no right to waive the provisions of the law. . . . The obvious intention of the legislature was to make contracts for persons that they would not in all cases make for themselves, and to forbid the making of contracts that they would make. The laborer may be the chief sufferer. His labor may be the only means of supplying himself and family, but by this law he is denied the right to work, and another the right to employ him, unless he can be paid once a week. Any law or policy that disables the citizen from making a contract whereby he may find lawful, needed, and satisfactory employment is unreasonable. It may be that the workman will desire and request his employer, as conducive to economy and saving, to keep back all wages not needed for current necessities. Whether he leaves his surplus earnings with his employer, or deposits them with the building and loan association or with the savings bank, involves no public interest and affects no public concern. . . . The statute places the wage earners of the state under quasi guardianship. It classes them with minors and other persons under legal disability, by making their contracts void at the pleasure of a public officer. It tends to degrade them as citizens, by impeaching their ability to take care of themselves. It is paternalism, pure and simple, and in violent conflict with the liberty and equality theory of our institutions.

As to the legal requirement of payment of wages in money there is very much the same difference of view. A decision of more than ordinary interest is Shaffer and Munn *v.* Union Mining Co. The interest lies not so much in the fact that the opinion makes use of the conventional phrases about liberty and property, but rather that it adopts the point of view of the employee rather than that of the employer in the application of these phrases. Judge Irving of Maryland expressed the view of the court, in part as follows:

This statute was evidently conceived and enacted for the purpose of correcting some evil which had resulted to the employees of such corporations as are described in the Act, and perchance to the community also, from the mode in which these corporations had been wont to deal with their operatives. The statute was manifestly intended to be in the interest of the employees. We suppose it must have been intended to protect the employee from further exactions, extortion or over-reaching supposed to have affected them injuriously in the past. Being protective in its character, it cannot have been intended as restrictive of the employee's rights, except in so far as it prevents his colluding with the employer to do what the law forbade the corporation to do. The Legislature is always presumed to have intended a constitutional exercise of power; and laws will be so construed as to make their provisions lawful if possible. It cannot be supposed the Legislature intended to impose a restriction upon these employees, which would have been an unconstitutional invasion of their rights. . . .

To accord to this law the construction contended for by the appellee, and which was given it by the learned Judge who decided this case below, would be doing unwarranted violence to the rights of the employees over the fruits of their own labor. It would be preventing their use of their wages, which might have been accumulating in the employer's hands, in the purchase of property, real or personal, and taking conveyance therefor. If the employer should be slothful in payment it would prevent his employee, however straitened for the want of it, using his overdue wages by transfer as other people do their *choses in action*. It would have, also, the further effect of preventing other citizens investing their funds in the debts of such corporation, if they should so desire. Such cannot have been its intention, and ought not to be held its legitimate result.

The United States supreme court has expressed itself on this proposition, throwing the weight of its influence on the side of the reasonableness of the principle involved. The matter came before it in Knoxville Iron Co. *v.* Harbison, a case appealed from the supreme court of Tennessee. Justice Shiras wrote the opinion, following closely the views expressed by the Tennessee court and quoting freely from it. Quoting the Tennessee opinion:

> The legislature evidently deemed the laborer at some disadvantage under existing laws and customs, and by this act undertook to ameliorate his condition in some measure by enabling him or his bona-fide transferee, at his election and at a proper time, to demand and receive his unpaid wages in money rather than in something less valuable. Its tendency, though slight it may be, is to place the employer and employee upon equal ground in the matter of wages, and, so far as calculated to accomplish that end, it deserves commendation. . . .
>
> The act before us is, perhaps, less stringent than any one considered in any of the cases mentioned. It is neither prohibitory nor penal; not special, but general; tending towards equality between employer and employee in the matter of wages; intended and well calculated to promote peace and good order, and to prevent strife, violence, and bloodshed. Such being the character, purpose, and tendency of the act, we have no hesitation in holding that it is valid, both as general legislation,. without reference to the state's reserved police power, and also as a wholesome regulation adopted in the proper exercise of that power.

Following these quoted statements the court expresses more fully its view of the police power. This power "must be expected and allowed to expand, and take in new subjects from time to time; as trade and business advance, and new conditions arise." The final test is that of reasonableness. "It shall not arbitrarily or unreasonably affect the citizen in his life, liberty, and property." In the exercise of this right "a large discretion is necessarily vested in the legislature, which, in the first instance, is presumed to know, not only what the welfare of the public requires, but also what measures are necessary for its advancement." It is next pointed out that the right to contract is not without its limitations. Cases are cited where this right has been restricted. Applying these principles to the case, the conclusion is finally reached.

It is readily seen from the analysis already given that the limitation placed upon the right of contract by this act is not arbitrary and oppressive, but entirely just and reasonable. While in some sense qualifying certain contracts of the employer, it in no sense works a great hardship upon him. It only requires that in certain events he shall pay the wages of his employee in money, rather than in something less desirable. The legislature, as it thought, found the employee at a disadvantage in this respect, and by this enactment undertook to place him and the employer more nearly upon an equality. This alone commends the act, and entitles it to a place on the statute book as a valid police regulation.

Besides the amelioration of the employee's condition in the way mentioned, the act was intended and is well calculated to promote the public peace and good order, and to lessen the growing tendency to strife, violence, and even bloodshed in certain departments of important trade and business.

Finally, in the International Text-Book case we find again the court, expressing its view through Justice Dowling of Indiana, showing its appreciation of the laborers' side of the contention.

A large proportion of the persons affected by these statutes of labor are dependent upon their daily or weekly wages for the maintenance of themselves and their families. Delay of payment or loss of wages results in deprivation of the necessaries of life, suffering, inability to meet just obligations to others, and, in many cases, may make the wage-earner a charge upon the public. The situation of these persons renders them peculiarly liable to imposition and injustice at the hands of employers, unscrupulous trades-men, and others who are willing to take advantage of their condition. Where future wages may be assigned, the temptation to anticipate their payment, and to sacrifice them for an inadequate consideration, is often very great. Such assignments would, in many cases, leave the laborer or wage-earner without present or future means of support. By removing the strongest incentive to faithful service—the expectation of pecuniary reward in the near future—their effect would be alike injurious to the laborer and his employer. It is clear that the object of the act of 1899 was the protection of wage-earners from oppression, extortion, or fraud on the part of others, and from the consequences of their own weakness, folly, or improvidence. We cannot say that no just ground existed for such legislative interference for so commendable a purpose.

Turning to the cases that adopt the opposite view, there is Frorer *v.* People, a case widely cited and quoted by other courts. It was the opinion of the Illinois court in a case in which was tested the constitutionality of a law forbidding persons or corporations while in the business of mining or manufacturing to be interested in a truck store: meaning by "truck" "the payment of wages otherwise than in lawful money, or otherwise than to the full amount earned by the employee." This law the court held to be unconstitutional and Judge Scholfield wrote an elaborate opinion in justification of the conclusions reached.

The first objection is that

while the prohibition includes, by name, only the person, company, corporation, or association engaged in "mining or manufacturing," it includes equally within its effect their employees; for the employee is necessarily denied the right to contract with one who is forbidden by the law to possess, for the purpose of contracting with him, the articles about which he wishes to contract. It would therefore have added nothing to the legal meaning of this section if it had expressly prohibited the employees from contracting with their employer for the purchase of the property in which it is thus made unlawful for their employer to have any ownership.

A further objection to the law lies in the fact that manufacturers and miners are not the only employers of labor in the state. Thousands are employed in a large variety of occupations. In all these other industries "employers and employees are unaffected by this statute; and such employers may therefore, after as before its taking effect, engage or be interested in truck stores."

This leads next to the inquiry whether the keeping of a truck store by a manufacturer or a miner is "in substance and in principle" different from the keeping of one by any other employer of labor. The answer to the question is clear.

The purpose is, manifestly, the same in each case, namely, the sale by the employer to the employee of the articles designated, and it requires precisely the same elements to constitute a contract—including mental capacity in the parties contracting, and freedom from fraud and over-reaching—in the one case as it does in the others. The operator of a mine and the manufacturer have no other control over the employee than that which may result from employing him, or continuing him in employment, or refusing to do so; and every other employer of labor has precisely the same control over those who obtain or wish to obtain employment with him. There can be no reason why the miner or the operative in the manufactory will be more or differently influenced by his hopes and fears in these respects than will laborers in any other industries.

Dealing with the assertion that the workers affected by the law were more than ordinarily dependent upon their employers, the court asserts:

> It cannot truthfully be said that all operators in mines or manufactories are more dependent upon their employers than all laborers in any other branch of industry. . . . There are varying degrees of . . . presumed dependence. . . . And so it must follow that any difference between [mining and manufacturing and other branches of industry] cannot be one of principle, but must be purely one of degree, varying with the circumstances of particular cases.

It is recognized in this opinion that the legislature may regulate mining and manufacturing in matters that pertain to them, but in this case "the prohibition of the statute operates not directly upon the business of mining and manufacturing, but upon the individual, because of his participation in that business." The law is imposed "for the sole purpose of imposing disabilities in contracting as to tools, clothing and food,—matters about which all laborers must contract, and as to which all laborers in every other branch of industry are permitted to contract with their employers without any restriction."

Yet another consideration that was of apparent moment in the mind of the court is that

> The privilege or liberty to engage in or control the business of keeping and selling clothing, provisions, groceries, tools, etc., to employees is one of profit—of presumptive value; and thus, by the effect of these sections, what the employers in other industries may do for their pecuniary gain with impunity, and have the law to protect and enforce, the miner and manufacturer, under precisely the same circumstances and conditions, are prohibited from doing for their pecuniary gain. The same act, in substance and in principle, if done by the one is lawful, but if done by the other is not only unlawful, but a misdemeanor, punishable by fine.

The Kansas court, in State *v.* Haun, took a position that illustrates the same view. The law was one prohibiting to certain corporations the right of payment of wages in scrip. To Judge Smith who wrote the opinion this seemed to be an invasion of the right both of the corporations concerned and of the workingmen. On the first of these points the opinion states:

> If the classification attempted by this act is a constitutional one, it follows that the legislature might have made the law applicable only to corporations employing married men or persons over a certain age, or to corporations a proportion of whose employees were women, or applied to any other arbitrary or capricious means of distinction.

The classification must be based on a reasonable ground. Instead of this, it " makes a distinction between corporations identically alike in organization, capital, and all other powers and privileges conferred by law. It is arbitrary and wanting in reason. The act in question is class legislation of the most pronounced character."

On the second point, the welfare of the workingman, the opinion says:

> However much the employed might profit by the necessities of the employer desiring to exchange property for labor at a value advantageous to the former, all such beneficial agreements are prohibited by this law. In short, such legislation infringes upon natural rights and constitutional grants of liberty. It treats the laborer as a ward of the government, and discourages the employment of those talents which lead to success in the fields of commercial enterprise. Persons *sui juris* need no guardians. Those who seek to put a protector over labor reflect upon the dignity and independence of the wage earner, and deceive him by the promise that legislation can cure all the ills of which he may complain. Such legis-

lation suggests the handiwork of the politician rather than the political economist.

A similar view was held by the Missouri court as expressed in the opinion of Judge Black in State *v.* Loomis. The statute in question forbade miners and manufacturers from paying wages in store orders. Here again the court deals with the problem from the point of view of the rights of the corporation, and of the individual rights of the workingmen.

There can be no doubt but the legislature may regulate the business of mining and manufacturing so as to secure the health and safety of the employees; but that is not the scope of the two sections of the statute now in question. They single out those persons who are engaged in carrying on the pursuits of mining and manufacturing, and say to such persons: "You cannot contract for labor payable alone in goods, wares, and merchandise. The farmer, the merchant, the builder, and the numerous contractors employing thousands of men may make such contracts, but you cannot." They say to the mining and manufacturing employees: "Though of full age, and competent to contract, still you shall not have the power to sell your labor for meat and clothing alone, as others may." It will not do to say these sections simply regulate payment of wages, for that is not their purpose. They undertake to deny to the persons engaged in the two designated pursuits the right to make and enforce the most ordinary, every-day contracts—a right accorded to all other persons. . . .

Now, it may be that instances of oppression have occurred, and will occur, on the part of some mine owners and manufacturers, but do they not occur quite as frequently in other fields of labor? Conceding that such instances may and do occur, still that furnishes no reasonable basis for depriving all persons engaged in the two lawful and necessary pursuits of the right to make and enforce every-day contracts. Liberty, as we have seen, includes the right to contract as others may, and to take that right away from a class of persons following lawful pursuits is simply depriving such persons of a time-honored right which the constitution undertakes to secure to every citizen.

As opposing this view of Judge Black, Judge Barclay wrote a dissenting opinion, presenting the following view:

The lawmaker necessarily deals with conditions as he finds them. If he observes, and wishes to abate, some fraudulent practice or abuse of power prevailing only in some one line of business, the fact that, in legislating to correct it, he does not also include in his remedy all other phases of human affairs, can furnish no reason for stigmatizing his remedy as no law at all. If an act reaching only mining and manufacturing concerns is, on that account, not "due process of law," what must be held of statutes establishing special rules of liability, or business regulations, applicable to railroads only, to warehousemen, pawnbrokers, auctioneers, millers, and the many other classes of persons whose affairs form topics of treatment in separate laws? Are all such statutes void, because each relates to persons engaged only in the particular class of business named in it? Probably they would not be so held. Some of them are acted on and enforced almost daily. Yet if they are valid, what, let me ask, is there so exceptional about the truck system that precludes legislation applicable to those lines of business in which it prevails? . . . Its plain purpose is to put some restraint upon that sort of freedom which would permit the employer to contract for labor, payable in goods, and then place his own prices upon the goods delivered in payment. . . . It does not differ in principle from governmental regulations in the form of laws by which a person who has contracted to receive a yard of cloth or a bushel of corn is protected against the necessity of accepting such a short yard or light bushel as the seller may choose to impose upon him.

Two other brief extracts may be added in closing this section.

More than this, [the law] is an insulting attempt to put the laborer under a legislative tutelage, which is not only degrading to his manhood, but subversive of his rights as a citizen of the United States. He may sell his labor for what he thinks best, whether money or goods, just as his employer may sell his iron or coal; and any and every law that proposes to prevent him from so doing is an infringement of his constitutional privileges, and consequently vicious and void. (Godcharles *v.* Wigeman.)

The patrimony of the poor man lies in the strength and dexterity of his own hands; and to hinder him from employing these in what manner he may think proper, without injury to his neighbor, is a plain violation of this most sacred property. It is equally an encroachment both upon the just liberty and rights of the workman and his employer, or those who might be disposed to employ him, for the legislature to interfere with the freedom of contract between them. . . . The enjoyment or deprivation of these rights and privileges constitutes the essential distinction between freedom and slavery, between liberty and oppression. (State *v.* Goodwill.)

CHAPTER XV

PAYMENT OF WAGES—SCREENING COAL

ONE other line of legislation relating to wages has led to court opinions that are of interest. It is with reference to screening coal before weighing it as a basis for determining wages. The matter has been an important ground of contention between the employer and employee and in several states legislation has been enacted forbidding the screening of the coal before weighing where payment was made by weight. This legislation has found its way to the courts and several lengthy opinions have been handed down. They display the same contrast of views brought out in the last chapter. Yet the differences are such that a discussion of them will add to the understanding of the court's attitude.

The West Virginia court in Peel Splint Co. *v.* State takes the view, first, that doubt of the validity of a law is to be dissolved in favor of the legislative authority; and second, that the law deals with corporations. These corporations, says the opinion, enjoy unusual and extraordinary privileges which enabled them " to surround themselves with a vast retinue of laborers, who need to be protected against all fraudulent or suspicious devices in the weighing of coal or in the payment of labor," and further that these corporations are licensees under the general supervision of the state. Following this, the opinion seeks " still higher ground " for its decision.

We do not base this decision so much upon the ground that the business is affected by the public use, but upon the still higher ground, that the public tranquillity, and the good and safety of society, demand, where the number of employees is such that specific contracts with each laborer would be improbable, if not impossible, that in general contracts justice shall prevail as between operator and miner; and, in the company's dealing with the multitude of laborers with which the state has by special legislation enabled the owners and operators to surround themselves, that all opportunities for fraud shall be removed. The state is frequently called upon to suppress strikes, to discountenance labor conspiracies, to denounce boycotting as injurious to trade and commerce; and it cannot be possible that the same police power may not be invoked to protect the laborer from being made the victim of the compulsory power of that artificial combination of capital which special state legislation has originated and rendered possible. It is a fact worthy of consideration, and one of such historical notoriety that the court may recognize it judicially, that every disturbance of the peace of any magnitude in this state since the civil war has been evolved from the disturbed relations between powerful corporations and their servants or employees. It cannot be possible that the state has no police power adequate to the protection of society against the recurrence of such disturbances, which threaten to shake civil order to its very foundations. Collisions between the capitalist and the workingman endanger the safety of the state, stay the wheels of commerce, discourage manufacturing enterprises, destroy public confidence, and at times throw an idle population upon the bosom of the community. Surely the hands of the legislature cannot be so restricted as to prohibit the passage of laws directly intended to prevent and forestall such collisions. . . .

Down through the centuries, hand in hand, and consolidated into one police regulation, have come these conspiracy laws to protect capital, and these truck acts to protect labor, and both to protect society; and are we now to be told that the effect of adopting our free American constitution is to leave in full vigor the power to protect capital, but to destroy the concomitant and correlative power to protect labor? The two powers, associated in their exercise for centuries, have not been divorced by American institutions. Such an idea is not to be entertained for a moment.

The Arkansas court, in McLean *v.* State, disposes of the essential point in the case in a brief statement. " This legislation," it concludes, " is clearly within the scope of the police power. The manifest purpose of the statute is to prevent those who operate coal mines from perpetrating fraud upon laborers whom they have employed to mine coal by the quantity." This case was appealed to the supreme court of the United States, and a lengthy opinion was written by Justice Day. So far as freedom of contract is concerned, the court recognizes the principle. It has been upheld in many cases. Yet, " in many cases in this court the right of freedom of contract has been held not to be unlimited in its nature." Limitations in favor of public health, safety and welfare, " may be valid, notwithstanding they have the effect to curtail or limit freedom of contract." After citing several cases in which the right has been restricted the conclusion is stated. " It is, then, the established doctrine of this court that the liberty of contract is not universal, and is subject to restrictions passed by the legislative branch of the government in the exercise of its power to protect the safety, health, and welfare of the people." But likewise the police power is not unlimited, it " is subject to judicial review; and when exerted in an arbitrary or oppressive manner, such laws may be annulled as violative of rights protected by the constitution." The principle underlying this adjustment of power between the legislature and the judicial power is declared to be well settled. It is stated to be: " The legislature, being familiar with local conditions, is, primarily, the judge of the necessity of such enactments," and the fact that the court may not entertain the same view as to the necessity, "affords no ground for judicial interference, unless the act in question is unmistakably and palpably in excess of legislative power." These principles are then applied to the case at bar.

After an examination of opinions from the several state courts, of the evidence of the Industrial Commission as published in its report, and of the conditions presented in evidence in the case, the court concludes: "It is not for us to say whether these are actual conditions. It is sufficient to say that it was a situation brought to the attention of the legislature, concerning which it was entitled to judge and act for itself in the exercise of its lawful power to pass remedial legislation."

In the same year that the first case mentioned above was brought before the West Virginia court, the Illinois court considered Ramsey *v.* People. That court had just handed down its opinion in Frorer *v.* People in which it had held that the prohibition of miners and manufacturers from keeping truck stores was in violation of the constitutional right of freedom of contract. In Ramsey *v.* People the court declares that the case before it dealing with the weighing of coal before screening involves "in the main, the same constitutional principles." Because of the fullness with which the earlier case had been considered, "we need do little more than refer to what is said" in that opinion. The statute

> attempts to take from both employer and employee, engaged in the mining business, the right and power of fixing by contract the manner in which such wages are to be ascertained. . . . There is nothing in the business of coal mining which renders either the employer or employee less capable of contracting in respect to wages than in any of the other numerous branches of business in which laborers are employed under analogous conditions. There is no difference, at least

in kind, so far as this matter is concerned, between coal mining, on the one hand, and other varieties of mining, quarrying stone, grading and constructing railroads, and their operation when constructed, manufacturing in all its departments, the construction of buildings, agriculture, commerce, domestic service, and an almost infinite variety of other avocations requiring the employment of laborers, on the other hand. Upon what principle, then, can those engaged in coal mining be singled out, and subjected to restrictions of their power to contract as to wages, while those engaged in all these other classes of business are left entirely free to contract as they see fit? We think the attempt of the legislature to impose such restrictions is clearly repugnant to the constitutional limitation above referred to, and therefore void.

Although the court in Peel Splint Coal Co. *v.* State had decided unanimously in favor of the law, a re-hearing was allowed. The second time the court was divided in its view, two still holding to the former opinion and two dissenting. The views set forth in this dissenting opinion, held by half of the court, are important, though they did not prevail in determining the decision of the case. Objection to the law is based upon an analysis of the mining work which may be summarized as follows. The coal in the mine is the property of the operator; and it is immaterial whether the operator be a corporation or a single individual. The object is to obtain from the mine merchantable coal in as large quantities as possible. In mining it is necessary to have some slack, but the greater the skill of the miner the less percentage of slack there will be. The weighing of coal after it is screened is a truer test of the amount of coal that has been mined. Otherwise the unskilled miner who loads most slack upon his car will receive the larger pay. The question is then asked: Is not screening before weighing the proper method of giving to the skilled miner what he is entitled to by reason of years of experience, instead of placing him on a par with the beginner, or really below the beginner, who is able to produce a small percentage of merchantable coal, and sends out the residue in the shape of slack?

Further this dissent points out that with a less amount of merchantable coal, a less wage must be paid. The "inevitable result" of the law must be to depress wages, to take "bread from the family of the skilled miner, and give it to the family of the careless and unskilled one," to cause

the product of the mine to be received in such a condition that a large percentage thereof is worthless to him, and to that extent the coal property for which he has paid his money is taken from him without compensation. . . . What more complete confiscation of the operator's property could possibly be enforced than to have a large percentage of his coal mined and put out in a condition that would be utterly worthless to him, and in addition to that to be compelled to pay the miner for his labor in producing it in that condition?

Turning from the property consideration the opinion takes up the question of contract.

I fail to perceive in what manner the public is interested in the private contract made between the coal operator and his employees, as to the time when such employee shall have the product of his labor weighed and paid for. The labor of the employee is his own property, and he has a perfect right to fix a price upon it, let it be high or low, and the public has no right to say, "Why do you so?" Neither is the public welfare in any manner affected by the terms of the contract, any more than it is in that of the man who works by the day on the farm.

CHAPTER XVI

Hours of Labor—Mines and Smelters

The validity of laws regulating the hours of labor of men in mines and smelters has been tested in two states in cases that led to the writing of elaborate opinions. One of these cases was appealed to the United States supreme court by which a third opinion was handed down. These three opinions afford an excellent opportunity to study the two opposing views.

The first of these cases came before the supreme court of Utah as Holden *v.* Hardy and State *v.* Holden, one dealing with mines and the other with smelters. The appeal of the former case to the United States supreme court in Holden *v.* Hardy led to the opinion from that court. The third opinion was one handed down by the supreme court of Colorado, *In re* Morgan. These opinions were all written within three years and the conditions in the neighboring states were such as to make the cases very similar. There was, however, one difference that must not be passed by unnoticed. The constitution of Utah contained a clause not found in the constitution of Colorado which required the legislature to "pass laws to provide for the health and safety of the employees in factories, smelters and mines." It does not appear from the reasoning in the opinions, however, that this difference was the real cause for the opposite conclusions reached.

The opinion of the Utah court deals first with the relation of the provisions of the law in question to the clause of the constitution just referred to. Any doubt that the statute does not come within the constitutional provision must be dissolved in favor of the legislature. " The court must be able to see clearly that the law was not so connected before holding it void for that reason." The judgment of the legislature as to the necessity for the law must not be lightly set aside by the court. In this spirit the court raises the question: Is the statute limiting the period of employment of laboring men in mines to eight hours a day calculated to promote the health of such laboring men? After stating the difference in conditions of labor the court finally answers its own question. " The fact must be conceded that the breathing of pure air is wholesome, and the breathing of impure air is unwholesome. We cannot say that this law . . . is not calculated to promote health, that it is not adapted to the protection of the health of the class of men who work in underground mines."

But the opinion is made to rest on broader grounds than the specific clause of the state constitution. The provision " does not prohibit the legislature from enacting other laws affecting such classes, to promote the general welfare." To the contention that this is class legislation the court replies:

But some pursuits are attended with peculiar hazards and perils, the injurious consequences from which may be largely prevented by precautionary means, and laws may be passed calculated to protect the classes of people engaged in such pursuits. It is not necessary to extend the protection to persons engaged in other pursuits not attended with similar dangers. To them the law would be inappropriate and idle. So, if underground mining is attended with dangers peculiar to it, laws adapted to the protection of such miners from such danger should be confined to that class of mining, and should not include other employments not subject to them. And if men engaged in underground mining are liable to be injured in their health, or otherwise, by too many hours' labor each day, a law to protect them should be aimed at that peculiar wrong. In this way, laws are enacted to protect people from perils from the operation of railroads, by requiring bells to be rung and whistles sounded at road crossings, and the slacking of the speed of trains in cities. So, the sale of liquor is regulated to lessen the evils of the liquor traffic, and other classes of business are regulated by appropriate laws. In this way, laws are designed and adapted to the peculiarities attending each class of business. By such laws, different classes of people are protected by various acts and provisions. In this way, various classes of business are regulated, and the people protected, by appropriate laws, from dangers and evils that beset them; safety is secured, health preserved, and the happiness and welfare of humanity promoted. All persons engaged in business that may be attended with peculiar injury to health or otherwise, if not regulated and controlled, should be subject to the same law; otherwise, the law should be adapted to the special circumstances. The purpose of such laws is not advantage to any person or any class of persons, or disadvantage to any other person or class of persons. Necessary and just protection is the sole object. [Quoting the United States supreme court]: The specific regulations for one kind of business, which may be necessary for the protection of the public, can never be the just ground of complaint because like restrictions are not imposed upon other business of a different kind. The discriminations which are open to objection are those where persons engaged in the same business are subject to different restrictions, or are held entitled to different privileges under the same conditions. It is only then that the discriminations can be said to impair that equal right which all can claim in the enforcement of the laws.

As a further justification of the law, the court introduces the police power. This power exists "to the protection of the lives, health, and property of the citizens, and to the preservation of good order and the public good."

These objects " are to be attained and provided for by such appropriate means as the legislative discretion may devise."

In State *v.* Holden the provision dealing with smelters was tested. The court pointed out that while conditions in mines were different than in smelters, yet it is true that

> poisonous gases, dust, and impalpable substances arise and float in the air in stamp mills, smelters, and other works in which ores containing metals, combined with arsenic or other poisonous elements or agencies, are treated, reduced, and refined; and there can be no doubt that prolonged effort day after day, subject to such conditions and agencies, will produce morbid, noxious, and often deadly effects in the human system. Some organisms and systems will resist and endure such conditions and effects longer than others. It may be said that labor in such conditions must be performed. Granted that, the period of labor each day should be of a reasonable length. Twelve hours per day would be less injurious than fourteen, ten than twelve, and eight than ten. The legislature has named eight. Such a period was deemed reasonable.

While the state constitution makes mandatory legislation to protect the health of such workmen, yet we do not " wish to be understood as intimating that the power to pass the law does not exist in the police powers of the state. The authority . . . undoubtedly is found in such police powers."

The United States supreme court endorsed fully the views and conclusions of the Utah court, as shown by the fact that a large portion of these views is directly incorporated in its opinion. In addition to the long quotations from the Utah court, Justice Brown adds other reasons in support of the law.

> But if it be within the power of the legislature to adopt such means for the protection of the lives of its citizens, it is difficult to see why precautions may not also be adopted for the

protection of their health and morals. It is as much for the interest of the state that the public health should be preserved as that life should be made secure. . . .

Upon the principles above stated, we think the act in question may be sustained as a valid exercise of the police power of the state. . . .

The legislature has also recognized the fact, which the experience of legislators in many states has corroborated, that the proprietors of these establishments and their operatives do not stand upon an equality, and that their interests are, to a certain extent, conflicting. The former naturally desire to obtain as much labor as possible from their employees, while the latter are often induced by the fear of discharge to conform to regulations which their judgment, fairly exercised, would pronounce to be detrimental to their health or strength. In other words, the proprietors lay down the rules and the laborers are practically constrained to obey them. In such cases self-interest is often an unsafe guide, and the legislature may properly interpose its authority.

The law enacted in Colorado carried practically the same provision, limiting the hours of work in mines and smelters to eight a day. The question before the court as stated in the opinion was " does the act . . . violate any constitutional provision?" At the outset it is made clear that " decisions of other jurisdictions, defining the limits of legislation under their constitutions," are not binding in Colorado. " We have no constitutional provision," states the opinion, " which authorizes the legislature to single out workingmen in underground mines and smelters, and impose upon them restrictions as to the number of hours they shall work at these industries, from which workingmen in all other departments of industry are exempt." The attitude is taken that since the constitution does not prescribe such work the legislature is not warranted in entering upon it, the principle being that, " when authority to do a particular thing is given [the regulation of mines] and the mode of doing it [ventilation, escape shafts and other safety devices] is prescribed, all other modes are excluded."

The real argument, however, is on other lines, the reason given for the change being that "we prefer to put our decision upon impregnable grounds." These "impregnable grounds" are stated at considerable length. The extracts that follow will indicate the line of argument.

> The act is equally obnoxious to the provisions of our bill of rights, set out in the statement, which guarantee to all persons their natural and inalienable right to personal liberty, and the right of acquiring, possessing, and protecting property. Liberty means something more than mere freedom from physical restraint. It includes the privilege of choosing any lawful occupation for the exercise of one's physical and mental faculties which is not injurious to others. The right to acquire and possess property includes the right to contract for one's labor. The latter is essentially a property right. . . . That this act infringes both the right to enjoy liberty and to acquire and possess property seems too clear for argument.

To the contention that the law comes within the police power of the state, the opinion replies:

> Following the authorities, we may say that it [the police power] extends to the protection of the public health. It is upon the specific ground that limiting the time a workingman may labor in a smelter to eight hours a day conduces to and preserves the health of the laborer himself that this act is sought to be upheld.

The court's view of the scope of this power is then stated more at length. Authorities are cited to show that the real scope of the power is not so broad. Citations in support of the broader scope of the police power, the court insists, come from " unguarded expressions of text writers or in judicial opinions," but they are " contrary to every well-considered decision."

To show that the provisions of the law do not come within its interpretation of the police power, the following analysis is presented:

Its supporters do not claim that its real and primary object is to protect the public health, or the health of that portion of the community in the immediate vicinity, or affected by the operation, of smelters. If that purpose is present at all, it is only so inferentially, and the means employed to secure it are neither adequate nor appropriate. The smelting of ores is a continuous process, night and day, the year through. It is not claimed that the business is injurious to public health. It would be absurd to argue that, while the process itself is continuous, limiting the hours of those laboring in a smelter in any wise conduces to preserve the health of any portion of the public. That is to say, three shifts of laborers, working eight hours each, would affect the public health to the same extent, if at all, as would two shifts at twelve hours each. It is not contended that the business of smelting is unlawful; nor is it claimed that the act was passed to prevent employers from perpetrating fraud upon employees, or to protect the latter from trespasses. Indeed, the only object that can rationally be claimed for it is the preservation of the health of those working in the smelters. Were the object of the act to protect the public health, and its provisions reasonably appropriate to that end, it might be sustained; for in such a case even the constitutional right of contract may be reasonably limited. But the act before us is not of that character. In selecting a subject for the exercise of the police power, the legislature must keep within its true scope. The reason for the existence of the power rests upon the theory that one must so use his own as not to injure others, and so as not to interfere with or injure the public health, safety, morals, or general welfare. How can one be said injuriously to affect others, or interfere with these great objects, by doing an act which confessedly visits its consequences on himself alone? And how can an alleged law, that purports to be the result of an exercise of the police power, be such in reality, when it has for its only object, not the protection of others, or the public health, safety, morals, or general welfare, but the welfare of him whose act is prohibited, when, if committed, it will injure him who commits it, and him only? . . .

In this we must not be understood as limiting the legislature, where the facts justify apparent discrimination, in passing health laws affecting only certain classes. . . . What we mean to decide is that in a purely private, lawful business, in which no special privilege or license has been granted by the state, and the carrying on of which is attended by no injury to the general public, it is beyond the power of the legislature, under the guise of the police power, to prohibit an adult man who desires to work thereat from working more than eight hours a day, on the ground that working longer may, or probably will, injure his own health. . . .

If the theory is correct, the state would be justified in prescribing the most minute details for the regulation of the personal conduct of individual citizens, as to things in no wise affecting the great public interests. Whenever a man fails in business, or loses a fortune by some great calamity, or droughts or floods destroy his crops, the legislature could levy a tax or make an appropriation, and therefrom establish him in business or make good the loss. The practical application of the theory would destroy the fundamental principles upon which our government is founded.

Let us make some further applications of this principle, and see to what such legislation would lead. It is, of course, no objection to this act to say that hereafter the legislature may pass another act that is invalid. But if the principle of the decision by which the present one is saved, in its logical extension, will protect others that every rational mind will declare void, it is well to stop for reflection; for it is a question of power, and not discretion, we are now considering. The business of operating smelters and working underground mines is purely a private business. It is not affected with a public interest, or devoted to a public use. Even here the general and better rule is that regulations of such businesses are confined to their public side, and do not descend to interference in contracts and strictly private dealings between employers and employees. Hence smelting does not come within the operation of the principle of those decisions in which have been upheld reasonable regulations of a business affected by a public interest. If, to protect the health of workmen engaged in these two occupations, the legislature may limit them to eight hours' labor per day, it may hereafter, upon the ground that idleness, resulting from short hours of labor, leads to drunkenness and gambling, and industry, promoted by longer hours, to happiness and health, enact that workmen must labor at these occupations 14 or 16 hours per day; and, by extending the same principle to other occupations, it may say, to use an illustration employed in argument, that a man weighing 120 pounds or less shall not work in a stone quarry, because only large and powerful men can safely work therein; that only men free from a tendency to tuberculosis shall work at indoor occupations, because those so afflicted need more pure air and sunshine than they can get if excluded from the open air; that only persons not needing the aid of eye-glasses shall become makers or repairers of watches, because labor, with such mechanical aids, upon delicate mechanisms, tends to destroy vision; or that those suffering from sluggish livers shall not engage in sedentary occupations, because their health demands active, muscular effort. Then it is only one step further to provide by law the style and quality of garments the citizens may wear, the quantity and quality of food he may eat, and the beverage he may drink. And, because one cannot support and properly educate his family for less than a certain amount of money, the legislature may declare that, to promote the general welfare, no employer shall contract to pay, or pay, an employee less than an arbitrary wage, so fixed as to produce the required sum. Such and other illustrations that readily suggest themselves are germane, and each and every supposed act could be sustained upon the same principle that would make the act before us valid. If counsel's contention be sound, that, to promote the general welfare and protect the public health or safety, the legislature is above the constitution, and brooks no restraint, if it is the sole judge, not merely of the exigency, but also of the subjects, for the exercise of the police power, and its reasonableness—then, indeed, all these, and almost all other conceivable, regulations of private affairs are permissible. If we stop to consider the form of government under which we live, and what pains the framers of our organic acts took to protect the rights of the individual citizen, we would naturally expect to find that measures passed for the alleged protection of the citizen against the consequences of his own acts would clash with constitutional safeguards inserted therein to conserve the inalienable rights of man. . . .

On the contrary, it is a distinct and emphatic return—a retrogression—to that period in English history when parliament busied itself in passing numerous acts interfering with the freedom of conscience in religious matters, and in prescribing minute regulations of the personal conduct of the individual, against which our ancestors rebelled, and which was one among other causes that prompted them to found here a government under which it would be impossible thus to interfere with the purely private affairs of the citizen.

Our conclusion as to the invalidity of this act is grounded upon principle. Let it now be tested by the authorities. . . .

This summary review of the leading authorities shows clearly to our minds that the great weight of authority, as well as reason, supports the conclusion which we have reached. The result of our deliberation, therefore, is that this act is an unwarrantable interference with, and infringes, the right of both the employer and employee in making contracts relating to a purely private business, in which no possible injury to the public can result; that it unjustly and arbitrarily singles out a class of persons, and imposes upon them restrictions from which others similarly situated and substantially in the same condition are exempt; and that it is not, under our constitution, a valid exercise of the police power of this state, either in the subject selected or in the reasonableness of the regulation.

CHAPTER XVII

Hours of Labor—Women

For more than thirty years the validity of legislative restrictions upon the employment of women has divided the minds of American jurists. Private rights, the sanctity of freedom of contract, equality before the law have stood over against sex differences, social well-being and the proper exercise of the police power. To express in abstract terms the relation between these points of view would not be a task of insuperable difficulty. To group special cases consistently under the one or the other has proven a task that our courts have not been able to perform with uniform satisfaction.

Many of the early cases that came before the state courts turned upon the employment of women as waitresses in saloons. In 1881, a California law forbidding women to work as waitresses in saloons was brought before the supreme court of that state. The court pronounced the law unconstitutional as being in violation of the rights of adult citizens of that state.[1] In 1884, an ordinance of the city of Cleveland established the same restriction within the municipal limits. The supreme court of Ohio pronounced the ordinance valid, but on the special ground that the power to regulate the sale of liquors is expressly delegated to cities in that state.[2]

[1] Case of Mary Maguire, 57 Cal., 604.

[2] Bergman *v.* Cleveland, 39 Ohio, 651.

Although these are among the earlier cases, they are not the earliest; and other cases, because of their greater importance, have attracted more attention. The restriction of the hours of labor to be undertaken by women in manufacturing industries has been contested in several states. Here there are two clearly defined lines of argument, each one of which has been so ably developed that neither has yet been completely and finally driven from the field.

The earliest opinion, recognized as the leading one on the one side of the question, was written by Judge Lord of the supreme judicial court of Massachusetts in 1876. (Commonwealth *v.* Hamilton Mfg. Co.) The law under consideration was one limiting to ten hours a day the legal workday of minors under eighteen and of all women. The decision is a brief one. It does not assume that an elaborate argument is necessary. It rather takes the attitude that the burden of proof rests upon those who undertake to show that the law is unconstitutional. On behalf of the corporations it was asserted that the act of incorporation was a contract with the commonwealth, and that the law impaired that contract. This the court would not admit. A considerable portion of the opinion is taken up with a consideration of this question, concluding with the statement: "The law, therefore, violates no contract." Taking up other points, the court continues:

> [The law] merely provides that in an employment, which the legislature has evidently deemed to some extent dangerous to health, no person shall be engaged in labor more than ten hours a day or sixty hours a week. There can be no doubt that such legislation may be maintained either as a health or police regulation, if it were necessary to resort to either of those sources for power. This principle has been so frequently recognized in this commonwealth that reference to the decisions is unnecessary.

It is also said that the law violates the right of Mary Shirley to labor in accordance with her own judgment as to the number of hours she shall work. The obvious and conclusive reply to this is, that the law does not limit her right to labor as many hours per day or per week as she may desire; it does not in terms forbid her laboring in any particular business or occupation as many hours per day or per week, as she may desire; it merely prohibits her being employed continuously in the same service more than a certain number of hours per day or week, which is so clearly within the power of the legislature, that it becomes unnecessary to inquire whether it is a matter of grievance of which this defendant has a right to complain.

The reasoning is not complete enough to satisfy one who would like to know the full mind of the court upon a question that has become of so great importance. The decision was written at a date when the principles involved had not yet come to be regarded as of much consequence. At the same time the case is one of more than usual importance, being cited in other cases as authority for similar legislation.

After the lapse of twenty-six years two similar cases came up for adjudication. In these the scene was shifted to the West. A law enacted by the Nebraska legislature came before the supreme court of that state in 1902, and in the same year a similar law was brought before the supreme court of the state of Washington. The two statutes were similar to that upheld in Massachusetts in that they limited the hours of women's labor to ten a day. The Nebraska law added a clause forbidding night work. In the decision of these cases the points in controversy were discussed at greater length than in the earlier case, and the opinions of the two courts incorporated the line of argument which of late has been more fully developed.

In the first of these cases (Wenham *v.* State) Judge

Barnes, who wrote the opinion, refers to the importance of the relations existing between the departments of our government. "Courts should never usurp legislative functions. . . . If, after a careful consideration of the question in all of its bearings, the matter [of constitutionality] is left in doubt, we should resolve such doubt in favor of the law, and declare it valid." The court admits that the plaintiff's business is property and that the ability of the working women is also property.

It must be conceded, however, that every property holder is secured in his title thereto and holds it under the implied rule and understanding that its use may be so regulated and restricted that it shall not be injurious to the equal enjoyment of others having the equal right to the enjoyment of their property, or to the rights of the community in which he lives. All property in this state is held subject to rules regulating the common good and the general welfare of our people.

The limitation upon such rights should of course be reasonable, but the reasonableness is to be determined by the legislature as a matter of expediency. This question the legislature is well fitted to answer.

The members of the legislature come from no particular class. They are elected from every portion of the state, and come from every avocation and from all the walks of life. They have observed the conditions with which they are surrounded, and know from experience what laws are necessary to be enacted for the welfare of the communities in which they reside.

Justification of the law is found in the fact that "women and children have always, to a certain extent, been wards of the state." While they may own property, yet they have no voice in the enactment of the laws. These considerations were evidently of importance to the court, but a consideration of greater weight follows.

[Women] are unable, by reason of their physical limitations, to endure the same hours of exhaustive labor as may be endured by adult males. Certain kinds of work which may be performed by men without injury to their health would wreck the constitutions and destroy the health of women, and render them incapable of bearing their share of the burdens of the family and the home. The state must be accorded the right to guard and protect women, as a class, against such a condition; and the law in question, to that extent, conserves the public health and welfare.

In the matter of freedom of contract, the opinion goes on to say:

We may well declare a law unconstitutional which interferes with or abridges the right of adult males to contract with each other in any of the business affairs or vocations of life. The employer and the laborer are practically on an equal footing, but these observations do not apply to women and children. Of the many vocations in this country, comparatively few are open to women. Their field of remunerative labor is restricted. Competition for places therein is necessarily great. The desire for place, and in many instances the necessity of obtaining employment, would subject them to hardships and exactions which they would not otherwise endure. The employer who seeks to obtain the most hours of labor for the least wages has such an advantage over them that the wisdom of the law, for their protection, cannot well be questioned. No doubt, these considerations were the moving cause for the passage of the law in question.

Judge Dunbar in his opinion in the second of these two cases (State *v.* Buchanan) goes more directly to the point, although in general the line of reasoning is much the same. He was the first to emphasize the particular physiological reasons for such legislation.

It is a matter of universal knowledge with all reasonably

intelligent people of the present age that continuous standing on the feet by women for a great many consecutive hours is deleterious to their health. It must logically follow that that which would deleteriously affect any great number of women who are the mothers of succeeding generations must necessarily affect the public welfare and the public morals. Law is, or ought to be, a progressive science. While the principles of justice are immutable, changing conditions of society and the evolution of employment make a change in the application of principles absolutely necessary to an intelligent administration of government. In the early history of the law, when employments were few and simple, the relative conditions of the citizen and the state were different, and many employments and uses which were then considered inalienable rights have since, from the very necessity of changed conditions, been subjected to legislative control, restriction, and restraint. This all flows from the old announcement made by Blackstone that when man enters into society as a compensation for the protection which society gives to him he must yield up some of his natural rights, and, as the responsibilities of the government increase, and a greater degree of protection is afforded to the citizen, the recompense is the yielding of more individual rights. . . . The changing conditions of society have made an imperative call upon the state for the exercise of these additional powers, and the welfare of society demands that the state should assume these powers, and it is the duty of the court to sustain them whenever it is found that they are based upon the idea of the promotion and protection of society.

In 1906 the supreme court of Oregon examined and upheld a similar law in State *v.* Muller. This case was of particular importance, being appealed to the United States supreme court and eliciting the opinion of that court in Muller *v.* Oregon. The law in question provided that "no female [shall] be employed in any mechanical establishment or factory or laundry in this state more than ten hours during any one day," and that "any employer who shall require any female to work in any of the places mentioned [in excess of the permitted ten hours] shall be guilty of a misdemeanor." The court held that the labor contract is "subject to such reasonable limitations as are essential to the peace, health, welfare and good order of the community." The question to be determined, then, was the reasonableness of the law. The view of the court as expressed by Chief Justice Bean upon this point is found in its statement that the law was enacted

in order to conserve the public health and welfare by protecting the physical well-being of females who work in mechanical establishments, factories and laundries. Such legislation must be taken as expressing the belief of the legislature, and through it of the people, that the labor of females in such establishments in excess of ten hours in any one day is detrimental to health and injuriously affects the public welfare.

The more elaborate opinion handed down by the supreme court of the United States in its review of this case, as well as the high degree of authority accorded to the decisions of this tribunal, make Muller *v.* Oregon a case of the greatest importance. In developing the argument upon which its decision is based, the court manifests great caution. It asserts the legal equality rather than the legal inequality of women and men, and it admits that the "general right to contract in relation to one's business is part of the liberty of the individual, protected by the fourteenth amendment to the federal Constitution." Yet this liberty is not absolute: a state may restrict in many respects the individual's power to contract. And admitting the legal equality of men and women, it does not necessarily follow that there are not differences of sex sufficient to justify a different rule respecting the restriction of hours of labor. These differences are two, and may be expressed in the language of the court.

That woman's physical structure and the performance of maternal functions place her at a disadvantage in the struggle for subsistence is obvious. This is especially true when the burdens of motherhood are upon her. Even when they are not, by abundant testimony of the medical fraternity continuance for a long time on her feet at work, repeating this from day to day, tends to injurious effects upon the body, and, as healthy mothers are essential to vigorous offspring, the physical well-being of woman becomes an object of public interest and care in order to preserve the strength and vigor of the race. Still again, history discloses the fact that woman has always been dependent upon man. . . . It is still true that in the struggle for subsistence she is not an equal competitor with her brother. Though limitations upon personal and contractual rights may be removed by legislation, there is that in her disposition and habits of life which will operate against a full assertion of those rights. She will still be where some legislation to protect her seems necessary to secure a real equality of right. Doubtless there are individual exceptions, and there are many respects in which she has an advantage over him; but looking at it from the viewpoint of the effort to maintain an independent position in life, she is not upon an equality. Differentiated by these matters from the other sex, she is properly placed in a class by herself, and legislation designed for her protection may be sustained, even when like legislation is not necessary for men, and could not be sustained. It is impossible to close one's eyes to the fact that she still looks to her brother and depends upon him. Even though all restrictions on political, personal, and contractual rights were taken away, and she stood, as far as statutes are concerned, upon an absolutely equal plane with him, it would still be true that she is so constituted that she will rest upon and look to him for protection; that her physical structure and a proper discharge of her maternal functions—having in view not merely her own health, but the well-being of the race—justify legislation to protect her from the greed as well as the passion of man. The limitations which this statute places upon her contractual powers, upon her right to agrèe with her employer as to the time she shall labor, are not imposed solely for her benefit, but also largely for the benefit of all. Many words cannot make this plainer. The two sexes differ in structure of body, in the functions to be performed by each, in the amount of physical strength, in the capacity for long-continued labor, particularly when done standing, the influence of vigorous health upon the future well-being of the race, the self-reliance which enables one to assert full rights, and in the capacity to maintain the struggle for subsistence. This difference justifies a difference in legislation, and upholds that which is designed to compensate for some of the burdens which rest upon her.

The leading case in which the validity of such restrictive legislation is denied is Ritchie *v.* People. This case was decided by the supreme court of Illinois in 1895. At that time the Massachusetts case, decided nineteen years earlier, was the only important decision dealing with the subject. The Illinois law prohibited women employed in manufacturing establishments from working longer than eight hours in a day. It thus undertook to make the legal workday for women in such establishments two hours shorter that the workday established by the Massachusetts law. The opinion is long and goes fully into the points in controversy. First, Judge Magruder dwells upon the constitutional rights of citizens, emphasizing especially that "the right to contract is the only way by which a person can rightfully acquire property by his own labor." This principle applied to the provisions of the law leads at once to the conclusion that the act is unconstitutional unless it can be positively shown that there is some special ground for upholding it. No such ground is discovered.

Attention is directed to the fact that the prohibition is not placed upon all women. Those employed in manufactures are brought within the terms of the law, but not women employed in other occupations, as saleswomen, domestic servants, bookkeepers, stenographers, typewriters. These

are at liberty to contract for as many hours of labor in a day as they choose. The manner in which the section thus discriminates against one class of employers and employees and in favor of all others places it in opposition to the constitutional guaranties hereinbefore discussed, and so renders it invalid.

But the objection to the particular and discriminating character of the law is not the leading objection. Of fundamental importance is the fact that the enactment is "a purely arbitrary restriction upon the fundamental rights of the citizen to control his or her own time and faculties. It substitutes the judgment of the legislature for the judgment of the employer and employee in a matter about which they are competent to agree with each other." This restriction is a burden that is "unreasonable and unnecessary;" and even though it were imposed upon all citizens or classes of citizens, it would transcend the authority of the legislature.

The contention that the act of the legislature may be upheld as an exercise of police power is very positively discountenanced. That power, it is admitted, is very broad and far-reaching, but it is not without its limitations. It is not above the constitution; and its exercise, moreover, must have some relation to the comfort, welfare or safety of society. This the law under consideration does not have. "It is not the nature of the things done, but the sex of the persons doing them, which is made the basis of the claim that the act is a measure for the promotion of the public health." The defense of the law based on the physical inferiority of women does not appeal to the mind of the court. "It will not be denied," the court replies, "that woman is entitled to the same rights, under the constitution, to make contracts with reference to her labor, as are secured thereby to men." The fourteenth amendment fully protects persons and citizens.

> Woman is both a "citizen" and a "person" within the meaning of this section. . . . As a "citizen," woman has the right to acquire and possess property of every kind. As a "person," she has the right to claim the benefit of the constitutional provision that she shall not be deprived of life, liberty or property without due process of law. Involved in these rights thus guaranteed to her is the right to make and enforce contracts. The law accords to her, as to every other citizen, the right to gain a livelihood by intelligence, honesty and industry in the arts, the sciences, the professions or other vocations. Before the law, her right to a choice of vocations cannot be said to be denied or abridged on account of sex. The tendency of legislation in this state has been to recognize the rights of woman in the particulars here specified.

Legislation is cited in evidence of this attitude. The opinion then continues:

> But inasmuch as sex is no bar, under the constitution and law, to the endowment of woman with the fundamental and inalienable rights of liberty and property, which include the right to make her own contracts, the mere fact of sex will not justify the legislature in putting forth the police power of the state for the purpose of limiting her exercise of those rights, unless the courts are able to see that there is some fair, just, and reasonable connection between such limitation and the public health, safety, or welfare proposed to be secured by it.
>
> Counsel for the people refer to statements in the text-books recognizing the propriety of regulations which forbid women to engage in certain kinds of work altogether. Thus it is said

in Cooley on Constitutional Limitations, that "some employments . . . may be admissible for males and improper for females, and regulations recognizing the impropriety, and forbidding women engaging in them, would be open to no reasonable objection." Attention is also called to the above-mentioned act of March 22, 1872, which makes an exception of military service, and provides that nothing in the act shall be construed as requiring any female to work on streets or roads, or serve on juries. But, without stopping to comment upon measures of this character, it is sufficient to say that what is said in reference to them has no application to the act of 1893. The act is not based upon the theory that the manufacture of clothing, wearing apparel, and other articles is an improper occupation for women to be engaged in. It does not inhibit their employment in factories or workshops. On the contrary, it recognizes such places as proper for them to work in by permitting their labor therein during eight hours of each day. The question here is not whether a particular employment is a proper one for the use of female labor, but the question is whether, in an employment which is conceded to be lawful in itself, and suitable for women to engage in, she shall be deprived of the right to determine for herself how many hours she can and may work during each day. There is no reasonable ground—at least none which has been made manifest to us in the arguments of counsel—for fixing upon eight hours in one day as the limit within which woman can work without injury to her physique, and beyond which, if she work, injury will necessarily follow. But the police power of the state can only be permitted to limit or abridge such a fundamental right as the right to make contracts when the exercise of such power is necessary to promote the health, comfort, welfare, or safety of society or the public; and it is questionable whether it can be exercised to prevent injury to the individual engaged in a particular calling. [Quoting Tiedeman in his work on *Limitations of Police Power*]: "In so far as the employment of a certain class in a particular occupation may threaten or inflict damage upon the public or third persons, there can be no doubt as to the constitutionality of any statute which prohibits their prosecution of that trade. But it is questionable, except in the case of minors, whether the prohibition can rest upon the claim that the employment will prove hurtful to them. . . . There can be no more justification for the prohibition of the prosecution of certain callings by women because the employment will prove hurtful to themselves than it would be for the state to prohibit men from working in the manufacture of white lead because they are apt to contract lead poisoning, or to prohibit occupation in certain parts of iron-smelting works, because the lives of the men so engaged are materially shortened."

In conclusion the Judge quotes an extract from the New York court of appeals, *In re* Jacobs, expressly stating that the view is adopted by the Illinois court.

When a health law is challenged in the courts as unconstitutional on the ground that it arbitrarily interferes with personal liberty and private property, without due process of law, the courts must be able to see that it has at least in fact some relation to the public health, that the public health is the end actually aimed at, and that it is appropriate and adapted to that end. This we have not been able to see in this law, and we must, therefore, pronounce it unconstitutional and void. In reaching this conclusion, we have not been unmindful that the power which courts possess to condemn legislative acts which are in conflict with the supreme law should be exercised with great caution, and even with reluctance. But, as said by Chancellor Kent, "It is only by the free exercise of this power that courts of justice are enabled to repel assaults and to protect every part of the government and every member of the community from undue and destructive innovations upon their charter rights."

The second decision of importance, restricting on constitutional grounds legislation regarding hours of women's work, came from the court of appeals of New York in the case of People *v.* Williams. This opinion, written by Judge Gray, was handed down in 1907, the year intervening between the Oregon state court decision and that of the United States supreme court on the appealed case. While in a sense the principle was the same, yet the provisions of the law under consideration were different. The court had before it, so far as the principles are concerned, the two lines of argument fully developed, both with equal authority. Although the greater number of state court decisions was already on the side upon which the Oregon court had placed itself, the authority of the United States supreme court had not yet been added. The statutes considered in the cases already referred to had limited the length of the day to ten or eight hours. The New York statute prohibited night work for women, restricting their legal hours of labor in factories to the hours between six o'clock in the morning and nine o'clock in the evening. Between the two principles advanced in the other cases the New York court chose that of the Illinois decision as its own. Yet the reasoning is elaborated in a somewhat different temper.

In enacting the law in question the legislature, the court says,

> has overstepped the limits set by the constitution of the state to the exercise of the power to interfere with the rights of citizens. The fundamental law of the state, as embodied in its constitution, provides that "no person shall . . . be deprived of life, liberty or property without due process of law." Article I, sec. 6. The provisions of the state and of the federal constitutions protect every citizen in the right to pursue any lawful employment in a lawful manner. He enjoys the utmost freedom to follow his chosen pursuit, and any arbitrary distinction against, or deprivation of, that freedom by the legislature is an invasion of the constitutional guaranty. Under

our laws men and women now stand alike in their constitutional rights, and there is no warrant for making any discrimination between them with respect to the liberty of person or of contract.

Replying to the claim that the law was authorized as an exercise of the police power, the court says:

It is to be observed that it is not a regulation of the number of hours of labor for working women. The enactment goes far beyond this. It attempts to take away the right of a woman to labor before 6 o'clock in the morning, or after 9 o'clock in the evening, without any reference to other considerations. In providing that "no female shall be employed, permitted, or suffered to work in any factory in this state before six o'clock in the morning, or after nine o'clock in the evening of any day," she is prevented, however willing, from engaging herself in a lawful employment during the specified periods of the 24 hours. Except as to women under 21 years of age, this was the first attempt on the part of the state to restrict their liberty of person, or their freedom of contract, in the pursuit of a vocation. I find nothing in the language of the section which suggests the purpose of promoting health, except as it might be inferred that for a woman to work during the forbidden hours of night would be unhealthful. If the inhibition of the section in question had been framed to prevent the 10 hours of work from being performed at night, or to prolong them beyond 9 o'clock in the evening, it might more readily be appreciated that the health of women was the matter of legislative concern. That is not the effect, nor the sense, of the provision of the section with which alone we are dealing. It was not the case upon which this defendant was convicted. If this enactment is to be sustained, then an adult woman, although a citizen, and entitled as such to all the rights of citizenship under our laws, may not be employed, nor contract to work, in any factory for any period of time, no matter how short, if it is within the prohibited hours, and this, too, without any regard to the healthfulness of the employment. It is clear, as it seems to me, that this legislation cannot, and should not, be upheld as a proper exercise of the police power. It is, certainly, discriminative against female citizens, in denying to them equal rights with men in the same pursuit.

The right of the state, as *parens patriae,* to restrict, or to regulate, the labor and employment of children is unquestionable; but an adult female is not to be regarded as a ward of the state, or in any other light than the man is regarded, when the question relates to the business pursuit or calling. She is no more a ward of the state than is the man. She is entitled to enjoy, unmolested, her liberty of person, and her freedom to work for whom she pleases, where she pleases, and as long as she pleases, within the general limits operative upon all persons alike, and shall we say that this is valid legislation, which closes the doors of a factory to her before and after certain hours? I think not.

In closing the Judge felt called upon to utter a word of warning, as follows:

The courts have gone very far in upholding legislative enactments, framed clearly for the welfare, comfort, and health of the community, and that a wide range in the exercise of the police power of the state should be conceded, I do not deny; but when it is sought, under the guise of a labor law, arbitrarily, as here, to prevent an adult female citizen from working at any time of the day that suits her, I think it is time to call a halt. It arbitrarily deprives citizens of their right to contract with each other. The tendency of legislatures, in the form of regulatory measures, to interfere with the lawful pursuits of citizens, is becoming a marked one in this country, and it behooves the courts, firmly and fearlessly, to interpose the barriers of their judgments, when invoked to protect against legislative acts plainly transcending the powers conferred by the constitution upon the legislative body.

The line of argument followed in the first Ritchie case has been recently largely annulled by another decision of the Illinois supreme court. In April of 1910 that court handed down an opinion (Ritchie *v.* Wayman) in which it held that the establishment of a ten-hour day for women is within the police power of the state. The chief interest of this opinion lies in the fact that it makes a legal restriction on the hours of labor of women binding in an important jurisdiction in which such restriction had previously been declared unconstitutional. It contains no new arguments. The only point of novelty is the manner in which the court seeks to reconcile its present view with that taken fifteen years ago.

Some of the more significant sentences from the opinion follow:

> If, therefore, the public interest requires that the time which women shall be permitted to work in any mechanical establishment or factory or laundry should be limited to ten hours in any one day, we are unable to see why this statute is not constitutional. . . . The property rights of the citizen are always held and enjoyed subject to the reasonable exercise of the police power by the state. . . . It is known to all men (and what we know as men we cannot profess to be ignorant of as judges) that woman's physical structure and the performance of maternal functions place her at a great disadvantage in the battle of life. . . . It would therefore seem obvious that legislation which limits the number of hours which women shall be permitted to work to ten hours in a single day in such employments as are carried on in mechanical establishments, factories and laundries would tend to preserve the health of women and insure the production of vigorous offspring by them, and would directly conduce to the health, morals and general welfare of the public, and that such legislation would fall clearly within the police power of the state.

In referring to the court's former decision the opinion

contrasts the law of 1893 with that of 1909 in two particulars.

(1) There is nothing in the title of the act of 1893, or in the act itself, which indicates or suggests that the act was passed for the purpose of promoting the health of women, except, as might be inferred from the provisions of section 5, that it might be conducive to the health of women to prohibit them from working more than eight hours in any one day, while the act of 1909 expressly provides in its title that the limitation upon the number of hours which women shall be required or permitted to work in mechanical establishments or factories or laundries is passed with the view "to safeguard the health of such employees."

(2) The act of 1893 provides for an eight-hour day, while the act of 1909 provides for a ten-hour day in which women shall be permitted to work in mechanical establishments or factories or laundries. Can it be said that, if the limitation upon the number of hours which women were permitted to work in the designated callings in the act of 1893 had been fixed at ten hours instead of eight hours, the court would have held the act unconstitutional as an unreasonable exercise of the police power of the state or that the act would have been held obnoxious to the constitution as special or class legislation? We do not think it can be so said, as there is throughout the opinion a veiled suggestion which indicates that it was the opinion of the court that the limitation of the right to work longer than eight hours was an unreasonable limitation upon the right to contract, while the right to contract for a longer day, at least under some circumstances, might be a valid limitation upon the right to contract.

Reduced to their lowest terms, the opposing views expressed in the decisions that have been cited may be set off against each other in the following words:

(1) Women are to be regarded as citizens in precisely the same sense as men. All rights of citizenship expressed or

implied in the constitution and laws are to be maintained regardless of sex. Freedom of contract is implied in the guaranty of life, liberty and property, and the labor contract is to be treated like other contracts. The police power cannot be construed as covering such cases.

(2) Women are citizens, but not in precisely the same sense as men. Difference of sex is a sufficient justification for making a distinction in the maintenance of the constitutional rights of citizens. This is based on scientific authority. Freedom of contract, though derived from the guaranty of life, liberty and property, has not the same sanctity. Under the police power freedom of contract may be restricted. That power may be so construed as to include not only the welfare of the community now living, but also the welfare of the community yet unborn and its right to a good birth.

The increasing number of states that are enacting legislation protecting women makes it very probable that all our courts will yet be called upon to elect between these two positions. It is hardly possible that anything new can be said. The two principles stand in clear contrast. The present indications are that the decisions, in the absence of complicating technicalities, will follow those of the United States supreme court and of the other courts that have adopted the same position.

CHAPTER XVIII

Hours of Labor—Bakers

Among the cases involving the question of the constitutionality of laws restricting the hours of labor, none have attracted more attention than those concerning the bakers. At the time when these decisions were handed down, popular interest in the subject was keen. The press of the country took up the discussion and the public was fully informed in regard to the views expressed. Although the cases are thus so generally known it is necessary in order to set forth accurately the attitude of the courts to include them in our discussion.

In response to a sentiment aroused by an investigation and report upon the conditions in city bake-shops the legislature of New York enacted a law fixing standards which must be met in all the bakery and confectionery establishments in the state. These standards were set forth in considerable detail, and as an addition to them, another section of the law established a ten-hour day as a maximum for all bakers. The law was challenged in the courts of the state and the case carried up to the court of appeals and from it to the United States supreme court. The outcome in the state court was that the law was held valid. In the supreme court of the United States it was finally declared unconstitutional. A count of the judges of the various courts which passed upon the case shows that the total number was twenty-two. Of these twelve cast their vote in favor of the validity of the law. In the final hearing by the United States supreme court the decision was carried by a majority of one vote only. The closeness of the decision indicates how near to the border line the principles involved really were. In the New York court of appeals two opinions were written concurring with the opinion of the court and two dissenting from it. In the United States supreme court two dissenting opinions were written. It will not be necessary to follow each of these eight opinions through by itself, nor to keep prevailing and dissenting opinions separate, as the dissenting view of the New York court was in the main the prevailing view of the federal court. It is the difference in attitude and in importance attached to arguments that is of chief interest here.

The first argument in support of the validity of the law was urged by Chief Justice Parker and was very general in its scope. Discussing the Fourteenth Amendment and its relation to the law in question the Justice quotes an extract from the federal supreme court in another case. The constitution of the United States

> was made for an undefined and expanding future, and for a people gathered and to be gathered from many nations and of many tongues. . . . We shall expect that the new and various experiences of our own situation and system will mould and shape it into new and not less useful forms. . . . While the cardinal principles of justice are immutable, the methods by which justice is administered are subject to constant fluctuation, and that the Constitution of the United States, which is necessarily and to a large extent inflexible, and exceedingly difficult of amendment, should not be so construed as to deprive the states of the power to so amend their laws as to make them conform to the wishes of the citizens as they may deem best for the public welfare without bringing them into conflict with the supreme law of the land.

This view Chief Justice Parker characterizes as a "broad

minded view," and insists that it should be followed by the state courts whenever called upon to consider the constitutionality of a measure. In somewhat the same mind Justice Holmes expresses himself.

A constitution is not intended to embody a particular economic theory, whether of paternalism and the organic relation of the citizen to the state or of *laissez faire*. It is made for people of fundamentally different views, and the accident of our finding certain opinions natural and familiar, or novel, and even shocking, ought not to conclude our judgment upon the question whether statutes embodying them conflict with the Constitution of the United States.

Entering upon the consideration of the needs of such legislation, Justice Parker refers to the changed conditions of the present and their effect upon the manner of preparing food. The public generally are concerned in "having bakers' and confectioners' establishments cleanly and wholesome in this day of appreciation of, and apprehension on account of, microbes, which cause disease and death." Formerly baking was done in the family. Now "in a large percentage of the houses in cities and villages the baker is relied on to a large extent to furnish bread, biscuits, cake, and pie, as well as confectionery." "Indeed," continues the opinion of this judge, "it can be safely said that the family of today is more dependent upon the baker for the necessaries of life than upon any other source of supply." Such a change, then, becomes sufficient ground for justification of such an act as an exercise of the police power. Certainly this is true of some of the features of the law. Prohibiting the use of cellars for bakeries unless certain prescribed sanitary precautions are taken, providing that floors, ceilings and side walls shall be of such material as to be readily cleaned, providing for keeping flour and meal in dry and airy rooms,—such provisions are clearly for the purpose of protecting " the public from the use of the food made dangerous by the germs that thrive in darkness and uncleanness." If this is not doubted,

why should any one question the object of the legislature in providing in the same article, and as a part of the scheme, that " no employee shall be required or permitted to work " in such an establishment " more than sixty hours in any one week," an average of ten hours for each working day. It is but reasonable to assume from this statute as a whole that the legislature had in mind that the health and cleanliness of the workers, as well as the cleanliness of the workrooms, was of the utmost importance, and that a man is more likely to be careful and cleanly when well, and not overworked, than when exhausted by fatigue, which makes for careless and slovenly habits, and tends to dirt and disease. If there is opportunity —and who can doubt it?—for this view, then the legislature had the power to enact as it did, and the courts are bound to sustain its action as justified by the police power, as we see from the authorities referred to earlier in the opinion.

The reading of the statute convinces Justice Parker that the purpose of the legislature was to benefit the public. For that reason he is satisfied to find that its action is within the police power under the authority of both the federal and the state courts.

Justice Gray's opinion emphasized still further the connection between the wholesomeness of the product and the conditions of its preparation.

In this law, which restricts the working hours of employees in bakery and confectionery establishments, I think we may fairly perceive a statutory regulation reasonably promotive of the public health, because compelling the master of such an establishment to conduct it in a manner the least capable of affecting his product prejudicially. We may, not unreasonably, assume that an employee may work too long for his health under the conditions, and that an impaired vitality and the possible development of organic disease may be the result. If, to obviate the possible consequences to the consumer of the food manufactured, the legislature determines to interfere by limiting, among other regulations, the hours of the workman, I do not think we should hold the interference to be without reason.

The next consideration of weight in the minds of the judges was the danger to health on the part of those engaged in bakeshop work. Here is shown evidence that medical authorities were consulted and their conclusions adopted. Work in bakers' or confectioners' establishments is classed by such authorities with potters, stonecutters, file grinders, and other workers " whose occupation necessitates the inhalation of dust particles, and hence predisposes its members to consumption." Even if other evidence in support of this legislation were wholly wanting, Judge Parker declares,

the published medical opinions and vital statistics bearing upon that subject standing alone fully justify the section under review as one to protect the health of the employees in such establishments, and it is the duty of this court to assume that the section was framed not only in the light of, but also with full appreciation of the force of the medical authority bearing upon, the subject—authority which reasonably challenges the attention and stimulates the helpfulness of the philanthropist.

Judge Vann attaches such great importance to the effect of this employment upon the health of those engaged in it that he was of opinion that unless the regulation could be sustained upon such grounds it could not be sustained at all. He says:

If such an occupation is unhealthy, the legislature has the right to prohibit employers from requiring or permitting their employees to spend more than a specified number of hours per day or week in the work, because such a command would be in the interest of the public health, and would promote the general welfare.

Upon consulting these authorities the Judge finds that "bakers and confectioners, who, during working hours, constantly breathe air filled with the finest dust from flour and sugar have a tendency to consumption, the most terrible scourge known to modern civilization, and resulting in more deaths than any other disease." To support this conclusion there are inserted in the opinion quotations from a variety of sources to show that the occupation is a dangerous one. This investigation leads the Judge to express his conclusion as follows:

While the mortality among those who breathe air filled with minute particles of flour is less than among those who work in stone, metal, or clay, still it seems to be demonstrated that it is greater than in avocations generally. The dust-laden air in the baker's or confectioner's establishment is more benign and less liable to irritate than particles of stone or metal, hence, while bakers are classified with potters, stonemasons, file grinders, etc., still they are regarded as less liable to pulmonary disease than other members of the class. The evidence, while not uniform, leads to the conclusion that the occupation of a baker or confectioner is unhealthy, and tends to result in diseases of the respiratory organs. . . . So I think an act is valid which provides that in an employment which the legislature deems, and which is in fact, to some extent detrimental to health, no person, regardless of age or sex, shall be permitted or required to labor more than a certain number of hours per day or week. Such legislation, under such circumstances, is a health law, and is a valid exercise of the police power.

The opinion which the majority of the New York court reaches is that

> from an examination of the statute in the light of the authorities cited, [it follows] that the purpose of article 8, and every part of it, including the provision in question, is to benefit the public; that it has a just and reasonable relation to the public welfare, and hence is within the police power possessed by the legislature.

Justice Harlan was of the opinion that the legislation in question had been enacted as expressing the belief of the people of New York that it was wise and necessary. The only question for the federal court then was "whether the means devised by the state are germane to an end which may be lawfully accomplished and have a real or substantial relation to the protection of health, as involved in the daily work of the persons, male or female, engaged in bakery and confectionery establishments." He was not willing to admit that the statute "has no appropriate or direct connection with that protection to health which each state owes to her citizens;" or that it "is not promotive of the health of the employees in question;" or that "the regulation prescribed by the state is utterly unreasonable and extravagant or wholly arbitrary;" or that it is "beyond question, a plain, palpable invasion of rights secured by the fundamental law." He was of opinion that in bakery and confectionery establishments "as all know, the air constantly breathed by workmen is not as pure and healthful as that to be found in some other establishments or out of doors." This opinion he supports by quotations from various sources.

The entire question of fixing the hours of labor is a difficult one, urges the Justice, one that has been "for a long period, and is yet, a subject of serious consideration among civilized peoples, and by those having special knowledge of the laws of health." It is probable, he urges, that a law prohibiting more than eighteen hours' work a day in bakeries would not raise any question of legislative authority. The present law fixes ten hours, and this "may be said to occupy a middle ground in respect of the hours of labor." Yet the best course for the state to pursue in connection with such regulations need not be determined with absolute certainty. Interference with industrial freedom always opens debatable ground.

It is enough for the determination of this case, and it is enough for this court to know, that the question is one about which there is room for debate and for an honest difference of opinion. There are many reasons of a weighty, substantial character, based upon the experience of mankind, in support of the theory that, all things considered, more than ten hours' steady work each day, from week to week, in a bakery or confectionery establishment, may endanger the health and shorten the lives of the workmen, thereby diminishing their physical and mental capacity to serve the state and to provide for those dependent upon them.

Turning to the expression of the views upon which the opposite opinion is based, it is found that here again several considerations were important. The one of perhaps greatest weight was expressed by Justice Peckham in writing the prevailing opinion of the federal court.

The mandate of the statute that "no employee shall be required or permitted to work" is the substantial equivalent of an enactment that "no employee shall contract or agree to work" more than ten hours per day; and, as there is no provision for special emergencies, the statute is mandatory in all cases. It is not an act merely fixing the number of hours which shall constitute a legal day's work, but an absolute prohibition upon the employer permitting, under any circumstances, more than ten hours' work to be done in his establishment. The employee may desire to earn the extra money which would arise from his working more than the prescribed time, but this statute forbids the employer from permitting the employee to earn it.

The statute necessarily interferes with the right of contract between the employer and employees, concerning the number of hours in which the latter may labor in the bakery of the employer. The general right to make a contract in relation to his business is part of the liberty of the individual protected by the 14th Amendment of the Federal Constitution. . . .

The question whether this act is valid as a labor law, pure and simple, may be dismissed in a few words. There is no reasonable ground for interfering with the liberty of person or the right of free contract, by determining the hours of labor, in the occupation of a baker. There is no contention that bakers as a class are not equal in intelligence and capacity to men in other trades or manual occupations, or that they are not able to assert their rights and care for themselves without the protecting arm of the state, interfering with their independence of judgment and of action. They are in no sense wards of the state. Viewed in the light of a purely labor law, with no reference whatever to the question of health, we think that a law like the one before us involves neither the safety, the morals, nor the welfare of the public, and that the interest of the public is not in the slightest degree affected by such an act. . . .

We think the limit of the police power has been reached and passed in this case. There is, in our judgment, no reasonable foundation for holding this to be necessary or appropriate as a health law to safeguard the public health, or the health of the individuals who are following the trade of a baker. If this statute be valid, and if, therefore, a proper case is made out in which to deny the right of an individual, *sui juris,* as employer or employee, to make contracts for the labor of the latter under the protection of the provisions of the Federal

Constitution, there would seem to be no length to which legislation of this nature might not go. . . .

We think that there can be no fair doubt that the trade of a baker, in and of itself, is not an unhealthy one to that degree which would authorize the legislature to interfere with the right to labor, and with the right of free contract on the part of the individual, either as employer or employee. In looking through statistics regarding all trades and occupations, it may be true that the trade of a baker does not appear to be as healthy as some other trades, and is also vastly more healthy than still others. To the common understanding the trade of a baker has never been regarded as an unhealthy one. Very likely physicians would not recommend the exercise of that or of any other trade as a remedy for ill health. Some occupations are more healthy than others, but we think there are none which might not come under the power of the legislature to supervise and control the hours of working therein, if the mere fact that the occupation is not absolutely and perfectly healthy is to confer that right upon the leigslative department of the government. It might be safely affirmed that almost all occupations more or less affect the health. There must be more than the mere fact of the possible existence of some small amount of unhealthiness to warrant legislative interference with liberty. It is unfortunately true that labor, even in any department, may possibly carry with it the seeds of unhealthiness. But are we all, on that account, at the mercy of legislative majorities? . . . No trade, no occupation, no mode of earning one's living, could escape this all-pervading power, and the acts of the legislature in limiting the hours of labor in all employments would be valid, although such limitation might seriously cripple the ability of the laborer to support himself and his family. . . .

It is also urged, pursuing the same line of argument, that it is to the interest of the state that its population should be strong and robust, and therefore any legislation which may be said to tend to make people healthy must be valid as health laws, enacted under the police power. If this be a valid argument and a justification for this kind of legislation, it follows that the protection of the Federal Constitution from undue interference with liberty of person and freedom of contract is visionary, wherever the law is sought to be justified as a valid exercise of the police power. Scarcely any law but might find shelter under such assumptions, and conduct, properly so called, as well as contract, would come under the restrictive sway of the legislature. Not only the hours of employees, but the hours of employers, could be regulated, and doctors, lawyers, scientists, all professional men, as well as athletes and artisans, could be forbidden to fatigue their brains and bodies by prolonged hours of exercise, lest the fighting strength of the state be impaired. We mention these extreme cases because the contention is extreme. We do not believe in the soundness of the views which uphold this law. . . . The act is not, within any fair meaning of the term, a health law, but is an illegal interference with the rights of individuals, both employers and employees, to make contracts regarding labor upon such terms as they may think best, or which they may agree upon with the other parties to such contracts. Statutes of the nature of that under review, limiting the hours in which grown and intelligent men may labor to earn their living, are mere meddlesome interferences with the rights of the individual, and they are not saved from condemnation by the claim that they are passed in the exercise of the police power and upon the subject of the health of the individual whose rights are interfered with, unless there be some fair ground, reasonable in and of itself, to say that there is material danger to the public health, or to the health of the employees, if the hours of labor are not curtailed. If this be not clearly the case, the individuals whose rights are thus made the subject of legislative interference are under the protection of the Federal Constitution regarding their liberty of contract as well as of person; and the legislature of the state has no power to limit their right as proposed in this statute. . . .

Adding to all these requirements a prohibition to enter into any contract of labor in a bakery for more than a certain number of hours a week is, in our judgment, so wholly beside the matter of a proper, reasonable, and fair provision as to run counter to that liberty of person and of free contract provided for in the Federal Constitution. . . .

In our judgment it is not possible in fact to discover the connection between the number of hours a baker may work in the bakery and the healthful quality of the bread made by the workmen. The connection, if any exist, is too shadowy and thin to build any argument for the interference of the legislature. If the man works ten hours a day it is all right, but if ten and a half or eleven, his health is in danger and his bread may be unhealthy, and, therefore, he shall not be permitted to do it. This, we think, is unreasonable and entirely arbitrary. . . .

It is manifest to us that the limitation of the hours of labor as provided for in this section of the statute under which the indictment was found, and the plaintiff in error convicted, has no such direct relation to, and no such substantial effect upon, the health of the employee, as to justify us in regarding the section as really a health law. It seems to us that the real object and purpose were simply to regulate the hours of labor between the master and his employee (all being men, *sui juris*) in a private business, not dangerous in any degree to morals, or in any real and substantial degree to the health of the employees. Under such circumstances the freedom of master and employee to contract with each other in relation to their employment, and in defining the same, cannot be prohibited or interfered with, without violating the Federal Constitution.

Two other opinions, those of Judges O'Brien and Bartlett, are interesting for the light they throw upon their authors' knowledge of present industrial conditions. Judge O'Brien alludes to the antiquity of the bakers' vocation, and also to its universality. It is a process found in every home in the land, as well as in places called bakeries, where bread is made for sale to the public. It has never been supposed that it was a trade or vocation that was or might be dangerous to health, morals, or good order, or that there was any thing about it to justify legislation restricting the right of the master and servant to make their own contracts, express or implied, with respect to hours of work or the terms of employment. There is nothing in the record before us from which it can be inferred that there was any ground for the passage of the statute as a police regulation for the protection of health, morals, or good order, and hence it cannot be upheld as an exercise of the police power. It is a plain discrimination against a limited class of people who happen to be obliged to employ labor in the manufacture of bread, biscuit, or confectionery in those places called bakeries. This relatively small class is restricted by the statute to the regulations there prescribed with respect to the hours of labor by their employees, and is prohibited from agreeing with them as to the time they are to work, even though extra pay should be given for overwork—a right which the law gives to all other persons employing labor. If the legislature can do all this, then the right to enact what wages the servant shall receive per day or per hour must necessarily follow as an inevitable conclusion. A statute fixing the wages of the servant at such a sum as to enable him to live more comfortably could be defended as a health law by the same argument and authority adduced in support of the section of the present law, the violation of which is the only crime charged.

Judge Bartlett selects one of the extracts from the authorities cited on the matter of health and finds in that authority that the breathing of air filled with fine particles that come from grinding grain and loaf sugar may cause consumption. But evidence is not found by the Justice in the record warranting the conclusion that bakers in New York state are subject to any such peril, if any there be, as might result from grinding the articles they use. It is common experience that the baker, like the cooks in hotels, restaurants, and private families, has provided for him in his business flour, sugar, and the other ingredients duly prepared for immediate use. The claim that the compounding of these constituents, so prepared, in the business of a baker, is an unhealthy occupation, will surprise the bakers and good housewives of this state. The grinding of steel, like the needle grinding of Sheffield, England, and of other similar materials and substances, causing clouds of impalpable dust, is not to be confounded with the avocation of the family baker, engaged in the necessary and highly appreciated labor of producing bread, pies, cakes, and other commodities more calculated to cause dyspepsia in the consumer than consumption in the manufacturer. The country miller of fifty years ago, who passed a long and happy life amid the hum of machinery and the grinding process of the upper and nether stones, little dreamed of a coming day when the legislature, in the full panoply of paternalism, would rescue his successor from the appalling dangers of the life he led until old age summoned him to retire.

CHAPTER XIX

Hours of Labor—Barbers

The line of division between the trades that should and those that should not be regulated by legislation has been difficult to draw. If any trade were to be selected as the one most nearly on the border line, it would be that of the barber. Legislation applying to barbers has had reference chiefly to the keeping of barber shops open on Sunday. Concerning such laws the courts in the several states have expressed diverse opinions. Such laws have been passed and have led to judicial decisions in the courts of New York, Georgia, California, Illinois, and in the United States supreme court—all within the past fifteen years. Other state courts have also passed upon such legislation, though not in opinions that contain any new views of importance. In the states named two courts took an attitude favorable to the principle of such legislation and two unfavorable. The United States supreme court sided with the former. The two opinions which are based upon principles hostile to this legislation were both written in 1896, before the more favorable views had been expressed. The California court in its opinion (*ex parte* Jentzsch) emphasized that such legislation could not be regarded favorably " from a religious standpoint."

Under a constitution which guarantees to all equal liberty of religion and conscience, any law which forbids an act not in itself *contra bonos mores,* because that act is repugnant to the beliefs of one religious sect, of necessity interferes with the liberty of those who hold to other beliefs or to none at all.

Such laws, therefore, must be viewed as civil enactments. If declared valid at all, they must be upheld as a proper exercise of the police power.

Entering more fully into the arguments, Judge Henshaw continues:

Still it may be suggested in passing that our government was not designed to be paternal in form. We are a self-governing people, and our just pride is that our laws are made by us as well as for us. Every individual citizen is to be allowed so much liberty as may exist without impairment of the equal rights of his fellows. Our institutions are founded upon the conviction that we are not only capable of self-government as a community, but, what is the logical necessity, that we are capable, to a great extent, of individual self-government. If this conviction shall prove ill founded, we have built our house upon sand. The spirit of a system such as ours is therefore at total variance with that which, more or less veiled, still shows in the paternalism of other nations. . . .

In brief, we give to the individual the utmost possible amount of personal liberty, and with that guaranteed him, he is treated as a person of responsible judgment, not as a child in his nonage, and is left free to work out his destiny as impulse, education, training, heredity, and environment direct him. So, while the police power is one whose proper use makes most potently for good, in its undefined scope and inordinate exercise lurks no small danger to the republic, for the difficulty which is experienced in defining its just limits and bounds affords a temptation to the legislature to encroach upon the rights of citizens with experimental laws none the less dangerous because well meant. We think the act under consideration gives plain evidence of such encroachment.

The laboring barber, engaged in a most respectable, useful, and cleanly pursuit, is singled out from the thousands of his fellows in other employments, and told that, willy nilly, he shall not work upon holidays and Sundays after 12 o'clock noon. His wishes, tastes, or necessities are not consulted. If he labors, he is a criminal. Such protection to labor, carried a little further, would send him from the jail to the poorhouse. How comes it that the legislative eye was so keen to discern the needs of the oppressed barber, and yet was blind to his toiling brethren in other vocations? Steam car and street car operatives toil through long and weary Sunday hours, so do mill and factory hands. There is no Sunday period of rest, and no protection for the overworked employees of our daily papers. Do these not need rest and protection? The bare suggestion of these considerations shows the injustice and inequality of this law.

The Illinois court (Eden *v.* People) came to the same conclusion as that reached by the California court, though by a somewhat different process of reasoning. Under the laws of Illinois, the court asserts, every citizen is left perfectly free to labor and transact business on Sunday, or refrain from labor and business, as he may choose, so long as he does not disturb the peace and good order of society. The act in question attempts to inaugurate "a radical change in the law as to a class of the laboring element of the state, the barbers." The relation of this act to property right is explained in the following manner by Chief Justice Craig.

The owner of a place who carries on the business of a barber is prohibited from doing any business whatever during one day in the week. He may have in his employ a dozen men, and yet during one day in seven he is deprived of their labor, and also deprived of his own labor. The income derived from his place and his own labor and the labor of his employees is his property, but the legislature has by the act taken that property away from him. The journeyman barber who works by the day or week or for a share of the amount he may receive from customers for his services is by the law denied the right of laboring one day in the week. He may rely solely upon his labor for the support of himself and family, his labor may be the only property that he possesses, and yet this law takes that property away from him. His labor is his capital, and that capital is all the property he owns. Can a law which takes that from the laborer be sustained? The constitution of the United States says the state shall not deprive any person of property without due process of law, and our state constitution declares the same thing.

Due process of law, continues the opinion, comprehends laws that are general public laws, " binding upon all the members of the community, under all circumstances; and not partial or private laws, affecting the rights of private individuals or classes of individuals." The law in question is then tested by this formula. It does not affect merchants, clerks, restaurant keepers or employees, blacksmiths, those engaged in clothing houses, livery stables, street car lines, or in fact any branch of business except that of the barber. " He alone is required to close his place of business." " The barber is thus deprived of property without due process of law, in direct violation of the constitution of the United States and of this state."

The opinion then refers to the claim that this legislation thus dealing with the barber, this discrimination against that calling and that alone, may be justified as an act within the police power. It deals with this argument as follows:

It will not and cannot be claimed that the law in question was passed as a sanitary measure, or that it has any relation whatever to the health of society. As has been heretofore seen, as a general rule a police regulation has reference to the health, comfort, safety and welfare of society. How, it may be asked, is the health, the comfort, safety, or welfare of society to be injuriously affected by the keeping open a barber shop on Sunday? It is a matter of common observation that the barber business, as carried on in this state, is both quiet and orderly. Indeed, it is shown by the evidence incorporated in the record that the barber business, as conducted, is quiet and orderly, much more so than many other departments of business. In view of the nature of the business and the manner in which it is carried on, it is difficult to perceive how the rights of any person can be affected, or how the comfort or welfare of society can be disturbed. If the act was one calculated to promote the health, comfort, safety, and welfare of society, then it might be regarded as an exercise of the police power of the state. . . . If the public welfare of the state demands that all business and all labor of every description except work of necessity and charity should cease on Sunday, the first day of the week, and that day shall be kept as a day of rest, the legislature has the power to enact a law requiring all persons to refrain from their ordinary callings on that day . . . and in order that Sunday may be kept as a day of rest then all will be placed on a perfect equality, and no one can complain of an unjust discrimination. But when the legislature undertakes to single out one class of labor, harmless in itself, and condemn that, and that alone, it transcends its legitimate powers and its action cannot be sustained.

The reasoning followed in support of such legislation may be shown from the opinion of the New York court in People *v.* Havnor. The "vital question," declares Judge Vann, "is whether the real purpose of the statute under consideration has a reasonable connection with the public health, welfare, or safety." To the court the object of the act seemed to be to regulate the trade of the barber on Sunday. This regulation obviously had no reference to forcing the observance of Sunday as a holy day or to effecting a religious end in any way. This purpose being obvious, the justification for it is found on two grounds.

(1) The peculiar character of the first day of the week, not simply on account of the obligations of religion, but as a day of rest and recreation, has been recognized from time out of mind both by the legislature and the courts. Statutes passed upon the subject while we were a colony of Great Britain, as well as under the various constitutions in force since our organization as a state, have, so far as appears, been uniformly enforced by the courts. . . . The rule is believed to be general throughout the Union, although not generally enforced, that the ordinary business of life shall be suspended on Sunday, in order that thereby the physical and moral well-being of the people may be advanced. The inconvenience to some is not regarded as an argument against the constitutionality of the statute, as that is an incident to all general laws. . . . While works of charity and necessity have usually been excepted from the effect of laws relating to the Sabbath, and sometimes, also, those persons who keep another day of the week, still quiet pursuits have not, even when they can be carried on without the labor of others, because general respect and observance of the day, so far as practicable, have been deemed essential to the interest of the public, including, as a part thereof, those who prefer not to keep the day, as their health and morals are entitled to protection, even against their will, the same as those of any other class in the community. According to the common judgment of civilized men, public economy requires, for sanitary reasons, a day of general rest from labor, and the day naturally selected is that regarded as sacred by the greatest number of citizens, as this causes the least inconvenience through interference with business.

(2) It is to the interest of the state to have strong, robust, healthy citizens, capable of self-support, of bearing arms, and of adding to the resources of the country. Laws to effect this purpose, by protecting the citizen from overwork, and requiring a general day of rest to restore his strength and preserve his health, have an obvious connection with the public welfare. Independent of any question relating to morals or religion, the physical welfare of the citizen is a subject of such primary

importance to the state, and has such a direct relation to the general good, as to make laws tending to promote that object proper under the police power, and hence valid under the constitution, which "presupposes its existence, and is to be construed with reference to that fact." . . . The statute under discussion tends to effect this result, because it requires persons, engaged in a kind of business that takes many hours each day, to refrain from carrying it on during one day in seven. This affords an opportunity, recurring at regular intervals, for rest, needed both by the employer and the employed, and the latter, at least, may not have the power to observe a day of rest without the aid of legislation. As Mr. Tiedeman says, in his work on Police Powers: "If the law did not interfere, the feverish, intense desire to acquire wealth, . . . inciting a relentless rivalry and competition, would ultimately prevent not only the wage earners, but likewise the capitalists and employers themselves, from yielding to the warnings of nature, and obeying the instinct of self-preservation, by resting periodically from labor." As barbers generally work more hours each day than most men, the legislature may well have concluded that legislation was necessary for the protection of their health. We think that this statute was intended and is adapted to promote the public health, and thereby to serve a public purpose of the utmost importance, by promoting the observance of Sunday as a day of rest. It follows, therefore, that it does not go beyond the limits of legislative power by depriving any one of liberty or property within the meaning of the constitution.

To this line of reasoning, the United States supreme court gave its assent in the case appealed to it from the Minnesota court (Petit *v.* State). Chief Justice Fuller wrote the opinion, in which he cited with approval a passage written by Justice Field while he was a member of the California court. The requirement of the law, says Justice Field, is a cessation from labor. In its enactment the legislature has given the sanction of law to a rule of conduct which the entire civilized world recognizes as essential to the physical and moral well-being of society. Upon no subject is there such a concurrence of opinion, among philosophers, moralists, and statesmen of all nations, as on the necessity of periodical cessations from labor. One day in seven is the rule, founded in experience, and sustained by science. . . . The prohibition of secular business on Sunday is advocated on the ground that by it the general welfare is advanced, labor protected, and the moral and physical well-being of society promoted.

Justice Fuller then turns to the opinion that had been handed down by the Minnesota supreme court and cites the following extract:

Courts will take judicial notice of the fact that, in view of the custom to keep barber shops open in the evening as well as in the day, the employees in them work more, and during later, hours than those engaged in most other occupations, and that this is especially true on Saturday afternoons and evenings; also that, owing to the habit of so many men to postpone getting shaved until Sunday, if such shops were to be permitted to be kept open on Sunday, the employees would ordinarily be deprived of rest during half of that day.

In view of all these facts we cannot say that the legislature has exceeded the limits of its legislative police power in declaring that, as a matter of law, keeping barber shops open on Sunday is not a work of necessity or charity, while as to all other kinds of labor they have left that question to be determined as one of fact.

Commenting upon this view, the Chief Justice adds in closing:

We recognize the force of the distinctions suggested and perceive no adequate ground for interfering with the wide discretion confessedly necessarily exercised by the states in these matters, by holding that the classification was so palpably arbitrary as to bring the law into conflict with the Federal Constitution.

CHAPTER XX

Tenements

The regulation of sweat-shop work by law has been greatly affected by the view early taken by the New York courts. In 1885 an effort was made to put a stop to sweating by the enactment of a law prohibiting the making of cigars and other tobacco products in the tenement houses of cities of the first class. This law was taken to the highest court of the state and a decision secured adverse to the statute. The opinion written in this court has attracted wide attention and has had wide influence both on courts in reaching decisions on other cases and on legislatures in framing and passing laws for the removal of industrial evils. It has also called forth from sources both varied and weighty criticisms as vigorous as have been offered touching any decision since that in the Dred Scott case. To make the law effective it was found necessary to draw it up in a specific form embodying details that would make both its meaning and its application clear. The act was designated as "an act to improve the public health by prohibiting the manufacture of cigars and preparations of tobacco in any form in tenement houses in certain cases, and regulating the use of tenement houses in certain cases." To make the enforcement of the law possible, it was deemed necessary to state expressly that the manufacture was prohibited in any part of any floor of any tenement house if such part of such floor was occupied for living purposes. A tenement house was defined as any house occupied as a home by more than three families living independently. If there was a tobacco store on the first floor, the law was not to apply to that entire floor. The law visited a penalty upon any person found guilty either of violating or of causing another to violate the act. Justice Earl wrote the opinion of the court and there was no dissent.

The point of view of the court is shown in its answer to a question asked by itself: " What does this act attempt to do?" Its answer is:

In form, it makes it a crime for a cigar-maker in New York or Brooklyn . . . to carry on a perfectly lawful trade in his own home. Whether he owns the tenement house or has hired a room therein for the purpose of prosecuting his trade, he cannot manufacture therein his own tobacco into cigars for his own use or for sale, and he will become a criminal for doing that which is perfectly lawful outside of the two cities named—everywhere else so far as we are able to learn in the whole world.

He must either abandon the trade by which he earns a livelihood for himself and family, or, if able, procure a room elsewhere, or hire himself out to one who has a room upon such terms as, under the fierce competition of trade and the inexorable laws of supply and demand, he may be able to obtain from his employer. He may choose to do his work where he can have the supervision of his family and their help, and such choice is denied him. He may choose to work for himself rather than for a taskmaster, and he is left without freedom of choice. He may desire the advantage of cheap production in consequence of his cheap rent and family help, and of this he is deprived. In the unceasing struggle for success and existence which pervades all societies of men, he may be deprived of that which will enable him to maintain his hold, and to survive. He may go to a tenement house, and finding no one living, sleeping, cooking or doing any household work upon one of the floors, hire a room upon such floor to carry on his trade, and afterward some one may commence to sleep or to do some household work upon such floor, even without his knowledge and he at once becomes a criminal in consequence of another's act. He may go to a tenement house, and finding but two families living therein independently, hire a room, and afterward by subdivision of the families, or a change in their mode of life, or in some other way, a fourth family begins to live therein independently, and thus he may become a criminal without the knowledge, or possibly the means of knowledge that he was violating any law. It is, therefore, plain that this law interferes with the profitable and free use of his property by the owner or lessee of a tenement house who is a cigarmaker, and trammels him in the application of his industry and the disposition of his labor, and thus, in a strictly legitimate sense, it arbitrarily deprives him of his property and of some portion of his personal liberty. . . .

Property may be destroyed, or its value may be annihilated. It is owned and kept for some useful purpose and it has no value unless it can be used. Its capability for enjoyment and adaptability to some use are essential characteristics and attributes without which property cannot be conceived, and hence any law which destroys it or its value, or takes away any of its essential attributes, deprives the owner of his property. . . .

If the legislature has the power under the constitution to prohibit the prosecution of one lawful trade in a tenement house, then it may prevent the prosecution of all trades therein.

The law further infringes upon the right of liberty. To deprive of liberty actual imprisonment is not necessary. One may be deprived of liberty in other ways.

Liberty, in its broad sense as understood in this country, means the right, not only of freedom from actual servitude, imprisonment or restraint, but the right of one to use his faculties in all lawful ways, to live and work where he will, to earn his livelihood in any lawful calling, and to pursue any lawful trade or avocation. All laws therefore which impair or trammel these rights, which limit one in his choice of a trade or profession, or confine him to work or live in a specified locality, or exclude him from his own house, or restrain his otherwise lawful movements (except as such laws may be passed in the exercise by the legislature of the police power, which will be noticed later), are infringements upon his fundamental rights of liberty, which are under constitutional protection.

As to the police power, the court agrees that it is very broad and comprehensive and may be used in the interests of public health, comfort, safety and welfare. Liberty and property may be regulated by it. But broad as this power is, it is not limitless. It is not above the Constitution. In its exercise "the legislature must respect the great fundamental rights guaranteed by the Constitution." Otherwise there would be no limitation at all upon the legislature, and "every right of the citizen might be invaded and every constitutional barrier swept away" by an assumed relation of the act to public health, welfare, or safety. This relation between means and end must be apparent.

Personal rights and private property cannot be arbitrarily invaded, and the determination of the legislature is not final or conclusive. If it passes an act ostensibly for the public health, and thereby destroys or takes away the property of a citizen, or interferes with his personal liberty, then it is for the courts to scrutinize the act and see whether it really relates to and is convenient and appropriate to promote the public health. It matters not that the legislature may in the title to the act, or in its body, declare that it is intended for the improvement of the public health. Such a declaration does not conclude the courts, and they must yet determine the fact declared and enforce the supreme law. . . . It may be difficult sometimes to determine whether a use is public or private.

Although the legislature may declare it to be public, that does not necessarily determine its character, it must in fact be public, and if it be not, no legislative fiat can make it so, and any owner of property attempted to be taken for a use really private can invoke the aid of the courts to protect his property rights against invasion. . . . These citations are apt to show how the police power may and how it ought not to be exercised, and how far its exercise is subject to judicial inquiry.

After stating these principles that govern the exercise of police power, the application is made to the law itself. " What possible relation," it asks, " can cigarmaking in any building have to the health of the general public?" And again " If the legislature had in mind the protection of the occupants of tenement houses, why was the act confined in its operation to the two cities only?" " What possible relation to the health of the occupants of a large tenement house could cigarmaking in one of its remote rooms have?" The answers to these questions are stated so clearly in the opinion as to leave no doubt of the view that was held. The law, it insists, does not deal with tenement houses as such; it does not regulate their population nor the method of their construction. It deals mainly with the preparation of tobacco and the manufacture of cigars. " Judicial notice " is then taken of the " nature and qualities of tobacco." Here is set forth its general use among civilized men, and the extent of the industry by which it is prepared for the market. The process of the manufacture is not one that is injurious to the health of those engaged in it, much less to the public health. These matters are taken up in some detail. Following this more general consideration, the opinion proceeds:

To justify this law it would not be sufficient that the use of tobacco may be injurious to some persons, or that its manipulation may be injurious to those who are engaged in its preparation and manufacture; but it would have to be injurious to the public health. This law was not intended to protect the health of those engaged in cigar-making, as they are allowed to manufacture cigars everywhere except in the forbidden tenement houses. It cannot be perceived how the cigar-maker is to be improved in his health or his morals by forcing him from his home and its hallowed associations and beneficent influences, to ply his trade elsewhere. It was not intended to protect the health of that portion of the public not residing in the forbidden tenement houses, as cigars are allowed to be manufactured in private houses, in large factories, and shops in the two crowded cities, and in all other parts of the state. What possible relation can cigar-making in any building have to the health of the general public? Nor was it intended to improve or protect the health of the occupants of tenement houses. If there are but three families in the tenement house, however numerous and gregarious their members may be, the manufacture is not forbidden; and it matters not how large the number of occupants may be if they are not divided into more than three families living and cooking independently. If a store is kept for the sale of cigars on the first floor of one of these houses, and thus more tobacco is kept there than otherwise would be, and the baneful influence of tobacco, if any, is thus increased, the floor, however numerous its occupants, or the occupants of the house, is exempt from the operation of the act. What possible relation to the health of the occupants of a large tenement house could cigar-making in one of its remote rooms have? If the legislature had in mind the protection of the occupants of tenement houses, why was the act confined in its operation to the two cities only? It is plain that this is not a health law, and that it has no relation whatever to the public health. Under the guise of promoting the public health the legislature might as well have banished cigar-making from all the cities of the state, or confined it to a single city or town, or have placed under a similar ban the trade of a baker, of a tailor, of a shoemaker, of a woodcarver, or of any other of the innocuous trades carried on by artisans in their own homes. The power would have been the same, and its exercise, so far as it concerns fundamental, constitutional rights, could have been justified by the same arguments. . . . Such governmental interferences disturb the normal adjustments of the social fabric, and usually derange the delicate and complicated machinery of industry and cause a score of ills while attempting the removal of one.

When a health law is challenged in the courts as unconstitutional on the ground that it arbitrarily interferes with personal liberty and private property without due process of law, the courts must be able to see that it has at least in fact some relation to the public health, that the public health is the end actually aimed at, and that it is appropriate and adapted to that end. This we have not been able to see in this law, and we must, therefore, pronounce it unconstitutional and void.

CHAPTER XXI

CONDITIONS VERSUS PRECEDENT

THE opinions that are here grouped together under the general heading, Legislation, have a common element notwithstanding the diversity of the measures which called them forth. The cases are on the border line between what is demanded by the *laissez faire* policy and social legislation; between the policy which confines the activity of government within the narrowest bounds and that which imposes restrictions upon the liberty of the individual in the interest of a larger social freedom.

Strict adherence to the *laissez faire* policy has passed quite entirely into the realm of history. Factory legislation, numerous in its items and varied in its requirements, is an accepted fact. Courts do not question the right to enact such statutes in the interest of public health, morals, safety and welfare. Sanitary conditions, safety devices, fire escapes, child labor, tenement-house conditions,—these suggest the broad field which is included in the term "factory laws" and in which legal regulation is universally recognized as valid. The related lines of legislation that have been considered are not so generally accepted as valid. Such laws are in the border land between strict factory laws and laws that do not so clearly contribute to public health, morals, safety or welfare. It is to this group of laws and the opinions which they have called forth that consideration has been restricted. A comparison of the principles upon which the various opinions are based shows a few broad generalizations running through the cases, and it is over these that the leading differences of view arise.

The first point that impresses the student is the lack of consistency in these decisions. The differences are of course due in part to the novelty of the questions involved and to the varying degrees of importance attached to the several propositions by the various judges. This inconsistency is not confined to differences of view on the part of different courts upon questions essentially the same in principle, such as screening coal, scrip payment or hours of labor in mines. It extends to the attitude assumed by the same court on questions the underlying principles of which are not essentially unlike.

The United States supreme court allows the validity of a law restricting the hours of labor of women in factories to ten a day and refuses approval of a law imposing a similar restriction upon labor in bakeries. The New York court insists that the restriction of hours of labor for bakers is valid but declines to approve a law prohibiting night work for women. This same New York court which insists that women must be protected in their right to work at night endorses a law preventing barbers from working on Sundays. Concerning barbers, this court declares:

> It is to the interest of the state to have strong, robust, healthy citizens, capable of self-support, of bearing arms, and of adding to the resources of the country. Laws to effect this purpose, by protecting the citizen from overwork, and requiring a general day of rest to restore his strength and preserve his health, have an obvious connection with the public welfare.

In rejecting the law preventing night work for women the same court said: " It might be observed that working in a factory in the night hours is not the only situation of menace to the working women."

Such instances as these will indicate the essential newness of the situation to the courts. The differences of view and the inconsistency will doubtless disappear in time. Reversals of opinion, though infrequent, are not unknown; and changing conditions are becoming so evident to all that they will very probably prove to be determining in these cases and cause views that are now rejected to be generally accepted.

The most striking contrast afforded by the various opinions is in the extent to which some courts cling to precedent and to an historic reading of certain familiar constitutional phrases, while others give full recognition to prevailing conditions and declare precedents inapplicable to the new situation. The degree of emphasis placed upon one or the other of these different attitudes leads to conclusions that are of vital importance. It means the acceptance or the rejection, the constitutionality or the unconstitutionality, of laws enacted by legislative bodies when such laws were enacted with the evident intent to meet some real want or to afford relief from an undesirable situation. It is of inestimable importance whether courts attach greater significance to changing conditions as reasons for new legislation or to judicial precedents as reasons for rejecting such legislation.

To indicate the importance of this difference in attitude on the part of the judges some of the contrasts shown in the different decisions may be recalled here. First there is that difference of attitude which is due to changes extending over a considerable period of time. Two hundred years or so ago it was the accepted legal view that wages could be fixed so as to correspond with the just wage. Neither party was supposed to have any direct influence. In England the fixing was to be done by the justice of the peace. That these justices were often employers, or of the class whose interests were most nearly akin to those of the employers, did not seem to strike any one as incongruous except occasionally the laborers themselves. The latter were helpless because the law stood directly in the way of their expressing in any effective way their dissatisfaction. Wages were thus fixed largely in the interest of employers. When, however, organizations of laborers were made lawful and some of their efforts to determine wages were recognized as legal it began to appear that wages should be fixed only by competition. When the laborers began to fix wages by strikes the courts were appealed to. These found in favor of competition. The whole view changed and the arbitrary fixing of wages was no longer approved. So long as the employer stood the better chance in the competition, competition seemed to the employing class the most satisfactory basis. Where labor legislation and labor organization have succeeded in strengthening the hands of the laborer in his bargaining activities, there has come the severest test of the attitude that the court should assume. Should the principles of competition in harmony with a philosophy of individualism obtain or should they yield to the principles of organization and coöperation in harmony with a philosophy of socialization?

Not to trace this development through all of its phases, for the story is a long one, it may be illustrated in a typical instance. It is that of laws in which is inserted the "require or permit" clause. Whether applied to hours of labor, payment of wages or to conditions to be regulated in special trades the question arises: is a law forbidding an employer either to require or to permit the employee to do the thing dealt with in the law a violation of the employee's right to contract? On the face of it, it certainly seems as if there were such a restriction. Experience in a variety of laws has shown however that such a phrase in the law is quite necessary to the accomplishment of the purpose intended.

Earlier laws sought to accomplish the object and at the same time to leave the freedom of contract undisturbed. In Illinois the law of 1867 established eight hours as the legal working day in certain employments, but added the clause " where there is no special contract or agreement to the contrary." A second section of this law contained the further statement: " nor shall any person be prevented by anything herein contained from working as many hours overtime or extra hours as he or she may agree." In New York the experience was much the same. The law of 1867 read: " eight hours of labor, between the rising and setting of the sun, shall be deemed and held to be a legal day's work, in all cases of labor and service by the day, where there is no contract or agreement to the contrary." In 1870 the measure was extended so as to include laborers for the state. It then read: " eight hours shall constitute a legal day's work for all classes of mechanics, working men and laborers, excepting those engaged in farm and domestic labor; but overwork for an extra compensation by agreement between employer and employee is hereby permitted." In Pennsylvania a law of 1875 provided for the payment by weight for mining coal, and added to its other provisions a clause further providing that the act should not apply to operators who should make a contract with their employees for some other manner of compensation. Commenting upon the practical working of this statute the Anthracite Coal Strike Commission says:

It may seem strange, but from all the evidence before the Commission the undoubted fact appears to be, that the requirements of this law have never been complied with. It is alleged by the counsel for the operators that they have never been applicable for the reason that the situation came within the purview of the last proviso of the section quoted which exempts from its provisions all cases where the employer shall by contract agree with his miners otherwise than is provided in the said statute for their compensation.[1]

A striking instance of this failure on the part of the court to comprehend the real situation and to enter into an appreciation of the reasons that led the legislature to enact the law is found in the experience of California.[2] The "truck system" and the "time check" system prevailed as a method of wage payment. The evils early attracted the attention of the State Labor Commissioner. In 1885 he reported that in the construction of the San Francisco sea wall "only patrons of the company boarding house could retain their places with a certain firm." The lumber industry, because of its isolation, was among the worst offenders. The several published reports of the Labor Commissioner show that

> some of the lumber companies have availed themselves of every possible opportunity to rob their employees systematically. Not satisfied with profits of the company store, boarding-house, and bar, an even more effective means of extortion was discovered. The monthly wages of the men were paid with time-checks due in thirty, sixty, or even ninety days. Those who had families to support, or needed ready money for other purposes could obtain it only by cashing these checks at a heavy discount.

In 1891, a law was enacted requiring payment of wages at regular intervals, either weekly or monthly as the company should elect, but specifying the time definitely. The corporations evaded the intent of the law by using time-checks. In the Labor Commissioner's report of 1895-96 these time-checks are referred to as a "dreadful curse," and further

[1] Bul. U. S. Bureau of Labor, No. 46, pp. 483, 484.

[2] Eaves, *History of California Labor Legislation*, pp. 257, 258.

legislation is urged. Finally the law was enacted requiring payment of wages in lawful money payable monthly. No corporation could require and no employee could make an agreement for a longer period of payment. The law was then taken to the court. There it was declared unconstitutional on the ground that it was class legislation inasmuch as it required of corporations what it did not require of individuals. The conditions that prevailed, the injustices imposed upon the men working for these corporations, and the very direct and obvious relation between such conditions and relations and the law seem not to have impressed the court as of any importance compared with the fact that corporations, who were the offenders in the matter, were being treated in a special manner.

In several opinions the practical necessity of these words is recognized. In other cases they constitute a stumbling block over which the court has fallen into the error of misjudging the real situation. It was the United States supreme court that held in the Bakeshop case that

> the mandate of the statute, that " no employee shall be required or permitted to work," is the substantial equivalent of an enactment that " no employee shall contract or agree to work " more than ten hours per day. [The statute is] an absolute prohibition upon the employer permitting, under any circumstances, more than ten hours' work to be done in his establishment. The employee may desire to earn the extra money which would arise from his working more than the prescribed time, but this statute forbids the employer from permitting the employee to earn it.

In earlier times beyond question long hours of labor have been sought by laborers in many instances where the advantages accrued quite entirely to the laborer. That such is the case now it seems almost incredible that anyone could believe. The employees of today are not in fact looking for long hours or any other conditions of labor that are to them unfavorable. The employer on the other hand is anxious for such conditions. All that the employer has needed in order to secure the working conditions most acceptable to him is to have the employee left free to work long hours. With the unequal bargaining power that characterizes the situation it has been an easy matter for him to induce the worker to agree to work for any length of day or under any conditions of payment that satisfied the employer. The practical effect of the position taken by the courts has been that they have come to the assistance of employers with the doctrine of personal liberty and the employers' ends have been gained. The entire force of the statute was in the word "permit." Without it the law was of no consequence. With it the law was of importance in actually tending to equalize the conditions of bargaining.

Efforts so persistently made by organized labor to discourage overtime work take on a meaning not always attributed to them when viewed in the light of this conflict. It is briefly expressed in a resolution adopted by the American Federation of Labor and published in the *American Federationist*.[1] "We advise strongly against the practice which now exists in some industries of working overtime, beyond the established hours of labor. . . It is an instigator of the basest selfishness, a radical violation of union principles, and . . . it tends to set back the general movement for an eight hour day." A further comment upon the same situation comes from the report of the Committee of One Hundred on National Health in its *Bulletin on National Vitality*.[2] Writing under the general heading, "Things Which Need to be Done," the following

[1] Vol. iv, p. 187.

[2] P. 128.

statement is made: "In industrial and commercial establishments employers may greatly aid the health movement . . . by providing . . . physiological (generally shorter) hours of work."

What shall be done, it may be asked, when such movements, kept within reasonable limits and undertaken for the benefit of those classes who know their own interests but are unable to protect them in the field of freedom of contract, are blocked by the courts.

In the New York Tenement House case two conflicting principles were brought face to face which the court failed to adjust. As a result of the decision but one of the principles could survive. There was the principle of right to private property and its use which the constitution protected. The manufacture of cigars was an enterprise that had won for itself a standing in the industrial world. To prohibit such manufacture in the rooms of a tenement house was a restriction upon the pursuit of a legal occupation and upon the use of property, and for this restriction the court could not be convinced of any need. That the law was a protection to home life, that tenement house conditions and the solution of tenement house problems had anything to do with the law, the court could not appreciate. On the contrary the court insisted that the law was an invasion of the home life. It forced those who wished to work to leave home and go to the factory. Perhaps the climax of the opinion is reached when the judge so far misunderstands the home of the tenement house where cigars are made and other sweatshop work is done as to insist that he cannot perceive how the cigar maker "is to be improved in his health or his morals by forcing him from his home and its hallowed associations and beneficent influences."

The conclusion in this case was so evidently reached

wholly without reference to conditions in tenement houses, and the opinion has been so pointedly and so justly criticized by others that it will not be necessary to urge it further as evidence of the attitude under consideration.

The New York Bakeshop case is even more important and has been quoted at length in the preceding pages. In the several opinions written, the influence of both precedent and conditions is clearly seen. The New York court seems to have been less bound by precedent in this case than the federal court. It was precedent that led to the overthrow of a law which had seemed so necessary to the people of New York state that it had been passed by the legislature and approved by the state court as a legitimate exercise of the police power in the interests of public welfare. The dangers to health from bakeshop work and the extensive citations of evidence in support of the fact could not be made to outweigh in the judges' minds the belief that the trade of the baker was as old as civilization itself and that "it has never been supposed that it was a trade or vocation that was or might be dangerous to health, morals or good order," and that the "claim that the compounding of these constituents, so prepared, in the business of a baker, is an unhealthy occupation, will surprise the bakers and good housewives of this state." The majority of the members of the Federal court, however, were ready to admit in face of the evidence that the trade of a baker was an unhealthy one but would not concede that it was unhealthy "to that degree which would authorize the legislature to interfere with the right to labor, and with the right of free contract on the part of the individual, either as employer or employee. . . . To the common understanding the trade of a baker has never been regarded as an unhealthy one."

In addition to these two important cases a number of

others may be added. Judge Cooper of California (Johnson *v.* Goodyear Mining Co.) argued that a law requiring payment of wages at the end of every month prohibited the corporation and the employee from making any other contract for the payment of wages. That the workingmen did not need any such legislation seems to the judge quite certain.

> The working man of intelligence is treated as an imbecile. Being over twenty-one years of age, and not a lunatic or insane, he is deprived of the right to make a contract as to the time when his wages shall become due. . . . The parties, being able to contract and willing to contract and desiring for the good of each other to contract, are by this statute forbidden to do so.

Considering an Indiana law requiring weekly payment of wages in cash, Judge Hadley takes much the same view. The Attorney General had argued before the court that conditions demanded the law. This he based on the claim that "wage earners are not upon an equal footing with employers, and opportunities for oppression and consequent public suffering ensue" and further that "thrift being beneficial to the community, it should be encouraged by enabling workmen to pay cash for current demands, which can only be done by requiring frequent payment of wages." To these considerations growing out of conditions that seemed evident, the court in the opinion answers:

> Assuming all these things to be true, they do not of themselves justify the arbitrary invasion of the personal rights and liberty of the citizen. Liberty to contract on one's own terms, to decide for himself his own employment, to buy and sell, to exchange one belonging for another, are among his most valuable and cherished rights.

Frorer *v.* People was a case that has had wide influence.

Its opinion has been quoted in other states in a number of cases where the same principle was involved. The law forbade mining companies to keep truck stores. This seemed to the Illinois court as altogether beyond the province of the legislature. The court could see the justification of laws which would affect the mechanical processes of mining and manufacturing. But this law, says the court, operates upon the individual, because of his participation in the business.

It is not imposed for the purpose of rendering mining and manufacturing less perilous or laborious, nor to restrict or regulate the duties of employer and employee in respects peculiar to those industries, but for the sole purpose of imposing disabilities in contracting as to tools, clothing and food—matters about which all laborers must contract, and as to which all laborers in every other branch of industry are permitted to contract with their employers without any restriction.

In a similar way the Missouri court in State *v.* Loomis admitted the right of the legislature to regulate the business of mining and manufacturing so as to secure health and safety of employees. It could not, however, single out persons engaged in carrying on these pursuits and forbid them from contracting to work for such form of payment as they might choose. Every law, declares Judge Gordon of Pennsylvania, that proposes to prevent the laborer from selling his labor for what he thinks best "is an infringement of his constitutional privileges and consequently vicious and void." Finally the opinion in *In re* Morgan may be referred to for the same purpose. Here, wholly without regard to conditions of labor and effect upon health, it is declared that the right of miners to work must not be interfered with. An act which would limit the hours of work in underground mines and smelters is "obnoxious to the provisions of our bill of rights . . . which guarantee to all persons their natural and inalienable right to personal liberty, and the right of acquiring, possessing and protecting property." Later in the opinion it is argued that since the smelting process is a continuous process it can make no difference to the public health whether the work be done by two shifts working twelve hours each or by three shifts working eight hours each. "The only object," says the judge, "that can rationally be claimed for it is the preservation of the health of those working in the smelters." This does not characterize the act as one dealing with the public health and therefore the act cannot stand.

While such views as the above are expressed by some of the judges other views find their way into the opinions from other courts. These show clearly that real conditions are taken into consideration and that they may even outweigh the force of precedent as expressed in earlier interpretations of certain constitutional phrases. Of this attitude the instances are numerous. Some of the more important have been chosen as illustrative of the much larger number.

In his dissenting opinion in Adair *v.* United States Justice Holmes refers particularly to the conditions as he sees them,—conditions of inequality of bargaining power as to wages and conditions of employment. It seems to him that the section of the law in question "simply prohibits the more powerful party to exact certain undertakings, or to threaten dismissal or unjustly discriminate on certain grounds against those already employed." As to the reality of individual rights secured by the Fifth Amendment, it seems that the real truth of the situation is, to the mind of the Justice, expressed in his statement that "the notion of a choice of persons is a fiction and wholesale employment is necessary." Such conditions it is proper to control by statute.

In State *v.* Brown & Sharpe Manufacturing Co. (weekly payment of wages by corporations) Judge Rogers elaborated the view that the corporation has the advantage over the individual in bargaining power. "It is a matter of common knowledge," he insists, "that while corporations . . . are the richest and strongest bodies, as a rule, in the state, their employees are often the weakest and least able to protect themselves, frequently being dependent upon their current wages for their daily bread." To the claim that each individual should be left free to follow his personal choice, the reply is that "poverty and weakness can wage but an unequal contest with corporate wealth and power" and that a recognition of these facts may well form a basis of reason for the legislative act of "minimizing corporate power to drive hard bargains with their employees, who, too often in the sharp and bitter competition for work, have to submit to such terms and conditions as their employers see fit to prescribe."

In Knoxville Iron Co. *v.* Harbison, a test of the law regulating truck stores and payment of wages in cash, Justice Shiras gave the chief consideration to conditions.

The legislature, as it thought, found the employee at a disadvantage in this respect [bargaining about the manner in which wages should be paid] and by this enactment undertook to place him and the employer more nearly upon an equality. This alone commends the act and entitles it to a place on the statute book as a valid police regulation. [It is calculated to] promote the public peace and good order, and to lessen the growing tendency to strife, violence, and even bloodshed in certain departments of important trade and business.

Justice Dowling in considering a similar principle expresses an opinion very much the same. After discussing the conditions in which wage earners live making frequent cash payments necessary to their welfare, he adds that it is clear that the object of the law "was the protection of wage-earners from oppression, extortion, or fraud on the part of others, and from the consequences of their own weakness, folly or improvidence. We cannot say that no just ground existed for such legislative interference for so commendable a purpose."

Speaking from the United States supreme court bench Justice Brown points out that in the statute (restricting hours of labor in mines and smelters) the legislature had recognized

> the fact, which the experience of legislators in many states has corroborated, that the proprietors of these establishments and their operatives do not stand upon an equality, and that their interests are, to a certain extent, conflicting. . . . The proprietors lay down the rules and the laborers are practically constrained to obey them. In such cases, self-interest is often an unsafe guide, and the legislature may promptly interpose its authority. [If the legislature has power to adopt means for the protection of life] it is difficult to see why precautions may not also be adopted for the protection of their health and morals. It is as much for the interest of the state that the public health should be preserved as that life should be made secure. The fact that both parties are of full age and competent to contract does not necessarily deprive the state of the power to interfere where the parties do not stand upon an equality, or where the public health demands that one party to the contract shall be protected against himself.

Justice Lucas in a long opinion on the statute regulating the screening of coal departs from the usual contract-right considerations and argues on the basis of the conditions that prevail. The opinion is not based "so much upon the ground that the business [of mining] is affected by the public use," but upon "the still higher ground,"

> that the public tranquillity, and the good and safety of society, demand, where the number of employees is such that specific contracts with each laborer would be improbable, if not impossible, that in general contracts justice shall prevail as between operator and miner; . . . that in the company's dealing with the multitude of laborers . . . all opportunities for fraud shall be removed.

That strikes, labor conspiracies, boycotts, and other serious labor disturbances do occur is a fact of such notoriety, urges this opinion, "that the court may recognize judicially" that every disturbance of any magnitude since the civil war

> has been evolved from the disturbed relations between powerful corporations and their servants or employees, [which] endanger the safety of the state, stay the wheels of commerce, discourage manufacturing enterprise, destroy public confidence, and at times throw an idle population upon the bosom of the community. Surely the hands of the legislature cannot be so restricted as to prohibit the passage of laws directly intended to prevent and forestall such collisions.

Of this opinion Judge Cooper of the California supreme court said (Johnson *v.* Goodyear Mining Co.): "The opinion while lengthy is not convincing." Of the same opinion Professor Ely has said, that it "takes the position —a true one—that wise legislation of this sort is calculated to prevent industrial strife . . . and to maintain the public peace." [1]

Justice Day (McLean *v.* State of Arkansas) refers to the variety of opinion as expressed by several state courts (on the screening of coal). These are matters, he says, which of course each state must decide for itself. As evidence of the conditions that exist, the report of the Industrial Commission is referred to. While it is recognized that there was

[1] *Evolution of Industrial Society,* p. 416.

not entire unanimity of opinion on the part of the witnesses examined by the Commission, yet it is pointed out that

> a number of witnesses expressed opinions, based upon their experience in the mining industry, that disputes concerning the introduction and use of screens had led to frequent and sometimes heated controversies between the operators and the miners. This condition was testified to have been the result, not only of the introduction of screens as a basis of paying the miners for screened coal only, but, after the screens had been introduced, differences had arisen because of the disarrangement of the parts of the screen, resulting in weakening it, or in increasing the size of the meshes through which the coal passed, thereby preventing a correct measure of the coal as the basis of paying the miner's wages.

In the face of the evidence set forth in the report of this Commission, and in the knowledge that such legislation had been deemed necessary by the legislatures in several of the states, the court declared itself " unable to say . . . that this law had no reasonable relation to the protection of a large class of laborers in the receipt of their just dues in the promotion of the harmonious relations of capital and labor engaged in a great industry in the state."

On the question of laws restricting hours of labor for women, there are instances where the conditions were of importance in shaping the opinion. In Wenham *v.* State Judge Barnes touches on this. Even admitting that in certain industries the employers and employees are practically on an equal footing when they are adult males, " these observations do not apply to women and children. . . . The employer who seeks to obtain the most hours of labor for the least wages has such an advantage over them that the wisdom of the law for their protection cannot well be questioned." The opinion also recognizes fully the difference in strength between the sexes and accepts fully a distinction in law based upon well established facts of science. Judge Dunbar in State *v.* Buchanan reasons that while the

> principles of justice are immutable, [yet] changing conditions of society and the evolution of employment make a change in the application of principles absolutely necessary to an intelligent administration of government. In the early history of the law when employments were few and simple, the relative conditions of the citizen and the state were different, and many employments and uses which were then considered inalienable rights have since, from the very necessity of changed conditions, been subjected to legislative control, restriction and restraint.

One other instance may be cited from this same class of legislation. The federal supreme court, speaking through Justice Brewer, laid great emphasis upon the conditions and the facts established by science. These opinions, he asserts, quoted from scientific sources

> may not be, technically speaking, authorities, and in them is little or no discussion of the constitutional question presented to us for determination, yet they are significant of a widespread belief that woman's physical structure and the functions she performs in consequence thereof justify special legislation restricting or qualifying the conditions under which she should be permitted to toil.

The court will not admit that constitutional questions are to be settled by "even a consensus of present public opinion," for written constitutions place limitations on legislatures in an unchanging form and thus give "permanence and stability to popular government which otherwise would be lacking." Even in face of this general principle of great importance, the court admits that when a question of fact is debated and debatable, and the extent to which a special constitutional limitation goes is affected by the truth in respect to that fact, a widespread and long-continued belief concerning it is worthy of consideration. We take judicial cognizance of all matters of general knowledge.

That differing degrees of importance are attached to the weight of precedents is beyond question. In many cases precedent is followed and helpful legislation declared void. In others the conditions dealt with are deemed of sufficient weight to overcome the obstacle of precedent in the case and to justify the law. The former tendency gives little ground for hopefulness, but the latter justifies a good deal of optimism as to the future. A further discussion of this situation involves considerations of such fundamental importance that it will be postponed to the concluding chapter.

CHAPTER XXII

Conclusions

Underlying all the confusion of interpretation and all the differences of legal opinion revealed in the decisions that have been reviewed are certain fundamental facts. These facts explain to a large extent the cause of the differences. If the differences, the confusion, the conflicting decisions and the general feeling of dissatisfaction are to any extent to be removed these facts must be realized.

First, it is undeniable that a certain theory underlies the legal view which is not generally accepted outside of legal circles. This theory is that law is based on certain principles of justice that are eternal and immutable. It leads to the idea that legal right is an unchanging concept. Inasmuch as those legal authorities now universally accepted wrote in the age when social-contract ideas prevailed, these principles and theories were expressed in terms of the social contract and of natural rights. Judges, lawyers and text-book writers continue to use the phrases. A consequence is that the common law brought over from the past into the present is expressed quite entirely in phrases that have but little if any present application.

We find ourselves, however, in this state [New York] at the beginning of the twentieth century substantially where we were at the beginning of the nineteenth century so far as the great body of our legal principles is concerned. The same situation exists in the great majority of the other states of the union.[1]

A second great fact is that of industrial change. This is so generally recognized as to make anything more than the mere statement of it unnecessary. Such declarations as that nothing is done today as it was a quarter century ago and that the past century has witnessed greater changes than all preceding centuries combined have ceased to be startling. They are taken for granted. This change in all our activities is due largely to transitions in industry that have forced the establishment of new relations between the various industrial factors. The world at the beginning of the twentieth century is a world undreamed of a century ago. Complexity and dependence have everywhere taken the place of simplicity and independence. The acts of individuals become everywhere matters of social concern. Isolation is impossible. Interdependence is unavoidable. Here is a contrast of almost immeasurable importance. Legal development lagging so far in the rear of industrial expansion gives rise to a situation that is well nigh impossible of practical adjustment. The situation has not escaped comment. Many writers refer to "the well-known but unfortunate fact, so often commented on, that our law has not kept pace in its development with our industrial evolution."[2]

Closely related to these two great facts are two others of practical importance. The first relates to our written constitutions, state and federal. These constitutions took form at a time when the individualist philosophy dominated men's minds. The tenets of individualism were woven into

[1] Hornblower, "A Century of 'Judge-Made' Law," *Columbia Law Rev.*, vol. 7, p. 457, Nov., 1907.

[2] Ely, *Monopolies and Trusts*, p. 29.

its structure. Constitutional phrases remain that have their whole meaning in the philosophy of individualism, held in an environment in which the ideal was social and industrial, as well as political, equality. They prevailed at a time when the terms liberty, equality, justice, natural and inalienable rights were freely used and seldom defined, and when competition was regarded as the great saving factor of society, particularly in industry.

The second of this group is the fact that while these written constitutions remain practically unchanged the entire foundation of philosophy and social thought upon which at first they rested so securely has been materially altered. Individualism as expressed in the extreme *laissez faire* policy has been abandoned. Socialization and the recognition of social solidarity and social interdependence have taken its place. Greater caution prevails in the use of such terms as liberty, equality, justice and rights, and more definite meanings are demanded. Competition is no longer a word of such talismanic charm. Industrial organization is now characterized rather by coöperation and organization. The great corporations and the trusts on the one side and the great trade and labor organizations on the other are now patent facts.

Bringing these facts together,—fixed theory of the law and changing conditions of society, written constitutions based on early philosophy and industrial and social structure based on a later philosophy,—the real underlying nature of the difficulty appears. Judges are trained primarily in the law and are bound by habits of thought to follow the beaten paths marked out by the precedents of earlier years. Laws upon which they pass opinions are on the contrary essentially adapted to present-day conditions.

What is sometimes overlooked is that to our judges falls the very difficult task of reconciling elements that are almost irreconcilable. To abandon the position taken as a result of their legal training seems quite impossible to some, and is not to be expected of all of them at once. To comprehend the spirit of the times and to understand the bearing of modern conditions are quite out of the question for them until they have altered their point of view.

If the common law bore the same relation to the masses of people today that it did in former times, the situation would be relieved of much of its seriousness. This is not the case. The situation has been concisely pointed out in the following words.

> To-day for the first time the common law finds itself arrayed against the people; for the first time instead of securing for them what they most prize they know it chiefly as something that continually stands between them and what they desire. . . There is a feeling that [the common law] prevents everything and does nothing. . . . It exhibits too great a re-respect for the individual and for the intrenched, position in which our legal and political history has put him, and too little respect for the needs of society when they come in conflict with the individual to be in touch with the present age.[1]

A gleam of hope appears in Judge Dunbar's statement (State *v.* Buchanan): "While the principles of justice are immutable, changing conditions of society and the evolution of employment make a change in the application of principles absolutely necessary to an intelligent administration of government." The relic of the oldtime view may be overlooked in face of the very intelligent application that is made in this case. Interest in the truth or falsity of the statement that "the principles of justice are immutable" may be left to the realm of the academic, if the proper

[1] Pound, "Do We Need a Philosophy of Law?" *Columbia Law Rev.*, vol. v, p. 344, May, 1905.

application of these immutable principles be made. A greater feeling of security results however from the consideration that whatever "justice" may be in itself man's conception of justice must of necessity change. So long as this fact is recognized and allowed to influence opinions, it is of no practical importance whether the principles of justice be immutable and their application subject to change with changing conditions or the principles of justice themselves be mutable.

That there is a distinct tendency in legal minds to regard constitutions as unchanging and unchangeable is everywhere apparent. No clearer evidence of the point could be furnished, perhaps, than the citations that are brought together by a writer in the *Green Bag*.[1]

As long as it [the constitution] continues to exist in its present form it speaks not only in the same words, but with the same meaning and intent with which it spoke when it came from the hands of its framers. (Chief Justice Taney in Dred Scott case.)

It is evident when one considers the nature of a rigid or supreme constitution that some method of altering it so as to conform to altered facts and ideas, is indispensable. . . . Since modifications or developments are often needed, and since they can rarely be made by amendment, some other way of making them must be found. The ingenuity of lawyers has discovered one method in interpretation; while the dexterity of politicians has invented a variety of devices whereby legislation may extend, or usage may modify the express provisions of the apparently immovable and inflexible instrument. . . . The interpretation which has thus stretched the constitution to cover powers once undreamt of, may be deemed a dangerous resource. But it must be remembered that even the con-

[1] Amidon, "The Nation and the Constitution," *Green Bag*, vol. xix, pp. 594, 595, Oct., 1907.

stitutions we call rigid must take their choice between being bent and being broken. The Americans have more than once bent their constitution in order that they might not be forced to break it. . . . And it has stood because it has submitted to a process of constant though sometimes scarcely perceptible change which has adapted it to the conditions of the new age. (James Bryce.)

A constitution is not to be made to mean one thing at one time, and another at some subsequent time, when the circumstances may have so changed as, perhaps, to make a different rule in the same case seem desirable. A principal share of the benefit expected from written constitutions would be lost if the rules they established were so flexible as to bend to circumstances or be modified by public opinion. . . . A court or legislature which should allow a change in public sentiment to influence it in giving to a written constitution a construction not warranted by the intention of its framers, would be justly chargable with reckless disregard of official oath and public duty. (Cooley, *Constitutional Limitations.*)

No instrument can be the same in meaning to-day and forever and in all men's minds. As the people change so does their written constitution change also. They see it in new lights and with different eyes; events may have given unexpected illumination to some of its provisions, and what they read one way before they read a very different way now. . . . We may think we have the constitution all before us, but for practical purposes the constitution is that which the government in its several departments, and the people in the performance of their duties as citizens, recognize and respect as such, and nothing else is. Cervantes says: "Every one is the son of his own work." This is more emphatically true of an instrument of government than it can possibly be of a natural person. What it takes to itself, though at first unwarrantable, helps to make it over into a new instrument of government, and it represents at last the acts done under it. (Cooley, *History of Michigan.*)

To these views may be added that of the United States supreme court: "Constitutional questions, it is true, are not settled by even a consensus of present public opinion, for it is the peculiar value of a written constitution that it places in unchanging form limitations upon legislative action, and thus gives a permanence and stability to popular government which otherwise would be lacking." (Muller *v.* Oregon.)

In such a situation as has been outlined, it is impossible to secure with any promptness a satisfactory adjustment between the opinions of courts and the needs of a live industrial society.

The practical nature of the difficulty appears again when one considers the functions of courts in our system of government. It will be generally agreed that if these functions are to be stated briefly they will be declared to be the regulation of legislation in such a way as to keep it consistent with the constitution. The constitutions state the fundamental principles. The laws make application of these principles to the detailed work of social activity. Consistency must be maintained between these laws and the fundamental or constitutional law. This court function is not difficult to perform in a satisfactory manner so long as the fundamental principles are such as enable the society to do what it aims to do. The forcing of minor matters into accord with those of major importance may occasion some hardship but not to such an extent as to interfere seriously with the necessary adjustment. When, however, fundamental or constitutional principles cease to be in accordance with and expressive of social aims the clash becomes a serious one. With this important work to perform, no one can deny the pre-eminence of the courts in our political system. As an agency for preserving the basic principles of a civilization the courts deserve all the recognition and all the honor that they receive. So far as they keep these basic principles alive and make them a vital force, the courts do their work well. So far, however, as they cling to old forms that have lost their vitalizing qualities the courts cease to help. They become hindrances and to that extent dangerous.

The marked position of advantage that courts now occupy with reference to legislation has not failed to attract attention. It may be an open question as to what definite rôle courts were intended to play in the general scheme of legislation. Much discussion is now current on this topic. Whether or not courts were intended to become third houses of legislation, it cannot be doubted that they are in a position to assume such a rôle and much evidence exists of their tendency to take advantage of that position. Whenever the question of constitutionality arises, the court is the final arbiter. Further the court decides whether or not such a question does exist. Thus the question of constitutionality is entirely in the court's hands. It is its own referee concerning questions to which it is a party.

It does not come within the scope of this work to discuss fully the problems that arise from the considerations thus stated. That such discussions are being engaged in offers basis of hope. That they are being carried on among those skilled in the law, court procedure and the principles of political science is a matter of great significance. The current law periodicals have during the past three or four years contained articles as pointedly critical of the courts and their attitude toward social and economic questions as anyone could wish. That such articles are deemed of sufficient importance to call for replies promises further discussion. Even a casual reading of them is sufficient to show how necessary a changed attitude on the part of the courts appears to be to the minds of some of the best trained lawyers of the country.

An immediate need is that courts shall come to see and to recognize the importance of conditions as determining the needs for legislation. New relations peculiar to present day industry call as loudly for legislation relating to them as ever did the conditions attendant upon the first stages of the development of factories call for new laws a century ago. But courts cannot go to the factories and mills and see the conditions of work, then to the homes and see there the life impelled by such conditions, then to the hospitals, asylums, almshouses, saloons and houses of prostitution and witness again their direct results. They cannot go out to see at first hand these things. Commissions have been appointed to reveal such facts to legislatures. These revelations have been sufficient to convince legislators of the need for the laws. But in too many cases when such laws have been brought to the courts, the arguments from facts have been laid aside and support for the law has been sought in legal principles or in an effort to convince the court that because the police power is indeterminate and can be extended where there is need for it, it may be extended to cover the case. On such grounds as these the conservative temper of the court is very apt to lead to a finding against the law. One experiences some difficulty in explaining why the evidence which has been convincing to legislators has not been more freely used in arguing before the courts. Legal training is probably largely responsible. Citations from economists, sociologists, publicists, philanthropists, are seldom popular and almost never convincing to the legally trained mind. They cannot stand well against the good old common law and the time honored expressions of jurists who wrote a century or more ago.

The exceptions to the course usually followed in such trials and their favorable outcome point a lesson that should be learned more thoroughly. When courts are shown beyond doubt the necessity inherent in the situation with which the legislation deals, the realization of such necessity has its favorable effect. Professor Seager after a study of several cases in 1904 stated as his conclusion:

> Confused and conflicting as are these decisions, it is believed that a study of them justifies the contention that in the field of labor restrictions the courts will sustain any measure which they think really calculated to promote the public welfare. . . . The constitutional and the economic aspects of the question are so intimately related that we may be certain that a court which believes a protective law economically desirable will find it legally admissible.[1]

Concerning the well-remembered opinion of the New York court in the Tenement House case the comment of Mrs. Kelley in *Some Ethical Gains Through Legislation* has left nothing more to be said. That decision was based upon personal liberty. Its result has been to perpetuate the tenement house problem. Had that earliest statute been sustained, " it is safe to assert that the odious system of tenement manufacture would long ago have perished in every trade in every city of the Republic." Because the court was not made to see the facts upon which the need for the law rested, personal liberty was made the deciding factor, with the result that " for the convenience of the powerful, the weakest industrial factors in the community . . . have been invaded by industry and by inspectors." It cannot be repeated too often in connection with the opinion in that case that the court so far misunderstood tenement house conditions and so far confused the situation with the

[1] "The Attitude of American Courts Toward Restrictive Labor Laws," *Political Science Quarterly*, vol. xix, pp. 589, 593, 601, Dec., 1904.

thought of the ideal "home" as to insert in the opinion the statement that the law intruded upon the sacred right of the cigar maker not to be forced by an act of the legislature "from his home and its hallowed associations and beneficent influences to ply his trade elsewhere." An opinion in which the court in all seriousness talks of the hallowed associations and beneficent influences of tenement house life is certainly a case that must ever stand as an instance of how not to do it in matters of labor legislation before the courts.

The New York Bakers' case before the United States supreme court met with a similar fate and for much the same reason. If that case, Professor Ely has declared, "had been presented from the standpoint of industrial hygiene it would not have been lost. It would have appeared reasonable."[1]

The Bakers' case was before the court in 1905. In 1908 the same court heard Muller *v.* Oregon. That case was presented in an entirely different manner. Conditions as they existed and the latest facts of science were brought before the court in a convincing way, with a result altogether satisfactory. In the opinion, as though to justify the court in departure from the usual line of consideration, an explanation is made.

The legislation and the opinions of experts contained in the elaborate brief prepared for the court, says the Justice,

> may not be, technically speaking, authorities, and in them is little or no discussion of the constitutional question presented to us for determination, yet they are significant of a widespread belief that [the conditions of the case] justify special legislation. . . . Constitutional questions, it is true, are not settled by even a concensus of present public opinion, for it is the peculiar value of a written constitution that it places in

[1] At Council Meeting of the American Association for Labor Legislation, Chicago, April, 1909.

unchanging form limitations upon legislative action, and thus gives a permanence and stability to popular government which otherwise would be lacking. At the same time, when a question of fact is debated and debatable, and the extent to which a special constitutional limitation goes is affected by the truth in respect to that fact, a widespread and long-continued belief concerning it is worthy of consideration. We take judicial cognizance of all matters of general knowledge.

The elaboration of the brief which was the means to obtaining the favorable opinion in this last mentioned case for use before the Illinois court secured not only a favorable decision but a virtual reversal by that court of its former opinion in a similar case.

Here is a way out of some of the difficulties. When lawyers presenting such cases shall avail themselves of like methods the chances of success will be greatly increased. The method may be carried further with advantage by adopting a suggestion coming informally from several sources. The plan is given the form of a definite suggestion by Mr. Mornay Williams of the New York Bar [1] in connection with the discussion of the decision of the New York court in the new Workmen's Compensation Act. The plan as suggested proposes the appointment of a referee by the court to take testimony of facts concerning the actual conditions. This report made by a disinterested referee could then serve as a guide to the judges in estimating the importance to be attached to the industrial facts with which the law aims to deal. The advantages of such a plan are apparent. It would bring before the court a conclusion based upon evidence of fact to supplement the involved legal argument based upon general principles. This conclusion based upon fact would not be weakened by being drawn by counsel for one

[1] *The Survey*, vol. xxvi, p. 127.

side from such facts as he might choose to present, and being contradicted by opposing counsel as not presenting the whole truth. Such *ex parte* statements would be weighed by the referee and presented to the court as a balance of conclusion. Even such a plan would not altogether escape, however, the difficulties that now make so many decisions unsatisfactory. The referee would be a lawyer if not a judge. Probably he would be chosen from a list of judges. That would leave standing every objection that is so real and so valid growing out of legal training and legal habits of mind. To such methods of trial must be added further plans. Among these are two that are of immediate importance. The changing of law courses as at present organized in law schools is a topic already receiving much attention among lawyers themselves. The changes urged lie along the line of a revision of text books so that statements now rejected everywhere else shall not continue to be taught to law students. One writer urges that the remedy is to be found

> in our law schools . . . in training the rising generation of lawyers in a social, political and legal philosophy abreast of our time. [The present law course] preserves an old legal philosophy and prevents the best educated of our bar from becoming children of the present. . . . In view of his relation to the state wherein the most intimate problems of sociology and economics are tried in actions of trespass and suits to enjoin repeated trespasses, must not a philosophy of law founded on a sound knowledge of the elements of the social and political science of to-day form part—and a necessary part—of the equipment of a trained lawyer? [1]

The second necessary development is a larger recognition

[1] Pound, "Do We Need a Philosophy of Law?" *Columbia Law Rev.*, vol. v, p. 353, May, 1905. See also Pound, "The Need of a Sociological Jurisprudence," *Green Bag*, vol. xix, p. 607, Oct., 1907.

of the authority of the expert opinion of special students of social and industrial conditions. Economics and sociology seldom receive cordial treatment at the hands of courts. The principles of these newer sciences which bear such a direct relation to the important things of life play but a very minor rôle in shaping decisions on many of life's most perplexing problems. After an examination of a late volume of United States supreme court decisions an investigator concludes:

> Of discussions essentially economic and of subjects upon which economists could throw so much light this volume contains an abundance. There is in this volume by the most liberal enumeration but a single reference to an economic writing. The most effective and frequently cited authority [in the Income Tax cases] was an extract from Coke upon Littleton, concluding, "For what is the land but the profits thereof?" Adam Smith, Turgot and a few other standard writers were accorded equal rank with the best English dictionaries in defining a "direct tax" and two casual references to Mill and one to Seligman were made incidentally. These are all the references to economic writings contained in the 339 pages covered in the reports by these cases.

Another illustration of the same point is given by the same writer. In reply to the opposing counsel's citations from economic writers a lawyer sought to dismiss them all with a wave of his hand and the remark: "What we want to get at, may it please the court, is the good old English Common Law as it has existed from the days of Magna Charta." The writer adds: "So far as any direct influence upon our courts is concerned, our modern text books on economics might as well be written in Chinese." [1] That the charges

[1] Humble, "Economics From a Legal Standpoint," *American Law Rev.*, vol. xlii, pp. 379, 382, May-June, 1908.

made by this writer are true cannot be doubted. One will search in vain through the almost unending pages of court opinions in cases which involve social and industrial interests to find references to economics or sociology that are given weight. There have come to some of our courts most recently men who begin to realize this fault. From these more may be expected. Their opinions are often dissenting, yet they have in them germs of development that will bear fruit in the future. From one of this small group, Mr. Justice Holmes, has come these words: "In my opinion, economists and sociologists are the people to whom we ought to turn more than we do for instruction in the grounds and foundations of all rational decisions."[1]

The value of expert economic advice is being recognized more and more. When commissions appointed by legislatures were composed largely of lawyers their reports were generally such as to secure legislation acceptable to courts but not well adapted to benefit society. More recently economic experts have been appointed either as members of such commissions or as consulting experts. The reports of such commissions are among our most valuable documents. Legislation enacted as a result of their work has usually been well adapted to benefit society but has often not been acceptable to courts. Commissions have revealed through their investigations and reports the need for legislation restricting the hours of labor for women in Illinois, the need for the regulation of the hours of labor in bakeries in New York, the need for the regulation of tenement work in New York, the need for workingmen's compensation to take the place of the old relation of legal liability. When these cases came to the courts the industrial conditions and the economic principles were alike brushed aside. When

[1] Ely, *Evolution of Industrial Society*, p. 415, note.

such expert advice can be brought to bear upon the minds of judges a change may be expected similar to that occasioned by the use of such advice in legislative bodies.

While one cannot urge that courts shall ever depart from the traditional and constitutional attitude of protecting life, liberty and property it seems that the constitution itself cannot be made to accomplish all that it must have been intended to accomplish unless the content of its phrases be allowed to change with the changing social conditions. Doubtless the framers of our federal constitution were intent upon preserving for all time the advantages that had just been secured through the political struggle with England. No one can suppose that they intended that constitution to become a barrier to the gaining of other blessings for themselves and their posterity. The largest work that a court can do, and it is work that must be done by some one, is to keep a constitution up to date. Such expressions as "life, liberty and property," "life, liberty and pursuit of happiness" and "freedom of contract" must not be allowed to lose their importance. Yet it must be admitted that they have not a vital meaning as now often used by courts. When a court admits that conditions are such that "opportunities for oppression and consequent public suffering" may arise and that "wage earners are not upon an equal footing with employers" and then in face of such an admission insists that such things "do not of themselves justify the arbitrary invasion of the personal rights and liberties of the citizen;" and goes further and insists that "liberty to contract on one's own terms, to decide for himself his own employment . . . are among his most valuable and cherished rights" (Republic Iron and Steel Co. *v.* State), it is difficult to see that "freedom of contract" and "personal rights and liberties" are of any real value to those who are in need of constitutional protection.

The age in which our constitutional principles were given their present form of expression was an age of governmental non-interference. Such a policy was adopted as being the one that would secure the best results. *Laissez faire* was the natural political policy in the day of an extreme individualistic philosophy. The departure from such a policy has been a very real one. It finds its expression in the main in the factory laws. These laws were at first tolerated because of the imperative need for them that conditions imposed. Toleration has passed into a more willing sanction, and that in turn into a positive insistence that such laws are not a necessary evil, that they enable the constitution to do for citizens living under it what it was intended to do as stated in its preamble.

But this change has not been a sudden one effected by the cumbersome machinery of amendment. In the main the change has come about slowly. It has been accepted whereever conditions were revealed which made such changes necessary. It has not led to any violent strains in constitutional interpretation. Life, liberty, property, pursuit of happiness, freedom of contract, all are more really protected by our constitution because of such changes in interpretation. The constitution is stronger because of them. It always seems easier to realize that changes have occurred in the past than to appreciate that they are continuing in the very present. Nothing could be more true however. An adjustment of constitutional meaning in the past must be a part of similar adjustment in the present. Departure from Individualism in the direction of Socialization, departure from the industrial simplicity of the domestic system to the complexity of the factory system with the large industrial unit, the corporation, and the laboring "class,"—these are the changes of the present. Non-interference by government in industry is no longer held to be either wise or possible. Factory legislation is not sufficient to eliminate the evils of a twentieth century industry. Social legislation is imperative. The conditions demand it. Here, again, changes must be made in former meanings of our constitutional phrases or the constitution will lose its vitality. It cannot remain a vital factor in preserving amicable relations in a twentieth century society if it is to be allowed to have only the meaning of an eighteenth century philosophy expressed in terms of an eighteenth century civilization.

Twentieth century liberty, property and happiness are not those of two centuries ago. The same words carry quite a different content. We neither want nor need the kind of rights our great grandfathers had any more than we want or need the kind of stage coach they traveled in or the kind of tools they worked with. To the extent that the courts continue to insist upon our having such rights, society will be as seriously handicapped as it would be if stage coaches and hand sickles were forced upon us. A legislature is convinced that a law is needed to secure weekly payment of wages. This conviction is based on an economic advantage, the desire of workmen to have a weekly payday and the inability of such workmen to secure what they greatly desire because of the inequality of bargaining power. A court reviews the law. The court cannot see any economic advantage to the community from such payments. It does not seem to realize that the workingmen want it. It sees that employer and employee are both men, and being men they must be equal. This equality of right cannot exist, in the mind of the court, unless the workingman is left free to agree to work for irregular payments if he chooses. So the conclusion of the court is that such legislation is not in accord with the constitution inasmuch as it violates the workman's right to life, liberty, property, pursuit of happiness or freedom of contract. The court then overthrows the act of the legislature by a line of reasoning that has no reference to conditions and that deprives these phrases of any present meaning. To reduce such a case to its final terms it may be stated thus. If the law allows the master to employ only on terms of weekly payment, then the servant can find employment only on such terms. That is a restriction upon his "liberty." If the court saw the situation in its real light, it would be stated thus. If the employer finds it to his personal interest to employ the workman only upon terms of monthly payment, the workman, whatever his own personal interest may be, can find employment only on such terms. That is to say: If the employer is obliged by law to pay wages at the end of each week for services rendered, then the workman can find employment only on such terms. That is a distinct contribution to his welfare. Even at its worst it is a choice between liberty and welfare. And when one finds that the constitution forces upon the employee under the name of liberty something that he does not want and thereby deprives him of something that is a distinct contribution to his welfare, one wonders if our constitution must continue to be made an agency in accomplishing such an end.

What is true of this case as illustrative is true of a list of employments that is certainly not a short one. Does any one suppose that bakers want to work fourteen hours a day and seven days in a week? Do women work at night or during a twelve hour day or longer from choice? Is sweat shop labor voluntarily chosen in preference to other work? Is one to suppose that workmen with families to support are entirely indifferent to payday, or that they would exercise their freedom by deliberately insisting that wages should be paid at irregular intervals not oftener than ten or twelve times a year? Even ministers and college professors object to irregular payment of salaries or payment in ten installments. Physicians, lawyers and others whose income is in the form of fees complain that irregular payments make the problem of financing the family budget a difficult one. Do barbers insist upon their inalienable right to work all day Sunday as well as nearly all Saturday night? Every one of the questions here raised has received a serious affirmative answer at the hand of some judicial tribunal. The court has then come to the rescue of the rights of such persons by sweeping away the acts of an oppressive legislature and restoring to them their constitutional right of freedom of contract and opening for them the way to pursuit of happiness. When the Wisconsin legislature enacted a law providing for closing barber shops on Sunday, the supreme court of the state upheld the law. The extent to which barbers regarded the law as an invasion of their rights as citizens of the state may be seen in their attitude toward the decision. "General rejoicing prevails," says the *Journeyman Barber*,[1] "amongst the barbers of Wisconsin and especially Milwaukee where the barbers have been slaves to Sunday work ever since this city had barber shops."

Freedom of contract is one of the rights most strongly insisted upon by courts in general. This insistence leads to difficulties often more serious than those sought to be avoided by its means. That the constitution nowhere guarantees directly freedom of contract is a fact more generally admitted than acted upon. That freedom to contract is derived from constitutional rights expressly stated affords reason for refusing to regard it as a right of the same degree of sanctity as life or liberty. The right to limit freedom of contract is so widely recognized that opinions do not generally stop to discuss it. Numerous limitations placed

[1] Vol. v, p. 372, Nov., 1909.

upon this right in the interests of public welfare leave no doubt of the error of any assumption of an unqualified right to freedom of contract. Yet the burden of proof always lies with the party that contends for a further restriction. To Sir George Jessel has been credited the formulation of a statement in 1875 that has had "more influence at court than volumes of economic writing or even of evidence of conditions." [1] It concerns freedom of contract and is as follows: "If there is one thing more than another which public policy requires, it is that men of full age and competent understanding shall have the utmost liberty of contracting and that such contracts shall be enforced by courts of justice." The expression itself is of as much importance today as it ever was, if rightly understood. If not so understood, however, it can result only in harm. Conditions show that masses of men "of full age and competent understanding" have not the "utmost liberty of contracting." They have in fact nothing whatever to say about what agreement they shall work under. Employed in wholesale numbers in a manner wholly impersonal, their choice is to take work on the terms offered or let it alone. Clearly every whit of freedom of contract lies with the employer. There are opinions that cannot be carefully read without giving the reader the impression that the employer's freedom to make a contract suitable to himself was a consideration in the judge's mind more weighty than the workingman's freedom. Necessarily the employer's liberty must be limited as that of his employee is expanded. When a situation wherein the bargaining advantage lies so obviously on one side is sought to be remedied, the remedy cannot be effected without restricting the side that formerly had the

[1] Humble, "Economics From a Legal Standpoint," *American Law Rev.*, vol. xlii, p. 384, May-June, 1908.

advantage. In view of these facts it becomes evident that courts that take the technical legal view of the right of contract by seeking to perpetuate rights do in fact deprive of those rights the very ones whom they profess to help. An instance will make this clear. A law requiring wage payment in money was enacted in Missouri. This law, the court said, singled out workingmen in mines and manufacturing establishments and said to such: "You cannot contract for labor payable alone in goods, wares and merchandise." Others may make such contracts "but you cannot." "Though of full age, and competent to contract, still you shall not have the power to sell your labor for meat and clothing alone, as others may." That instances of oppression occur may be true, admits the court. Yet

> conceding that such instances may and do occur, still that furnishes no reasonable basis for depriving all persons engaged in the two lawful and necessary pursuits of the right to make and enforce every-day contracts. Liberty, as we have seen, includes the right to contract as others may, and to take that right away from a class of persons following lawful pursuits is simply depriving such persons of a time-honored right which the constitution undertakes to secure to every citizen.

Could any expression show more clearly the failure to appreciate conditions, failure to realize what scrip payment and truck stores mean, and the determination to enforce in modern conditions old meanings adaptable to surroundings that no longer exist. The employees are in fact deprived of the substance of liberty in order that they may have its semblance. The employers in fact are supported in a position of absolute dictators under cover of terms that imply equality. How striking is the contrast! The technical view as adopted by so many judges from old definitions and ancient precedents is that any law that prevents a laborer from selling his labor as he thinks best is an infringement of his constitutional privileges, especially his freedom to contract, and consequently is vicious and void. It deprives him of a right which the constitution undertakes to guarantee to every citizen. Public policy, indeed, requires that men shall have utmost liberty of entering freely and voluntarily into contracts. On the other hand the view is that in certain employments, unlike other employments in certain very important particulars, workingmen very much desire to have what they are totally unable to get. Their having or not having these things touches so many people in respects so fundamentally important that the matter becomes one of public interest. That these may have what is so necessary to their own welfare and to the welfare of the public, laws are enacted to provide for it. These laws, conditions very clearly indicate, are necessary to secure such liberty to all in an equal degree. In such a case such laws can be nothing else than constitutional since they protect men in their equality. They restore to some those rights which they have lost and which the constitution undertakes to secure to every one. In any condition where, in the absence of a law, a laborer is practically prevented from selling his labor as he thinks best, or from being on an equality in opportunity to contract, the presence of such a law is a protection to his constitutional privileges. It becomes a constitutional necessity. In any modernized interpretation of the Constitution, such a law must be constitutional. Without it the constitution is helpless. With it that document becomes real, alive and a positive force.

With the contract understood as it is, can there be any doubt as to what must be the final outcome of this conflict of view, if men are to continue to look to the constitution and to the courts for guidance as to their rights. Writing on this subject of the attitude of courts on the rights of contract, an author already quoted says of the decisions in general that they " serve to show that the right of the individual to contract as he pleases is upheld by our legal system at the expense of the right of society to stand between our laboring population and oppression." [1]

The situation so far as the contract relation is concerned reaches a conclusion so absurd as to be hardly believable. Clearly the employee class does not want long hours, irregular pay, or conditions of labor dangerous to health. To assume that workmen want such conditions is absurd. If, then, they do not want them it is scarcely less absurd to assume that they value the liberty which enables them to insist upon such terms. To the workman as a class such a freedom, judged by results, can be no freedom at all. Nor indeed are any cases to be found where the workmen are appealing to the courts for the protection of this right. The only indication that can be found is that in which employees appear as witnesses to testify that long hours, night work, irregular pay or some similar condition is necessary in order that they may make a living. The best instance illustrative of this is in the attack made by the employer upon the Illinois law restricting the hours of labor of women. Current discussion of the matter during the trial pointed out the real truth of the situation. One employee testified that she had been at work making paper boxes for thirty-two years, beginning when thirteen years old. She earned with this thirty-two years of experience sixteen cents an hour working from half past seven in the morning until five at night with one-half hour for lunch. In the busy season she worked again from six to nine o'clock in the evening. Another employee had been working for sixteen years having begun at sixteen years of age. One of these employees was

[1] Pound, " Do We Need a Philosophy of Law?" *Columbia Law Rev.*, vol. v, p. 345, May, 1905.

supporting a dependent sister. The other was the source of support for a father, a mother, a sister and a brother. Both of these employees testified that it was necessary for them to work longer than ten hours in order to earn enough to prevent running into debt. It was a simple matter for the skill of the lawyer to make it appear that because these employees had to work long hours to earn a living it was a violation of their right of contract to forbid them to do so. The connection between piece wages, long hours and net income has so often been pointed out that it is unnecessary to elaborate the suggestion raised in the discussion at the time, that is, why the wages paid are so small that injuriously long hours are a necessity.

These cases are almost uniformly brought to court by employers, who appear strangely solicitous of the rights of their employees. Yet this has not generally been apparent to the judges. It seems as if to their minds a right was a right no matter by whom it might be urged. Such a habit of viewing rights seems to have blinded courts to the real facts in a case where one seeks his own private ends through the court by appearing to champion the rights of others. In two instances has the real situation revealed itself to the court clearly enough to call for comment.

(1) It is a notable fact in this connection that the alleged constitutional right of the laborer to contract his labor at any price which seems to him desirable is not in this or any other reported case a claim urged by the laborer, but the earnest contention in his behalf is made by the contractors who are reaping the benefits of the violation of that contract in paying the laborer a less remuneration than he is entitled to under the statute. (*In re* Broad.)

(2) It may not be improper to suggest in this connection that although the prosecution in this case was against the employer of labor, who apparently under the statute is the only

one liable, his defense is not so much that his right to contract has been infringed upon, but that the act works a peculiar hardship to his employees, whose right to labor as long as they please is alleged to be thereby violated. The argument would certainly come with better grace and greater cogency from the latter class. (Holden *v.* Hardy.)

Although in no reported case is the claim that his rights are being destroyed urged by the laborer, and although in fact the laws are not only wholly acceptable to him and even urged by him upon the legislature, yet the courts continue to find in such legislation that the rights of the workingmen are being trampled upon. The employer is thus able to turn the very constitution itself into an instrument of inequality. Thus do courts blind their eyes to the conditions that prevail today and cling loyally to the ideas of a former day applying them to the positive injury of those very ones whom they are seeking to protect. To protect every man in the exercise of his own liberty to choose conditions in which he shall work results today in permitting to one party, the employer, the arbitrary dictation of conditions in which the other, the employee, must work or starve. That such a situation is frequently recognized by courts is among the hopeful signs. That it has been so often overlooked is a chief cause for the dissatisfaction with our courts evinced by large numbers of our population.

Unfortunately the reactionary cases may be of equal weight as precedents with the progressive decisions. In 1905 the United States supreme court annulled the New York Bakeshop law on the ground that it limited the rights of bakers to work longer than ten hours a day if they chose, and characterized it as "mere meddlesome interference with the rights of the individual." In 1909 the supreme court of Missouri (State *v.* Miksicek) adopted this opinion as authority in annulling a law of that state which did not place any limitation on the number of hours in a day that a baker should be allowed to work but which restricted his "right" to labor to six days in the week. Bakers in Missouri, on a principle deliberately adopted both by the supreme court of that state and by the United States supreme court, are thus fully protected in their inherent and inalienable right expressly granted by a written constitution to gratify their impulses to industry and thrift by working twenty-four hours a day and seven days in the week. The blessings of liberty are thus preserved to all citizens of these United States. One can hardly refrain from sympathizing with barbers in certain states because of their deprivation of rights in being denied the privilege of working while compelled to witness elsewhere their industrious brothers, the bakers, busy in industry.

An editorial first published in the Chicago *Evening Post* and copied in other papers emphasizes this point so clearly that it would be difficult to improve upon it. It was written at the time of the trial of the Illinois women's ten-hour-a-day law.

It must be a great comfort to the working women of Illinois to know that their interests are being so faithfully guarded by Dora Windeguth, Anna Kusserow and the W. C. Ritchie Company, paper-box manufacturers.

It is a blessed privilege indeed, that of "overtime," the very Beulah land, we understand from the Ritchie petition, of the woman who toils. Sweet is a twelve-hour day, but even sweeter is a thirteen or a fourteen, crowned with "supper money." There is a great zest and excitement about working after dark. The electric lights throw a brilliant glare over the shop that was dingy by daytime; the machines which hummed monotonously at noon now run into queer crescendos and diminuendos; cheeks that were pale are flushed and pretty; quitting time is far less boisterous.

And then there is the money consideration. What more

natural, in a business community governed strictly by pecuniary ideals, that we should pay a certain deference to the pecuniary point of view of the employee? When Dora Windeguth, her employer at her elbow, says that she cannot earn enough in ten hours to live, our whole chivalry rises to her defense; let her work twelve hours then. We have always contended that nobody need starve in America.

It is interesting to reflect that while Dora's feudal forebears fought for "the right to work," it has been left for Dora's generation to fight for the right to work overtime. But there is still a chance—if all stick together—to save this state from the fate of Massachusetts, Oregon, Missouri, Washington and half a score of other commonwealths which, given the choice between healthy womanhood and cheap paper boxes, are now going without paper boxes.

Opposition to the Factory Acts in England was based upon class interest plus the accepted principles of *laissez faire.* Opposition to similar legislation in this country is based upon class interest plus the accepted principle of individualism embodied in our constitutions.

In the determination of property right, the courts are not in a position that will stand careful examination. The fact that the expression life, liberty and pursuit of happiness in the Declaration of Independence becomes in the constitution life, liberty and property is a significant one. Property has in fact a sanctity in the minds of some judges that ranks it equal with life itself. It may be insisted by some that property has necessarily a personal side, that property right is only one form of personal right. A person's right in property is similar in kind to his right in life. This is clear so far as it goes. In its application the conclusion of the analysis is not always kept in mind. In fact, in the minds of many judges the difference between property right and personal right has become so great as to amount in reality to a difference in kind. Rights in property are set off against rights in life in such a way as to give the property right the decided advantage. How often is an act which affects the income of property construed as an act destructive of property. How seldom is it discovered that property is being so used as slowly to deprive one of life. There is not always the same clearness of vision in seeing on the one hand that destroying income of property is destroying property and is an invasion of the property right, and on the other that destroying means of livelihood is destroying life itself and pursuit of happiness, and is an invasion of the right to life. The right over property in a pistol does not include the right of its owner to point it at one and shoot, relying on that one's freedom of action to enable him to get out of the way. No more does the right over any property include the right of the owner to set certain conditions of labor and payment of wages and rely on the workingman's freedom of contract to refuse to accept the terms offered. To agree to pay a certain wage and then retain part of it by irregular or infrequent payments is lessening the wage-earner's income. This is just as much depriving him of the right to life as is the lessening of the income from property to that extent depriving the owner of the right to property. A comparison of the line of argument in these cases and in boycott cases, for example, is both interesting and instructive.

The more one reads the decisions the more he must necessarily be impressed with the fact that a number of opinions all too large are given over to the repetition of those time-honored phrases of an extreme individualism. Discussions often unnecessarily elaborate are to be found ringing the changes on " life, liberty and property," the " trinity of rights," the sacred right of " freedom of contract." Even granted that these views are obiter, their injection into the opinion reveals the attitude of the judge and further shows to what extent these obstructions loom up to obscure the real conditions out of which the case grows. They assume the appearance of an effort more or less blind to compel conformity of present conditions to past ideals through the persistent use of expressions brought forward from a former age. Liberty does not mean the same to-day that it did in 1809. The idea that the term carries with it is, if possible, of greater import than ever before. Read any of such general statements in the abstract and they have a ring of true Americanism that appeals to us. But read them in the light of present conditions with which they undertake to deal and take into consideration the conclusion to which they lead and one must confess that after all the ring that before seemed true comes to have a hollow sound.

If such use of these phrases were merely to no purpose at all, the situation would not be so serious. The courts are in fact so using them as to defeat the very purposes for which they exist. Liberty is so interpreted as to deprive of liberty those who stand in greatest need of real liberty. In one case a minority recognizes this in a dissenting opinion. The Missouri legislature prohibited the use of store orders in payment of wages. In the view of the majority of the court the legislature in doing this had taken away from such workingmen the liberty to contract as others may. This the court declared to be "depriving such persons of a time-honored right which the constitution undertakes to secure to every citizen." (State *v.* Loomis.) To the minority, however, this law seemed to secure a liberty rather than take one away. The court in annulling the law reduced to a shadow again the liberty which the legislature undertook to actualize. What the workmen most want and what they are compelled to give up if they are to have any employment at all, because of the superior bargaining power of the employer or because of the indefinite uncontrollable pressure of a community, is thus placed permanently beyond their reach in order that they may have their constitutional rights. Freedom of contract is in reality a means. It has received such emphasis, however, that it has come to be regarded as an end in itself. As such it is a serious obstacle in the way of the attainment of a higher end, industrial liberty. If legal protection of freedom of contract furthers real industrial liberty, it should be defended to the last. When, however, this is not the case, it loses its claim to protection in the larger interest in industrial liberty. When the further legal limitation on freedom of contract actually increases industrial liberty, such limitation cannot in reason be regarded as a violation of the real purpose and meaning of the constitution.

There is evidence that the courts themselves are inclined more and more to interpret constitutionality in terms of necessity. In other words public necessity as indicated by conditions of public morals, public health, public welfare, public safety determines the extent to which the individualism shall be limited. This necessity is the essence of police power. The definition of that expression lies with the court. Courts are slow to define it. They prefer, and doubtless wisely, to decide only whether any particular act does or does not come within its meaning. The police power is the expression of necessity. But it must not be forgotten that this necessity must be one that the judge sees. Professor Seager's conclusion already referred to is that "the courts will sustain any measure which they think really calculated to promote the public welfare. . . . The constitutional and the economic aspects of the question are so intimately related that we may be certain that a court which believes a protective law economically desirable will find it legally admissible." While no one will deny the advantage of this tendency, it must be admitted that it is not sufficient. Too much depends upon the method of presentation of the case to the court, and altogether too much upon the point of view of the judges. It must not be overlooked that the degree of necessity in a given case will not appear to be the same to all who sit on the case. Long training in the meaning of legal phrases and little schooling in interpreting economic principles and observing industrial conditions determine the judge's mental attitude. This makes the task of convincing a court that a protective law is economically so desirable that it should be held legally admissible a very difficult one. That the tendency is not uninterruptedly in the direction of the association of the economically desirable with the legally admissible has been shown in an unexpected way by the New York court of appeals in its opinion of the New York Workmen's Compensation Act. Professor Seager has more recently expressed his view of this decision.

> Impressed by the suffering and destitution which industrial accidents impose each year upon thousands of innocent persons; conscious of the inadequacy of damage suits under the employers' liability law to remedy these evils; recognizing the inequality in intelligence and financial resources of employer and employee; and perceiving the great interest which the state has in the subject, [the commission] confidently hoped that the courts would sustain an extension of the police power to this new field of legislation. The highest New York court has declared against such an extension. It has done so, it should be emphatically stated, not because it is opposed to the law on its merits, but merely because it feels bound by the constitution.[1]

To make this point clear, it is necessary to cite only a few

[1] *The Survey*, vol. xxvi, p. 185, April 29, 1911.

passages from the court's opinion. "In arriving at this opinion [of unconstitutionality] we do not overlook," insists the court, "the cogent economic and sociological arguments which are urged in support of the statute." The court shows by its further statement that the "theory of this law" is clearly understood. It admits the strength of the appeal that "our present system [of employers' liability] is uncertain, unscientific and wasteful, and fosters a spirit of antagonism between employer and employee which it is to the interest of the state to remove." The opinion of this court certainly argues for the economic desirability of this law. Yet it is not able to find it legally admissible.

> The statute, judged by our common-law standards, is plainly revolutionary. . . . The radical character of this legislation is at once revealed by contrasting it with the rule of the common law. . . . Under our form of government, however, courts must regard all economic, philosophical and moral theories, attractive and desirable though they may be, as subordinate to the primary question whether they can be moulded into statutes without infringing upon the letter or spirit of our written constitutions. . . . When our Constitutions were adopted it was the law of the land that no man who was without fault or negligence could be held liable in damages for injuries sustained by another. . . . It is conceded that [the liability in the new law] is a liability unknown to the common law and we think it plainly constitutes a deprivation of liberty and property under the Federal and State Constitutions. . . . If such economic and sociological arguments as are here advanced in support of this statute can be allowed to subvert the fundamental idea of property, then there is no private right entirely safe, because there is no limitation upon the absolute discretion of legislatures, and the guarantees of the Constitution are a mere waste of words. . . . The argument that the risk to an employee should be borne by the employer because it is inherent in the employment may be economically

sound, but it is at war with the legal principle that no employer can be compelled to assume a risk which is inseparable from the work of the employee and which may exist in spite of a degree of care by the employer far greater than may be exacted by the most drastic law.[1]

In this conclusion appears the whole difficulty of abiding in the hope that our judges will see the legal reasonableness of legislation even when its economic necessity is made to appear. In the first place it is often extremely difficult and even impossible to make an economic necessity real to a judge who is in such a mental attitude as to be able to see only legal phases of a question. In the second place, even when the economic necessity is made so real to the court that they admit it, there is then no assurance that they will feel in any sense bound to be governed by that necessity. To have to amend a state constitution in order to secure laws made necessary by industrial changes would necessitate a constant amending process and the amendment of state constitutions is slow and difficult. The amendment of any constitution so as to make possible laws arising out of economic necessity is not very clearly in accord with the principles of political science if distinctions are to be maintained between constitutional law and statute law. To have to amend the federal constitution in order to secure laws made necessary by industrial changes would necessitate the application of the continuous amendment process to a constitution that is generally regarded as practically unamendable.

Such is the situation that arises when the necessity for a law must be a necessity that the court can see; when courts insist upon being bound by written constitutions, "the charters which demark the extent and the limitations of

[1] These extracts are taken from the opinion as printed in the New York *Labor Bulletin*, March, 1911, pp. 59 *et seq.*

legislative power;" and when they further insist that they shall not be bound in any sense by "the frequent and violent fluctuations of that which, for want of a better name, we call public opinion." Courts take satisfaction in declaring that public opinion cannot enter into the determination of what the law is. Numerous expressions indicate the extent to which this view is held.

It is not universally held however. It was upon this fact that the New York Commission based its expectation of constitutionality. The supreme court of the United States has deferred in at least two important cases to views generally held in public opinion. One of these cases is that so frequently referred to,—Muller *v.* Oregon. The court there expressly recognized the necessity for the law based upon "a widespread and long-continued belief" that the needs of the case "justify special legislation." The other is the more recent utterance in a case not dealing with a question of labor legislation. The law in question was upheld under the police power on the ground that "strong and preponderant opinion" and "prevailing morality" hold the law "to be greatly and immediately necessary to the public welfare." With such a precedent and example in recognizing great and immediate necessity and widespread and long-continued belief, the New York court declares: "We cannot recognize them as controlling our construction of our own constitution."

Where such conclusions are reached as this typical one indicates, there is but one thing to do to meet the exigency. That is, of course, to secure an amendment. New York has passed through the experience before. It can do so again. But even the demonstration of the ability to amend a constitution every time it is found that legal conservatism and eighteenth century philosophy make it necessary does not end the matter.

If judges are to give an interpretation to the phrases of our constitution such that these phrases shall be adapted to modern society, if they are to be able to see the reasonableness of legislation for social welfare, if they are to adjust the law to society, it is not enough that they shall know the law. They must know society. They must be so trained for the bench that they shall have keen social insight as well as keen legal insight. They must add to a profound knowledge of things legal a comprehensive understanding of things social. If society changes from decade to decade, then judges must keep pace with such changes. Changing society must be accompanied by changing adjustment in the law. No jurist can lay claim to real greatness who holds the view that constitutional law is an unchanging rule of action for society to which society must forever conform. Law is for society not society for law. So also with constitutions; they are for society. Not all the advantages of written constitutions combined can be made to stand as an obstacle in the way of the normal development of social changes. That a written constitution is a mould that is forever to confine a society within the limits of its fixed lines is a conception that cannot stand the test of application. If the lines of the constitution are variable enough to admit of social development, then well and good. If, however, these lines are rigid and unyielding, there must sometime come a break. That society must conform to a constitution is a principle of very minor importance compared with the fundamental principle that constitutions must conform to societies.

The point at which this principle fails of recognition is in the judicial interpretation of concepts of liberty and justice. It is becoming more and more necessary that those upon whom is to fall the duty of interpreting our constitutions in terms of the present shall have the new appreciation of society. The importance of the word "social" as a qualifying adjective is constantly increasing. Social legislation is clearly the order of the day because the problems to be dealt with by legislation are social problems. Justice is ever the thing sought. It was so in earlier centuries; it is so in the twentieth century. Social justice is now sought as individual justice was sought a century and more ago. Individual justice was sought before it had been clearly defined. The quest for it aided in the definition of it. So we have not a generally accepted definition of social justice. Yet the pursuit of it is leading to a better understanding of its nature. The best formulation of a definition of social justice is found in the writings of three men who, approaching the problem from quite different points of view, arrive at very similar conclusions. Taking the three statements together they are fairly complete.

Justice consists in granting, so far as possible, to each individual the opportunity for a realization of his highest ethical self, . . . this involves, or rather is founded upon, the general duty of all, in the pursuit of their own ends, to recognize others as individuals who are striving for, and have a right to strive for, the realization of their own ends. In other words, there is a general ethical mandate to be a person, and to respect others as persons; to treat others as ends, never as mere means to one's own end.[1]

The true definition of justice is that it is the enforcement by society of an artificial equality in social conditions which are naturally unequal. By it the strong are forcibly shorn of their power to exploit the weak. . . . The civil and political inequalities of men have been fairly well removed by [civil justice]. Person and property are tolerably safe under its rule. It was a great step in social achievement. But society must

[1] Willoughby, *Social Justice*, p. 24.

take another step in the same direction. It must establish social justice.[1]

Justice may, then, be described as the effort to eliminate from our social conditions the effects of the inequalities of Nature upon the happiness and advancement of man, and particularly to create an artificial environment which shall serve the individual as well as the race, and tend to perpetuate noble types rather than those which are base.[2]

These general statements have already done much to modify the practical conception of justice. As they come to be more generally understood they will do more. They give expression to a new view. Social justice lays down for us a new rule. That new rule must become a part of our constitution. No constitutional amendments are necessary. All that is needed is to have the new meaning read into the present phrases. The new principle must be a guide for our courts as well as for our legislatures and our administrative departments. We are fast approaching the time when our progress must cease until this idea is embodied in our constitutional law. The practical application of these new lines of development will appear in a new interpretation of our constitutional phrases. Instead of saying, as did the New York court of appeals (People *v.* Coler), that "a law that restricts freedom of contract on the part of both master and servant cannot, in the end, operate to the benefit of either;" it may be held that as a matter of fact as industry is at present organized a law restricting freedom of contract on the part of both employer and employee may and often will in the end operate to the benefit of both. With this new view of the situation, legislation that forbids the employer from em-

[1] Ward, *Applied Sociology,* pp. 23, 24.

[2] Kelly, *Government or Human Evolution,* vol. i, p. 360.

ploying any one under certain prescribed conditions will no longer appear as an invasion of the freedom of the workmen but rather as an insurance to him of that freedom guaranteed to him in the constitution. Freedom of contract, to repeat, is not an end in itself. It is clearly a means to accomplishing an end. When this end is defeated by the very means that are intended to accomplish it, then it seems that the means may fairly be held to be unconstitutional. That end may be expressed as "life, liberty and pursuit of happiness," "life, liberty and property," or "social justice." They must be the same. If legal limitation of freedom of contract furthers the ends of social justice by equalizing the conditions of bargaining it cannot be in violation of the real purpose of the constitution. If the things of fundamental importance are to remain in our present industrial state and at the same time social justice be realized, competition must be preserved as a factor in distribution between employer and employee. Strengthening the employee should be allowed if in fact it equalizes the competition. This question of fact cannot be answered in generalizations from a discarded political philosophy.

Thus our view changes. Regulative laws heretofore held unconstitutional are in fact a protection to constitutional privileges and therefore they are a constitutional necessity. They are not only not positively unconstitutional; they are positively constitutional. They both modernize and vitalize these honored phrases with a new and a larger life. A new meaning is given to the constitution. The way is opened for it to do for twentieth century civilization what it has done for nineteenth century civilization.

INDEX